PENGUIN  CLASSICS

BUDDHIST SCRIPTURES

ADVISORY EDITOR: BETTY RADICE

EDWARD CONZE was born in London in 1904 and educated in Germany. He gained his Ph.D degree from Cologne University in 1928, and then studied Indian and European comparative philosophy at the Universities of Bonn and Hamburg. From 1933 until 1960 he lectured in psychology, philosophy and comparative religion at London and Oxford Universities. Between 1963 and 1973 he held a number of academic appointments in England. Germany and the U.S.A., and was also a Visiting Professor in the Department of Religious Studies at Lancaster, as well as Vice-President of the Buddhist Society. His books include *Buddhism* (1951), *Buddhist Wisdom Books* (1958). *Buddhist Thought in India* (1962), *Thirty Years of Buddhist Studies* (1967) and many translations from the Buddhist literature on Perfect Wisdom. Edward Conze died in 1979.

UNESCO COLLECTION OF REPRESENTATIVE WORKS

The Theravada texts in this volume have been accepted in the
series of translations from the literature of Burma, Ceylon,
India, the Khmer Republic, Laos and Thailand, jointly sponsored
by the United Nations Educational, Scientific and Cultural
Organisation (UNESCO), and the National Commissions for
UNESCO in these countries.

BUDDHIST SCRIPTURES

SELECTED AND TRANSLATED BY

Edward Conze

PENGUIN BOOKS

PENGUIN BOOKS

Published by the Penguin Group
Penguin Books Ltd, 27 Wrights Lane, London W8 5TZ, England
Viking Penguin, a division of Penguin Books USA Inc.
375 Hudson Street, New York, New York 10014, USA
Penguin Books Australia Ltd, Ringwood, Victoria, Australia
Penguin Books Canada Ltd, 2801 John Street, Markham, Ontario, Canada L3R 1B4
Penguin Books (NZ) Ltd, 182 190 Wairau Road, Auckland 10, New Zealand

Penguin Books Ltd, Registered Offices: Harmondsworth, Middlesex, England

This translation first published 1959
19 20 18

Copyright ⓒ Edward Conze, 1959
All rights reserved

Printed in England by Clays Ltd, St Ives plc
Set in Monotype Garamond

CONTENTS

Contents

Contents

Contents

ACKNOWLEDGEMENTS

THE thanks of the Editor and the publishers are due to the following, who have kindly granted permission for the inclusion of copyright material:

Bruno Cassirer Ltd, for two passages from *Buddhist Texts*, translated respectively by Dr D. L. Snellgrove and by the Editor of the present book; and for a passage from *The Buddha's Law Among the Birds*, also translated by the latter;

George Allen & Unwin Ltd, for a passage from the Editor's *Buddhist Meditation*;

Mr Christmas Humphreys, for a passage from D. T. Suzuki's *Manual of Zen Buddhism*;

The Pali Text Society, for a passage from Mr E. M. Hare's translation of the *Sutta-Nipata* (published as *Woven Cadences*);

Mr R. Trevor Leggett, for his kindness in permitting the use of two of his translations from the Japanese.

INTRODUCTION

BUDDHISM is divided into numerous traditional schools, each with its own set of Scriptures. Information about these schools, their divergences and agreements, can be found in my *Buddhism* (3rd edition, 1957), and its sequel, *Buddhist Texts*, an anthology which I edited in 1954, is arranged according to schools. This selection, by contrast, concentrates on the central tradition of Buddhism, at the expense of the more peripheral developments, on that which is common rather than that which separates. It contains very little that any Buddhist, of whichever school, would be prepared to reject.

The bulk of authoritative Buddhist writings is truly enormous, and covers tens and hundreds of thousands of pages. The Pali Canon, which is restricted to one single sect, fills 45 huge volumes in the complete Siamese edition, exclusive of commentaries. The Chinese and Tibetan Canons, on the other hand, include the work of all those schools which left their mark on China or Tibet. In its most recent Japanese edition the Chinese Scriptures consist of 100 volumes of 1,000 closely printed pages each, while the Tibetan extend to 325 volumes. This colossal mass cries out for selection, and at present no less than 17 anthologies have appeared in English alone. There is room for many more. Measured by the total wealth of the Buddhist tradition, each anthology is woefully inadequate and inevitably omits far more than it includes.

The available material would, of course, be very much reduced if we could restrict ourselves to the words of the Buddha himself, leaving aside all later accretions. Alas, this cannot be done. Buddhist tradition differs fundamentally from that of Christianity. In Christianity we can distinguish an 'initial tradition', embodied in the 'New Testament', from a 'continuing tradition', which consists of the Fathers and doctors of the Church, the decisions of councils and synods, and the pronouncements of various hierarchies. Buddhists possess nothing that corresponds to the 'New Testament'. The 'continuing tradition' is all that is clearly attested. The bulk of the selections in this book was written down between A.D. 100 and 400, in other words about 600 to 900 years after the Buddha's demise. For the first five hundred years the Scriptures were orally transmitted. They were written down only at the beginning of the Christian era, because at that time the decline in faith threatened their continued survival in the memories of the monks. Different schools wrote down different things. Much of it was obviously composed centuries ago, and some of it must represent the direct and actual sayings of the Buddha himself. At present we have, however, no objective criterion which would allow us to isolate the original gospel. All attempts to find it are based on mere surmise, and the discussion of the subject generally leads to nothing but ill will and fruitless disputes. Like the Common Law of England, the Buddhist Law continues to make itself all the time. In some periods, of course, the creative impulse is more evident than in others, and the years between A.D. 100 and 400 were the golden age of Buddhist literature.

A few words must now be said about the considerations which have governed my choice of the extracts, as well as their treatment. First of all, everything had to be readily intelligible. Generally I have preferred texts intended for laymen to those addressed to monks, on the assumption that the majority of my readers live in the world, and are denied the benefits of monastic seclusion. This selection therefore exhibits more of the humanity than of the profundity of the Scriptures. The 'Questions of King Milinda', for instance, explain the basic tenets of Buddhism in terms intelligible to the Greco-Bactrian king Menandros. The explanations are less overloaded with scholastic complications than the monkish treatises, but they also naturally go less deep. In fact, they pursue each subject about as far as the average reader will be willing to pursue it.

Further, aware that this is not the first attempt at a Buddhist anthology, I have taken some care not to duplicate the work of my predecessors. Other things being equal, I have been guided by the desire to break fresh ground. For instance, the *Dharmapada* ('Sayings on Dharma'), one of the most celebrated collections of sayings attributed to the Buddha, is extant both in Pali and Sanskrit. The Pali *Dhammapada* has so far been translated more than a dozen times. My two extracts (II 1, 4a, b) are, however, from the Sanskrit version (called *Udanavarga*), not because I believe it to be older, more beautiful or in any way more authoritative than the Pali, but simply because it is so much less known. Likewise, the Japanese Zen sect falls into two main branches, Rinzai and Soto. Prof. D. T. Suzuki's widely read works contain much information about Rinzai. The Soto branch has been less favoured. I have thought it useful to redress the balance by printing, with Mr T. Leggett's permission, two translations expounding the Soto point of view.

Buddhism is often described as a purely rational religion, which dispenses with faith, and for that reason appeals in our modern industrial age to men who are averse to the mythological, the miraculous and the occult. This assumption is not borne out by the actual writings of the Buddhists. The temptation to make Buddhism appear more attractive by including only those teachings which would not jar on the prejudices of the present age, has been manfully resisted, and the reader will find much to strain his belief. Likewise I did not feel called upon to present the authors as either more consistent or conclusive (see page 190) than they actually are. Obvious contradictions have been faithfully reproduced. A man who on page 203 was described as 'weak and decrepit' has on page 204 become 'strong, with powerful arms'. On page 45 the Bodhisattva says that his mother 'bore him with many pains', whereas on page 35 we learn that her pregnancy left her unaffected. Everything is there as I found it, warts and all.

Some decision had to be made about the length of the passages quoted. Very short extracts would have permitted me to cover many more sources and viewpoints than I have actually done. But to silence them almost the moment they have opened their mouths seems to me rather lacking in respect to these holy men. The communication of this sacred wisdom cannot be reduced to the level of a television performance, with each speaker allotted one or two 'holy minutes'. It would have pleased me best to include a few books in their entirety. The limitations of space forced me to adopt the compromise of drawing heavily on three books, composed in the first or second century of our era. The 'Questions of King Milinda' record a discussion with a half-European king, whose mentality is not unakin to our own. Five extracts, comprising one-eighth of my book, come from that source. Ashvaghosha was a poet who presented the message of the Buddha to the educated lay public of his time. One-fourth of my book has been given to his treatment of two central themes – the life of the Buddha (1 2) and the methods of Buddhist Meditation (II 2, 3).

The style of my translations will be much criticized. Buddhist texts have a characteristic diction of their own which must, I believe, to some extent be respected. Those who want to read about Buddhism in idiomatic English can do so by consulting books written by Englishmen. Here we listen to Asiatics speaking in their own idiom about sacred things. The translator ought, I think, to preserve some of the flavour of the original, and his language must also do justice to its sacred character, which sets it apart from the profane world and its ways. For Buddhists the founder of their religion is the 'Lord Buddha', a god-like being who has transcended the conditions of ordinary life, and his words are not those of a mere man, but a voice issuing from another world. It is therefore quite inconceivable that the Buddha should speak as ordinary people do. In these Scriptures the Buddha's utterances always have a numinous diction of their own, which departs from the standards of normal Indian usage. Galling as it may be to this democratic age, I would have regarded it as a sacrilege to reproduce His words in idiomatic English. The parallel with the New Testament is quite misleading. It is written in the *Koine*, the simple prose of the lower classes, whereas Buddhist writings, with few exceptions, are full of the artifices of Sanskrit rhetoric. The nearest parallel to Ashvaghosha's poem, for instance, would be Propertius or Lucan.

Nor must we forget that the excessive subtleties of Buddhist thought must on occasions lead to awkward English. To take just one example, on page 163 we are told that the Buddhas 'awake' to enlightenment. The present tense, 'awaken', would not do, because inapplicable to the past and future Buddhas. In addition, the word 'awaken' would give the impression that there was a time when the Buddhas were not yet awoken, that their 'awakening' is an action which took place at some time. Such an assumption would be in conflict with the finer points of Buddhist metaphysics. In search for a word which is, as it were, suspended above past, future and present, and which also implies neither action nor non-action, I have hit on 'awake' which is grammatically awkward, but does no violence to the sense.

Far more intractable is the difficulty presented by the technical terms which abound everywhere. In the original they are quite inconspicuous, but in all translations into non-Indian languages they stand out like so many foreign bodies. The Chinese either retained them in Sanskrit, or coined some strange neologism. I have marked them with capitals, and they are all explained in the Glossary at the end. The explanations there cannot, of course, go very far. The baffled reader is advised to read on without bothering overmuch about their exact meaning. Only years of study would, in any case, disclose that in its full precision.

Sanskrit words like Buddha, Nirvana, Bodhisattva and Dharma occur on every page. They cannot possibly be eliminated. The word 'Dharma', in particular, is deliberately ambiguous, with up to ten meanings. On page 198, for instance, we find 'dharmas' first used twice in the sense of 'properties'; at its third occurrence it means 'teachings'; two lines later the meaning has shifted to 'events', only to move on to 'true facts' a little later on. In this case it would have been simple to replace the term by its equivalents, but elsewhere two or three meanings are simultaneously intended (so at II 3, 3). The reader may sigh, and wish that Buddhists had been more unambiguous in their use of words. They obviously were not. In this respect, as in much else, they differ radically from contemporary 'linguistic analysts'. Buddhist thinkers had weighty reasons for preferring ambiguous, multivalent terms, and a mere translator must respect their preference. To rephrase their sayings would be commentary, not translation.

The authors of the Buddhist Scriptures were in fact unwilling, or unable, to state their message without a liberal use of technical terms. We may regret this, but to pulp the holy scriptures and regorge them in colloquial, strictly non-technical, English, would only turn precise spiritual teaching into vague and insipid uplift. The Scriptures as they stand cannot be read without some mental effort, and they demand a minimum of intellectual agility and attainment.

Where accuracy and readability conflict, I have chosen to be accurate. This may excuse such clumsy terms as 'conditioned co-production', or the rendering of *jñāna* by 'cognition'. Sanskrit has numerous words for 'knowledge', to which nothing corresponds in our own rather impoverished vocabulary. *Jñāna* is a knowledge which, motivated by the desire for emancipation, penetrates to the real nature of things. For an equivalent we must draw on Latin for 'cognition' or Greek for 'gnosis'. On page 206 it would have been more elegant to say of the father that he 'saved the lives' of his sons. But the text clearly has it that he 'presented them with life', and the spiritual message could be retained here and elsewhere only by a certain harshness of style. These works were intended for spiritual guidance rather than entertainment. All the Pali, Sanskrit, and Tibetan texts have been newly translated, partly to ensure uniformity in the rendering of the technical terms, and partly to bring them up to the standard of our present knowledge.

Much of the best Buddhist writing is in verse. Even a great poet would find it hard to reproduce it in English verse without considerable distortion. Occasionally I have tried to mark verse as such by using a rather hobbling loose rhythm. Mostly I have translated it as prose, thereby shirking the issue. In any case rhyme, unlike the Indian shloka, or the Greek and Latin hexameter, is not a suitable medium for didactic poetry of high quality. Pope's *Essay on Man* is almost the only example we can point to, and it is a warning example. A great deal of Indian thought, on the contrary, is enshrined in memorial verses of almost unbelievable precision.

The Introductory Notes to the different chapters are kept as brief as possible. They only indicate the theme and source of the extracts. Readers must then wrestle with them for themselves. An explanation in modern terms of what the Sages of old have to tell us would, once begun, soon crowd them out altogether.

As with all my books, Miss I. B. Horner, Hon. Secretary of the Pali Text Society, has selflessly helped me with the selection and translation of the Pali items. The kindness of Mr Trevor Leggett, of the Budokwai and Shanti Sadan, has enabled me to present Zen Buddhism from a new angle.

It is furthermore a pleasure to me to thank those publishers and authors who have appreciably lightened my burden by allowing me to reprint material which has appeared elsewhere before. Among them I must single out Daisetz Teitaro Suzuki, because to him I owe a debt of gratitude which can never be repaid. When, like others before me, in the middle of my journey through life I had strayed away from the right road, it was he who re-opened my eyes to the splendour of the Buddha's message. Whatever is good in this book is Suzuki's. The rest is my own.

EDWARD CONZE

London, June 1957

Part One

THE TEACHER

CHAPTER I

THE BUDDHA'S PREVIOUS LIVES

It is easy to see that we could not have any 'Buddhism' unless a Buddha had revealed it. We must, however, bear in mind that 'Buddha' is not the name of a person, but designates a type. 'Buddha' is Sanskrit for someone who is 'fully enlightened' about the nature and meaning of life. Numerous 'Buddhas' appear successively at suitable intervals. Buddhism sees itself not as the record of the sayings of one man who lived in Northern India about 500 B.C. His teachings are represented as the uniform result of an often repeated irruption of spiritual reality into this world.

Buddhists assume that there are two kinds of time – 'historical time' measured in years or centuries, and 'cosmic time' measured in aeons (see page 31 for the length of an aeon). A diagram will help to clarify the situation:

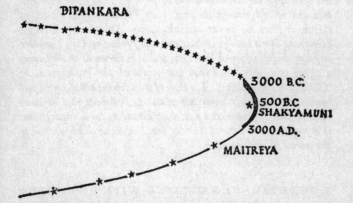

In this parabola the 'historical time', which I reckon as extending from roughly 3000 B.C. to A.D. 3000 (a few thousand years here or there make little difference), is shown by a thick line, not because it is the most real, but because it appears as more real to us in our present

perspective. Buddhas are marked by stars on the line of time. About 500 B.C. we have one 'historical Buddha', called Shakyamuni, who began to prepare himself for his task aeons ago under Dipankara, his twenty-fourth predecessor. He in his turn will be succeeded by Maitreya, about whom we shall hear more in III 2. Under Dipankara, Shakyamuni decided to become a Buddha, and thereby turned into what is known as a 'Bodhisattva'. The logic of the scheme is explained in our selection No. 3, which is taken from Nagarjuna's (c. A.D. 100) great commentary to the 'Perfection of Wisdom', although it does not give his own views, but those of the Sarvastivadin school, to the adherents of which he refers as 'the disciples of Katyayaniputra'.

Furthermore, I have illustrated the career of the Bodhisattva up to his last birth by a few typical events. (1) If the reader wishes to begin where the Buddha himself began, he must start with the turning point marked by the meeting with Dipankara, *of which we have many accounts. The one presented here is from the* Mahavastu, *'The Great Event', a biography of the Buddha due to a Hinayana school (the Lokottaravadins) which stood very near to the Mahayana. Then there are two famous episodes, the one illustrating the Bodhisattva's boundless generosity, the other his boundless patience. Both again have been told and re-told through the ages. (2a) The story of the* hungry tigress *is from the* Suvarnaprabhasa, *the 'Splendour of Gold', a Mahayana Sutra slowly composed over many centuries. (2b) The other story, of the* Preacher of Patience, *is told in the words of Aryasura, a gifted poet, who about A.D. 200 composed the* Jatakamala, *or 'Garland of Birth-stories'. The state of a Buddha is one of the highest possible perfection. It seems self-evident to Buddhists that an enormous amount of preparation over many lives is needed to reach it, and it is therefore only natural that our first chapter should be devoted to this period of slow gestation.*

1. SHAKYAMUNI'S MEETING WITH DIPANKARA

ONCE upon a time there lived a certain learned man who was well versed in brahminic lore, and who taught it to 500 young Brahmins. One of his pupils was Megha, a young Brahmin who was learned, wise, judicious, and of keen intelligence.

Before long he had learned all the mantras by heart. After completing his study of the Vedas, he left the Himalayas and went down into the country below, in order to find the fee due to his teacher. With his staff, water-pot, sunshade, sandals, and mantle he entered many villages, cities, and towns, and the confines of each became free of affliction and calamity through Megha's spiritual power. On his way he begged for money, and someone gave him 500 coins.

He then decided to go to the royal city Dīpavatī, in order to see the city of a universal monarch, made of the seven precious things, and delightful to behold. When he entered the city, he saw that it was in festive array. He wondered to himself, 'What holiday do we have here to-day, or what dramatic performance, or what festival? Perhaps king Arcimat has heard that the young Brahmin Megha, on completing his study of the Vedas, has come down from the Himalayas and is on his way to the royal city of Dīpavatī! Hence this gay adornment of the city!' And as he went on he looked for someone he could question.

Just then a young Brahmin girl came along, attractive, good-looking, reliable, gentle, and modest. She held a water jug and seven lotus flowers in her hands. Megha asked her, 'Is there a festival in the city to-day?' She replied with these verses:

> You cannot, young man, be a native of this place.
> A stranger from another city you must be.
> You do not know that there is coming to this town
> The Benefactor of the World, the Bringer of the Light!
> Dipankara, the leader of the world, the son
> Of king Arcimat, He, a greatly famous Buddha,
> Is drawing near. To honour him this city
> Is decked in gay and festive garb.

Megha asked her: 'How much did you pay for those seven lotus flowers?' She replied: 'Five of them I bought for 500 coins; two were given to me by a friend.' Megha said to her: 'I will give you 500 coins. You then give me those five lotuses, and with them I shall worship Dipankara, the Lord. You can honour him with the remaining two.' She replied:

21

'You can have those five lotuses, but only on condition that for all future time you take me for your wife. Wherever you may be reborn, there I shall be your wife, and you my husband.' Megha replied: 'My heart is set on supreme enlightenment. How can I think of marriage?' She answered: 'No need to desist from your quest! I shall not hinder you!' So Megha consented, and said, 'In exchange for those lotuses, I take you for my wife. I will be able to worship Dipankara, the Lord, and continue to strive for supreme enlightenment.' He gave her the 500 coins, and took the five lotus flowers. A sublime joy and exaltation had taken hold of his body when he had heard the maiden speak of the Buddha.

Meanwhile the Lord had set out for Dīpavatī, accompanied by 80,000 monks, and by king Arcimat with 80,000 of his vassals and with many thousands of noblemen, recluses and sectaries. Megha saw Dipankara, the Lord, coming from afar. The Lord's body had the thirty-two Marks of a superman, and was adorned with the eighty Subsidiary characteristics. He was endowed with the eighteen Special dharmas of a Buddha, mighty with the ten Powers of a Tathagata, and in possession of the four Grounds of self-confidence. He was like a great Naga, and had done all he had to do. His senses were turned inwards, and his mind did not turn to outer things. He had won the stable assurance of Dharma, his senses were calmed, his mind was calmed, he had reached perfect self-control and tranquillity, like a well-guarded Naga, who has conquered his senses, transparent as a pool, clear and unperturbed. He was beautiful and good to look at. No one ever got tired of seeing him, and there was nothing ungracious about him. The light which shone from his body extended to one league.

When he had seen the Buddha, Megha identified himself with him, and said to himself: 'I also will be a Buddha in the world.' He then recited these verses:

'Long is the time before this vision could arise.
Long is the time before Tathagatas appear.
Long is the time until my vow shall be fulfilled:
A Buddha I'll become, there is no doubt on that!'

Thereupon Megha, thrilled throughout his whole body, and his mind filled with sublime joy and exaltation, threw those five lotus flowers towards Dipankara, the Lord. The flowers remained suspended in the air, and formed a circle round the Lord's radiant head. The young Brahmin girl also threw her two lotuses. They also stood suspended in the air, and so did those thrown by other people. This was one of the miracles by which the Buddhas impress people, to make them listen to the truth. The Buddha sustained this canopy of flowers which stood above him in the air, so as to educate beings, and to bring joy and happiness to Megha, the young Brahmin. And this canopy was lovely and fair to behold, with four pillars and entrances, garlanded with strips of coloured cloth.

When Megha saw these lotus flowers standing all round the Lord's radiant halo, and how lovely and pleasing they were, his body was flooded with great joy and gladness, and a sublime decision arose in his mind. He put his water-pot on one side, spread out his deer-skin cloak, threw himself down at the feet of Dipankara, the Lord, wiped the soles of his feet with his hair, and aroused within himself the following thought: 'Ah! May I too at some future period become a Tathagata, with all the attributes of a perfect Buddha, as this Lord Dipankara is just now! May I too turn the wheel of the highest Dharma, as this Lord Dipankara does just now! Having crossed, may I lead others across; set free, may I free others; comforted, may I comfort others – as does this Lord Dipankara! May I become like him, for the weal and happiness of the many, out of compassion for the world, for the sake of a great multitude of living beings, for their weal and happiness, be they gods or men!'

Dipankara, the Lord, with a Buddha's supreme knowledge, knew how ready Megha, the young Brahmin, was to turn towards enlightenment. He knew that his past store of merit, as well as his recent vow, were without fault or defect, without blemish or scar. So he now predicted his future enlightenment, in these words: 'You shall be, young Brahmin, in a future period, after an immeasurable and incalculable

aeon, in Kapilavastu, the city of the Shakyans, a Tathagata by
the name of Shakyamuni, an Arhat, a fully enlightened
Buddha, perfect in knowledge and conduct, well-gone, a
world-knower, unsurpassed, a leader of men to be tamed, a
teacher of gods and men. Like me you will have a body
adorned with the thirty-two marks of a superman, and with
the eighty subsidiary characteristics. You will have the eighteen special dharmas of a Buddha, be mighty with the ten
powers of a Tathagata, confident with his four grounds of
self-confidence! Having crossed, you will lead others across;
freed, you will free others; comforted, you will comfort
others; having won final Nirvana, you will help others to win
it – as I do just now! You will turn the wheel of the highest
Dharma, preside over a harmoniously united body of Disciples, and both gods and men will listen to you and believe.
What I am now, that you will become one day – for the weal
and happiness of the many, out of compassion for the world,
for the sake of a great multitude of living beings, for their
weal and happiness, be they gods or men!'

2a. THE BODHISATTVA AND THE HUNGRY TIGRESS

The Buddha told the following story to Ananda: 'Once upon
a time, in the remote past, there lived a king, Maharatha by
name. He was rich in gold, grain, and chariots, and his power,
strength, and courage were irresistible. He had three sons who
were like young gods to look at. They were named Mahapranada, Mahadeva, and Mahasattva.

One day the king went for relaxation into a park. The
princes, delighted with the beauties of the park and the
flowers which could be seen everywhere, walked about here
and there until they came to a large thicket of bamboos. There
they dismissed their servants, in order to rest for a while. But
Mahapranada said to his two brothers: 'I feel rather afraid
here. There might easily be some wild beasts about, and they
might do us harm.' Mahadeva replied: 'I also feel ill at ease.

Though it is not my body I fear for. It is the thought of separation from those I love which terrifies me.' Finally, Mahasattva said:

> 'No fear feel I, nor any sorrow either,
> In this wide, lonesome wood, so dear to Sages.
> My heart is filled with bursting joy,
> For soon I'll win the highest boon.'

As the princes strolled about in the solitary thicket they saw a tigress, surrounded by five cubs, seven days old. Hunger and thirst had exhausted the tigress, and her body was quite weak. On seeing her, Mahapranada called out: 'The poor animal suffers from having given birth to the seven cubs only a week ago! If she finds nothing to eat, she will either eat her own young, or die from hunger!' Mahasattva replied: 'How can this poor exhausted creature find food?' Mahapranada said: 'Tigers live on fresh meat and warm blood.' Mahadeva said: 'She is quite exhausted, overcome by hunger and thirst, scarcely alive and very weak. In this state she cannot possibly catch any prey. And who would sacrifice himself to preserve her life?' Mahapranada said: 'Yes, self-sacrifice is so difficult!' Mahasattva replied: 'It is difficult for people like us, who are so fond of our lives and bodies, and who have so little intelligence. It is not at all difficult, however, for others, who are true men, intent on benefiting their fellow-creatures, and who long to sacrifice themselves. Holy men are born of pity and compassion. Whatever the bodies they may get, in heaven or on earth, a hundred times will they undo them, joyful in their hearts, so that the lives of others may be saved.'

Greatly agitated, the three brothers carefully watched the tigress for some time, and then went towards her. But Mahasattva thought to himself: 'Now the time has come for me to sacrifice myself! For a long time I have served this putrid body and given it beds and clothes, food and drink, and conveyances of all kinds. Yet it is doomed to perish and fall down, and in the end it will break up and be destroyed. How much better to leave this ungrateful body of one's own accord in good time! It cannot subsist for ever, because it is like urine which must come out. To-day I will use it for a sublime deed. Then it will act for me as a boat which helps me to cross the ocean of birth and death. When I have renounced this futile body, a mere ulcer, tied to countless becomings, burdened with urine and excrement, unsubstantial like foam, full of hundreds of parasites – then I shall win the perfectly pure Dharma-body, endowed with hundreds of virtues, full of such qualities as trance and wisdom, immaculate, free from all Substrata, changeless and without sorrow.' So, his heart filled with boundless compassion, Mahasattva asked his brothers to leave him alone for a while, went to the lair of the tigress, hung his cloak on a bamboo, and made the following vow:

'For the weal of the world I wish to win enlightenment, incomparably wonderful. From deep compassion I now give away my body, so hard to quit, unshaken in my mind. That enlightenment I shall now gain, in which nothing hurts and nothing harms, and which the Jina's sons have praised. Thus shall I cross to the Beyond of the fearful ocean of becoming which fills the triple world!'

The friendly prince then threw himself down in front of the tigress. But she did nothing to him. The Bodhisattva noticed that she was too weak to move. As a merciful man he had taken no sword with him. He therefore cut his throat with a sharp piece of bamboo, and fell down near the tigress. She noticed the Bodhisattva's body all covered with blood, and in no time ate up all the flesh and blood, leaving only the bones.

'It was I, Ananda, who at that time and on that occasion was that prince Mahasattva.'

2b. THE BODHISATTVA AS THE PREACHER OF PATIENCE

Nothing is indeed unbearable to those who have made forbearance all their own, and who are great in the correct appreciation of the true nature of things. This is shown by the following story: At one time the Bodhisattva was an ascetic, eminent for his moral conduct, his learning, his tranquillity, his self-discipline, and the control he had over his mind. He had understood that life in the home is indeed attended by a great many faults and calamities: that it is governed by a perpetual concern with material gain and sensual pleasure, and in consequence is not conducive to tranquillity; that it is constantly assailed by the dust and dirt of passions, such as greed, hate, delusion, impatience, anger, self-intoxication, conceit, and niggardliness; that it is apt to reduce the ability to maintain religious standards, and that it offers a field for covetousness and unfriendliness to others; and so, beset by opportunities for bad actions, it offers little scope for Dharma. The homeless life, on the other hand, he had found to be a happy one, for it is free from those faults, having abandoned all concern with material property and sense-objects. He had taken it upon himself to observe patience always and under all circumstances, he often spoke in praise of patience, and this was the virtue which he continually stressed in his expositions of Dharma. People in consequence invented for him the name 'Kshanti-vadin' ('Preacher of Patience'), and his original family name went quite out of use.

That great-souled man lived in the middle of a forest, in a place delightful for its solitude, and beautiful like a lovely garden – with flowers and fruits at all seasons and a pond of pure water adorned with pink and blue lotuses. And his presence conferred on this place the auspiciousness of a hermitage. The deities who inhabited that grove thought highly of him, and people often visited him in quest of spiritual bliss and spiritual virtue. And on this multitude of visitors he bestowed the supreme favour of expounding the subject of patience in suitable sermons which gladdened their ears as well as their hearts.

Now it so happened that the king of that part of the world, oppressed by the summer's heat, set his mind on playing in the water, a very pleasant thing to do at that time of the year. So with his harem he betook himself to that forest, which had all the qualities one looks for in a park, and amused himself to his heart's content. Then, tired from all this sporting about, and drowsy, he went to his splendid couch, which was luxuriously laid out, and fell asleep.

Thereupon the women, enchanted in their hearts by the beauties of the forest and unable to fill their eyes sufficiently with them, saw in the withdrawal of the king an opportunity to ramble about in casual groups, the noise of their rattling ornaments blending with the buzzing sound of their chatter. Roaming through the enchanting forest, the king's women came to Kshantivadin's hermitage, went into it, and their eyes fell on that most excellent sage, a sight making for peace and happiness. There he sat cross-legged under a tree, auspicious and meritorious to behold, the visible manifestation of Dharma. His deep profundity inspired awe, he shone with the lustre of his austerities, and he radiated a splendid stillness because, as a result of his diligent practice of trance, his senses remained unmoved even in the presence of sublime objects of meditation. The glow of his spirituality subdued the minds of the royal wives; when they saw him they at once shed their usual boisterousness, affectation, and frivolity, and adopted a disciplined, modest, and respectful demeanour. He in his turn addressed them with pleasant words of welcome, etc., and showed them the civility due to guests. Thereafter, he extended to them the hospitality of the Dharma, and, in response to their queries, talked to them in terms which womenfolk can easily grasp, careful to illustrate his meaning by examples and similes.

Meanwhile the king's sleep had dispelled his fatigue, and he woke up. With a frown on his face he asked the female attendants who guarded his couch, 'Where are my wives?' The attendants replied: 'They are now, your Majesty, embellishing some other part of this forest. They have gone off to see what else it contains.' On hearing this, the king rose from his couch, and, accompanied by his female warriors and eunuchs, marched off into the wood. To get to the hermitage he had only to follow the path which his wives had traced out in their juvenile wantonness, and which was marked by bunches of flowers, piles of twigs, and the red dye of betel leaves on the ground. But no sooner had the king seen Kshantivadin, that

great seer, surrounded by his royal wives, than he was seized
by frenzied wrath. This was due to the bias he felt against him
as a result of an enmity nursed during previous lives. In
addition, drowsiness still deranged his composure and jealousy
dulled his judgement. He had but little power to appreciate
the true nature of the situation, and in disregard of all the
rules of self-control and polite behaviour, he submitted to the
evils of anger. Sweat broke out over his body, his colour
changed, he trembled all over, he frowned, and his eyes, dark
red, became dull, revolved, and stared. Gone were all his
loveliness, grace, and charm. He shook his golden bracelets,
rubbed his be-ringed hands, and scoldingly said to the best of
Seers: 'Hey, you!

Who is it that scorns our Majesty, by lifting his eyes to our
harem wives?
Concealed in the garb of a Muni – a low-class meatseller's behaviour!'

And scornfully the king continued: 'Now you will have an
opportunity to show your passion for patience!' And, as one
cuts a lotus from its stalk, so he cut off with his sharp sword
the Sage's right hand, which in a prohibitive gesture was
slightly extended towards him, with its long and delicate
fingers raised aloft.

Though his hand was cut off, he yet felt no pain, so firm his
adherence to patience;
His pain lay in seeing the terrible fate this butcher, accustomed
to pleasure, would meet in the future.

But the Bodhisattva kept silent, because he regarded the
king as someone who was beyond help and who could not
possibly be won over by kindness. He sorrowed for him as
for a patient whom the doctors have given up. The king,
however, spoke to him in a threatening manner:

And so your body will be carved to pieces till you die!
Stop this pose of piety! Your roguish cunning shall be stopped!

But the Bodhisattva said nothing, because he knew him for
a person who could not be won over by affection, and recog-

nized that he would persist anyhow. So the king in the same
manner cut off the other hand of that great-souled man, and
thereafter both his arms, his ears and nose, and his feet.

> No sorrow and no anger felt the Muni, when that sharp sword
>   his frame demolished.
> This engine of the body must run down, he knew, and years of
>   practice had accustomed him to patience.
> And when he saw his limbs drop off, this holy man, unbroken,
>   firm and patient, felt but exaltation,
> No pain at all. What gave him anguish was to see the king so far
>   estranged from Dharma.
> Those who are great in true insight, whose minds are governed
>   by pity,
> Heed not the ill that befalls them, but that which troubles their
>   fellows.
> But the king, having done this terrible deed, forthwith succumbed
>   to a violent fever;
> He rushed from the garden, and the great earth, opening wide,
>   devoured him.

The best of Sages, however, who, thanks to his reliance on
forbearance, had throughout remained firm and unshaken in
his fortitude, ascended to heaven, as a temporary reward for
his patience.

3. OUTLINE OF A BODHISATTVA'S PROGRESS

The disciples of Katyayaniputra in their Abhidharma teach as
follows:

Q: What is a Bodhisattva?

A. Someone is called a Bodhisattva if he is certain to become a Buddha, a 'Buddha' being a man who has first enlightened himself and will thereafter enlighten others. The word
'Bodhi' refers here to that wisdom of holy men which has
reached the stage where the Outflows have dried up. A 'Bodhi-
being' is a being who is born of that wisdom, and is protected
and served by the wise.

The question now arises from what date onward he can

justifiably be called a 'Bodhisattva'. This change from an ordinary being to a Bodhi-being takes place when his mind has reached the stage when it can no longer turn back on enlightenment. Also, he has by then gained five advantages: he is no more reborn in the States of woe, but always among gods and men; he is never again born in poor or low-class families; he is always a male, and never a woman; he is always well-built, and free from physical defects; he can remember his past lives, and no more forgets them again.

Alternatively they teach that he deserves to be called a Bodhisattva from the time that he undertakes the deeds which lead to the production of the thirty-two marks of the super-man.

Q: When do these deeds take place?

A: After the three incalculable aeons which he has to go through first – in the aeons which follow on them.

Q: How long is an incalculable aeon?

A: 'Incalculable' is a number so high that neither human nor heavenly mathematicians can calculate it. It is, in any case, more than 10 followed by 27 noughts. In the first incalculable aeon he does not yet know whether he will become a Buddha, or not; in the second he knows he will be a Buddha, but does not dare to say so openly; in the third he knows for certain that one day he will be a Buddha, and fearlessly proclaims that fact to the world.

As for the Buddha Shakyamuni, in his first incalculable aeon he has honoured 75,000 Buddhas, beginning with the Buddha Maha-Shakyamuni and ending with Ratnashikhin. At the end of it the Bodhisattva was no more reborn as a woman. In his second incalculable aeon he honoured 76,000 Buddhas, the last of whom was Dipankara. At the end of it the Bodhisattva offered seven blue lotuses to the Buddha Dipankara, and protected him from the mud with the help of his antelope skin and his own hair. And the Buddha Dipankara on that occasion made this prediction: 'At a future time you will be a Buddha, by the name of Shakyamuni!' In the third incalculable aeon the Bodhisattva honoured 70,000 Buddhas, ending with Vipashyin. And after that, during the following hundred aeons he did the deeds which were later rewarded by the thirty-two Marks of the superman. Each one of these marks is due to a hundred acts of merit.

Q: How great is each of these (3,200) merits?

A: Some say that it equals the merit which gives a universal monarch his sovereignty over the four continents. Others say that it equals the merit which gave Shakra his sovereignty over the gods. Others say that it is as great as the merit which produces the happiness of all beings, with the exception of that of a Bodhisattva who is near enlightenment. Others again say that this merit is immeasurable, incalculable, and incomparable, and that only a Buddha can know it. Normally the Bodhisattvas take a hundred aeons to realize the thirty-two marks. Shakyamuni, however, succeeded in doing so after ninety-one aeons. During those ninety-one aeons, which go from the Buddha Vipashyin to the Buddha Kashyapa, he practised the six perfections.

Q: Which are these six perfections?

A: They are the perfections of giving, morality, patience, vigour, meditation, and wisdom. On numerous occasions the Bodhisattva gave away all he had, including his own body, without ever regretting it. As king Shibi he rescued a pigeon from a hawk, and to compensate the hawk joyfully gave him of his own flesh. He observed the moral rules, and lost his life rather than offend against them. This happened, for instance, when he was king Sutasoma, who kept his word to the Demon king, who had let him out on the promise that he would return. He showed his patience when he felt no ill-will whatsoever although men might insult, beat, or burn him, or cut him into pieces. When he was the Preacher of Patience, he remained inwardly unmoved when mutilated by the king's servants (as told on pp. 26–30). He also showed indefatigable energy, and the vigour of his mind never faltered. On one occasion, for instance, he praised the Buddha Pushya seven days and nights, standing on one leg and without moving his eye-lids. He became a master of all the trances. For instance, when he was the seer Shankhacarya his trance was so deep that his breath ceased to go in or out; his hair was then braided up like a conch shell, a bird laid her eggs in it, and the Bodhisattva deliberately remained immobile until the young could fly away. And finally his great mind became proficient in wisdom and attentive analysis. When he was the Brahmin Govinda, minister of a great king, he distributed after the king's death the kingdom evenly among his successors.

Under the Buddha Kashyapa the Bodhisattva, then called Jyotipala, led a religious life, strictly observed the moral rules, and as a result of his virtues was reborn in the Tushita heaven. There he decided on his last rebirth, and in due course descended from the Tushita heaven into his mother's womb.

CHAPTER 2

THE LEGEND OF THE BUDDHA
SHAKYAMUNI

We now come to the life of the 'historical Buddha', who is distinguished from other Buddhas as 'Shakya-muni', the 'Sage from the tribe of the Shakyas'. His biography, or legend, is an important constituent of Buddhist beliefs. It is curious that the canonical writings nowhere recount his life from birth to death. The first, and in many ways the finest, full-length biography is the work of the first century Indian poet Ashvaghosha. It is called the Buddhacarita, *or 'The Acts of the Buddha'.*

The first 13 cantos alone are preserved in Sanskrit; for the remaining 15 we must rely on the Tibetan translation, which I have consulted in Weller's edition, and the Narthang Tanjur of the India Office Library. The best English translation, which has superseded all the others, is that of E. H. Johnston (1936), though the second half is hidden away in a Danish periodical, the Acta Orientalia *(xv, 1937). The book's lengthy digressions are in keeping with Sanskrit poetical conventions. Canto v, for instance, describes in great detail the spectacle of the women sleeping in the palace, and Canto xii gives a valuable outline of the Samkhya system. I have condensed the whole into a manageable size, but have nearly always kept scrupulously to the author's words, though his way of expressing himself must strike our taste occasionally as rather artificial. The value of Ashvaghosha's account lies in its freedom from sectarian bias. Scholars still dispute which school he actually belonged to. I have concentrated on those scenes of the sacred drama which have impressed themselves most forcibly and extensively on the imagination of the Buddhist community, and which the art of Asia has over and over again depicted in stone, on silk and on canvas. To decide which of these events are credible or 'historical' was none of my functions, and would have been an unwarranted interference with the tradition.*

1. *The birth of the Bodhisattva*

There lived once upon a time a king of the Shakyas, a scion of the solar race, whose name was Shuddhodana. He was pure in conduct, and beloved of the Shakyas like the autumn-moon. He had a wife, splendid, beautiful, and steadfast, who was called the Great Maya, from her resemblance to Maya the Goddess. These two tasted of love's delights, and one day she conceived the fruit of her womb, but without any defilement, in the same way in which knowledge joined to trance bears fruit. Just before her conception she had a dream. A white king elephant seemed to enter her body, but without causing her any pain. So Maya, queen of that god-like king, bore in her womb the glory of his dynasty. But she remained free from the fatigues, depressions, and fancies which usually accompany pregnancies. Pure herself, she longed to withdraw into the pure forest, in the loneliness of which she could practise trance. She set her heart on going to Lumbini, a delightful grove, with trees of every kind, like the grove of Citraratha in Indra's Paradise. She asked the king to accompany her, and so they left the city, and went to that glorious grove.

When the queen noticed that the time of her delivery was approaching, she went to a couch overspread with an awning, thousands of waiting-women looking on with joy in their hearts. The propitious constellation of Pushya shone brightly when a son was born to the queen, for the weal of the world. He came out of his mother's side, without causing her pain or injury. His birth was as miraculous as that of Aurva, Prithu, Mandhatri, and Kakshivat, heroes of old who were born respectively from the thigh, from the hand, the head or the armpit. So he issued from the womb as befits a Buddha. He did not enter the world in the usual manner, and he appeared like one descended from the sky. And since he had for many aeons been engaged in the practice of meditation, he now was born in full awareness, and not thoughtless and bewildered as other people are. When born, he was so lustrous and stead-fast that it appeared as if the young sun had come down to earth. And yet, when people gazed at his dazzling brilliance, he held their eyes like the moon. His limbs shone with the radiant hue of precious gold, and lit up the space all around. Instantly he walked seven steps, firmly and with long strides. In that he was like the constellation of the Seven Seers. With the bearing of a lion he surveyed the four quarters, and spoke these words full of meaning for the future: 'For enlightenment I was born, for the good of all that lives. This is the last time that I have been born into this world of becoming.'

2. *Asita's visit*

Then Asita, the great seer, came to the palace of the ruler of the Shakyas, thirsting for the true Dharma. He knew of the birth of him who would put an end to birth, for in his trance he had perceived the miraculous signs which had attended it. In wonderment he looked upon the wondrous royal babe, and noticed that the soles of his feet were marked with wheels, that his fingers and toes were joined by webs, that a circle of soft down grew between his eyebrows, and that his testicles were withdrawn like those of an elephant. Lying on his nurse's lap the child seemed to Asita to be like Skanda, son of Agni, on the lap of his divine mother. With tears flickering on his eyelashes the seer sighed, and looked up to the highest heaven.

He then explained his agitation to the king in these words: 'It is not for him that I am perturbed, but I am alarmed because disappointed for myself. For the time has come when I must pass away, just when he is born who shall discover the extinction of birth, which is so hard to win. Uninterested in worldly affairs he will give up his kingdom. By strenuous efforts he will win that which is truly real. His gnosis will blaze forth like the sun, and remove the darkness of delusion from this world. The world is carried away in distress on the flooded river of suffering, which the foam of disease over-sprays, which has old age for its surge and rushes along with the violent rush of death: across this river he will ferry the world with the mighty boat of gnosis. The stream of his most excellent Dharma shall flow along with the current of wisdom, banked in by firm morality, cooled by Transic concentration, and holy works shall cover it like melodious ducks: the world of the living, tormented with the thirst of its cravings, will drink from this stream. To those who are tormented with pains and hemmed in by their worldly concerns, who are lost in the desert tracks of Samsara, he shall proclaim the path which leads to salvation, as to travellers who have lost their way. Creatures are scorched by the fire of greed, which feeds on sense-objects as its fuel: he will refresh them with the rain of the Dharma, which is copious like the rain from a mighty cloud when the summer's burning heat is over. With the irresistible hammer of the most excellent true Dharma he will break down the door which imprisons living beings with the bolt of craving and the panels of dark delusion, and thus he will enable them to escape. The world is entangled in the snares of self-delusion, it is overwhelmed by suffering, it has no refuge: after he has won full enlightenment this boy, then a king of Dharma, will free the world from its bonds.

'You, O king, have no reason to grieve for him. In this world of men we should grieve for those only who cannot hear this perfect Dharma, usually either because they are too deluded, or too intoxicated with sensuous pleasures. I myself fall short of the perfection required, and the final goal still eludes me. Through my proficiency in the trances I can take up my abode in the highest heaven. But even that I must regard as a misfortune, since I shall not be able to hear this Dharma.'

3. The Bodhisattva's youth and marriage

Queen Maya could not bear the joy which she felt at the sight of her son's majesty, which equalled that of the wisest seers. So she went to heaven, to dwell there. Her sister, his aunt, then brought up the prince as if he were her own son. And the prince grew up, and became more perfect every day.

His childhood passed without serious illness, and in due course he reached maturity. In a few days he acquired the knowledge appropriate to his station in life, which normally it takes years to learn. Since the king of the Shakyas had, however, heard from Asita, the great seer, that the supreme beatitude would be the prince's future goal, he tried to tie him down by sensual pleasures, so that he might not go away into the forest. He selected for him from a family of long-standing unblemished reputation a maiden, Yashodhara by name, chaste and outstanding for her beauty, modesty, and good breeding, a true Goddess of Fortune in the shape of a woman. And the prince, wondrous in his flashing beauty, took his delight with the bride chosen for him by his father, as it is told of Indra and Shaci in the Ramayana.

The monarch, however, decided that his son must never see anything that could perturb his mind, and he arranged for him to live in the upper storeys of the palace, without access to the ground. Thus he passed his time in the upper part of the palace, which was as brilliantly white as rain clouds in autumn, and which looked like a mansion of the Gods shifted to the earth. It contained rooms suited to each season, and the melodious music of the female attendants could be heard in them. This palace was as brilliant as that of Shiva on Mount Kailasa. Soft music came from the gold-edged tambourines which the women tapped with their finger-tips, and they danced as beautifully as the choicest heavenly nymphs. They entertained him with soft words, tremulous calls, wanton swayings, sweet laughter, butterfly kisses, and seductive glances. Thus he became a captive of these women who were well versed in the subject of sensuous enjoyment and indefatigable in sexual pleasure. And it did not occur to him to come down from the palace to the ground, just as people who in reward for their virtues live in a palace in heaven are content to remain there, and have no desire to descend to the earth.

In the course of time the fair-bosomed Yashodhara bore to the son of Shuddhodana a son, who was named Rahula. It must be remembered that all the Bodhisattvas, those beings of quite incomparable spirit, must first of all know the taste of the pleasures which the senses can give. Only then, after a son has been born to them, do they depart to the forest. Through the accumulated effects of his past deeds the Bodhisattva possessed in himself the root cause of enlightenment, but he could reach it only after first enjoying the pleasures of the senses.

4. *The awakening*

In the course of time the women told him how much they loved the groves near the city, and how delightful they were. So, feeling like an elephant locked up inside a house, he set his heart on making a journey outside the palace. The king heard of the plans of his dearly beloved son, and arranged a pleasure excursion which would be worthy of his own affection and royal dignity, as well as of his son's youth. But he gave orders that all the common folk with any kind of affliction should be kept away from the royal road, because he feared that they might agitate the prince's sensitive mind. Very gently all cripples were driven away, and all those who were crazy, aged, ailing, and the like, and also all wretched beggars. So the royal highway became supremely magnificent.

The citizens jubilantly acclaimed the prince. But the Gods of the Pure Abode, when they saw that everyone was happy as if in Paradise, conjured up the illusion of an *old man*, so as to induce the king's son to leave his home. The prince's charioteer explained to him the meaning of old age. The prince reacted to this news like a bull when a lightning-flash crashes down near him. For his understanding was purified by the noble intentions he had formed in his past lives and by the good deeds he had accumulated over countless aeons. In consequence his lofty soul was shocked to hear of old age. He sighed deeply, shook his head, fixed his gaze on the old man, surveyed the festive multitude, and, deeply perturbed, said to the charioteer: 'So that is how old age destroys indiscriminately the memory, beauty, and strength of all! And yet with such a sight before it the world goes on quite unperturbed. This being so, my son, turn round the horses, and travel back quickly to our palace! How can I delight to walk about in parks when my heart is full of fear of ageing?' So at the bidding of his master's son the charioteer reversed the chariot.

And the prince went back into his palace, which now seemed empty to him, as a result of his anxious reflections.

On a second pleasure excursion the same gods created a *man with a diseased body*. When this fact was explained to him, the son of Shuddhodana was dismayed, trembled like the reflection of the moon on rippling water, and in his compassion he uttered these words in a low voice: 'This then is the calamity of disease, which afflicts people! The world sees it, and yet does not lose its confident ways. Greatly lacking in insight it remains gay under the constant threat of disease. We will not continue this excursion, but go straight back to the palace! Since I have learnt of the danger of illness, my heart is repelled by pleasures and seems to shrink into itself.'

On a third excursion the same gods displayed a *corpse*, which only the prince and his charioteer could see being borne along the road. The charioteer again explained the meaning of this sight to the prince. Courageous though he was, the king's son, on hearing of death, was suddenly filled with dismay. Leaning his shoulder against the top of the chariot rail, he spoke these words in a forceful voice: 'This is the end which has been fixed for all, and yet the world forgets its fears and takes no heed! The hearts of men are surely hardened to fears, for they feel quite at ease even while travelling along the road to the next life. Turn back the chariot! This is no time or place for pleasure excursions. How could an intelligent person pay no heed at a time of disaster, when he knows of his impending destruction?'

5. Withdrawal from the women

From then onwards the prince withdrew from contact with the women in the palace, and in answer to the reproaches of Udayin, the king's counsellor, he explained his new attitude in the following words: 'It is not that I despise the objects of sense, and I know full well that they make up what we call the "world". But when I consider the impermanence of everything in this world, then I can find no delight in it. Yes, if this triad of old age, illness, and death did not exist, then all this loveliness would surely give me great pleasure. If only this beauty of women were imperishable, then my mind would certainly indulge in the passions, though, of course, they have their faults. But since even women attach no more value to their bodies after old age has drunk them up, to delight in them would clearly be a sign of delusion. If people, doomed to undergo old age, illness, and death, are carefree in their enjoyment with others who are in the same position, they behave like birds and beasts. And when you say that our holy books tell us of gods, sages, and heroes who, though high-minded, were addicted to sensuous passions, then that by itself should give rise to agitation, since they also are now extinct. Successful high-mindedness seems to me incompatible with both extinction and attachment to sensory concerns, and appears to require that one is in full control of one-self. This being so, you will not prevail upon me to devote myself to ignoble sense pleasures, for I am afflicted by ill and it is my lot to become old and to die. How strong and power-ful must be your own mind, that in the fleeting pleasures of the senses you find substance! You cling to sense-objects among the most frightful dangers, even while you cannot help seeing all creation on the way to death. By contrast I become frightened and greatly alarmed when I reflect on the dangers of old age, death, and disease. I find neither peace nor content-ment, and enjoyment is quite out of the question, for the world looks to me as if ablaze with an all-consuming fire. If a man has once grasped that death is quite inevitable, and if nevertheless greed arises in his heart, then he must surely have an iron will not to weep in this great danger, but to enjoy it.' This discourse indicated that the prince had come to a final decision and had combated the very foundations of sensuous passion. And it was the time of sunset.

6. *The flight*

Even amidst the allure of the finest opportunities for sen-suous enjoyment the Shakya king's son felt no contentment, and he could not regain a feeling of safety. He was, in fact, like a lion hit in the region of the heart by an arrow smeared with a potent poison. In the hope that a visit to the forest might bring him some peace, he left his palace with the king's consent, accompanied by an escort of ministers' sons, who were chosen for their reliability and their gift for telling entertaining stories. The prince rode out on the good horse Kanthaka, which looked splendid, for the bells of its bit were of fresh gold and its golden trappings beautiful with waving plumes. The beauties of the landscape and his longing for the forest carried him deep into the countryside. There he saw the soil being ploughed, and its surface, broken with the tracks of the furrows, looked like rippling water. The ploughs had torn up the sprouting grass, scattering tufts of grass here and there, and the land was littered with tiny creatures who had been killed and injured, worms, insects, and the like. The sight of all this grieved the prince as deeply as if he had witnessed the slaughter of his own kinsmen. He observed the ploughmen, saw how they suffered from wind, sun, and dust, and how the oxen were worn down by the labour of drawing. And in the supreme nobility of his mind he performed an act of supreme pity. He then alighted from his horse and walked gently and slowly over the ground, overcome with grief. He reflected on the generation and the passing of all living things, and in his distress he said to himself: 'How pitiful all this!'

His mind longed for solitude, he withdrew from the good friends who walked behind him, and went to a solitary spot at the foot of a rose-apple tree. The tree's lovely leaves were in constant motion, and the ground underneath it salubrious and green like beryl. There he sat down, reflected on the origination and passing away of all that lives, and then he worked on his mind in such a way that, with this theme as a basis, it became stable and concentrated. When he had won through to mental stability, he was suddenly freed from all desire for sense-objects and from cares of any kind. He had reached the first stage of trance, which is calm amidst applied and discursive thinking. In his case it had already at this stage a supramundane purity. He had obtained that concentration of mind which is born of detachment, and is accompanied by the highest rapture and joy, and in this state of trance his mind considered the destiny of the world correctly, as it is: 'Pitiful, indeed, that these people who themselves are helpless and doomed to undergo illness, old age, and destruction, should, in the ignorant blindness of their self-intoxication, show so little respect for others who are likewise victims of old age, disease, and death! But now that I have discerned this supreme Dharma, it would be unworthy and unbecoming if I, who am so constituted, should show no respect for others whose constitution is essentially the same as mine.' When he thus gained insight into the fact that the blemishes of disease, old age, and death vitiate the very core of this world, he lost at the same moment all self-intoxication, which normally arises from pride in one's own strength, youth, and vitality. He now was neither glad nor grieved; all doubt, lassitude, and sleepiness disappeared; sensuous excitements could no longer influence him; and hatred and contempt for others were far from his mind.

7. *The apparition of a mendicant*

As this understanding, pure and dustless, grew farther in his noble soul, he saw a man glide towards him, who remained invisible to other men, and who appeared in the guise of a *religious mendicant*. The king's son asked him: 'Tell me who you are', and the answer was: 'O Bull among men, I am a recluse who, terrified by birth and death, have adopted a homeless life to win salvation. Since all that lives is to extinction doomed, salvation from this world is what I wish, and so I search for that most blessed state in which extinction is unknown. Kinsmen and strangers mean the same to me, and greed and hate for all this world of sense have ceased to be. Wherever I may be, that is my home – the root of a tree, a deserted sanctuary, a hill or wood. Possessions I have none, no expectations either. Intent on the supreme goal I wander about, accepting any alms I may receive.' Before the prince's very eyes he then flew up into the sky. For he was a denizen of the heavens, who had seen other Buddhas in the past, and who had come to him in this form so as to remind him of the task before him.

When that being had risen like a bird into the sky, the best of men was elated and amazed. Then and there he intuitively perceived the Dharma, and made plans to leave his palace for the homeless life. And soon after returning to his palace he decided to escape during the night. The gods knew of his intention, and saw to it that the palace doors were open. He descended from the upper part of the palace, looked with disgust upon the women lying about in all kinds of disorderly positions, and unhesitatingly went to the stables in the outermost courtyard. He roused Chandaka, the groom, and ordered him quickly to bring the horse Kanthaka. 'For I want to depart from here to-day, and win the deathless state!'

8. *The dismissal of Chandaka*

They rode off, till they came to a hermitage, where the prince took off his jewels, gave them to Chandaka and dismissed him with this message to his father, king Shuddhodana: 'So that my father's grief may be dispelled, tell him that I have gone to this penance grove for the purpose of putting an end to old age and death, and by no means because I yearn for Paradise, or because I feel no affection for him, or from moody resentment. Since I have left for the homeless life with this end in view, there is no reason why he should grieve for me. Some day in any case all unions must come to an end, however long they may have lasted. It is just because we must reckon with perpetual separation that I am determined to win salvation, for then I shall no more be torn away from my kindred. There is no reason to grieve for me who have left for the homeless life so as to quit all grief. Rather should one grieve over those who greedily cling to those sensuous passions in which all grief is rooted. My father will perhaps say that it was too early for me to leave for the forest. But then there is no such thing as a wrong season for Dharma, our hold on life being so uncertain. This very day therefore I will begin to strive for the highest good – that is my firm resolve! Death confronts me all the time – how do I know how much of life is still at my disposal?'

The charioteer once more tried to dissuade the prince, and received this reply: 'Chandaka, stop this grief over parting from me! All those whom birth estranged from the oneness

The Legend of the Buddha Shakyamuni

of Dharma must one day go their separate ways. Even if
affection should prevent me from leaving my kinsfolk just
now of my own accord, in due course death would tear us
apart, and in that we would have no say. Just think of my
mother, who bore me in her womb with great longing and
with many pains. Fruitless proves her labour now. What am
I now to her, what she to me? Birds settle on a tree for a while,
and then go their separate ways again. The meeting of all
living beings must likewise inevitably end in their parting.
Clouds meet and then they fly apart again, and in the same
light I see the union of living beings and their parting. This
world passes away, and disappoints all hopes of everlasting
attachment. It is therefore unwise to have a sense of ownership
for people who are united with us as in a dream – for a short
while only, and not in fact. The colouring of their leaves is
connate to trees, and yet they must let it go; how much more
must this apply to the separation of disparate things! This
being so, you had better go away now, and cease, my friend,
from grieving! But if your love for me still holds you back,
go now to the king, and then return to me. And, please,
give this message to the people in Kapilavastu who keep their
eyes on me: "Cease to feel affection for him, and hear his
unshakeable resolve: 'Either he will extinguish old age and
death, and then you shall quickly see him again; or he will go
to perdition, because his strength has failed him and he could
not achieve his purpose'."'

9. The practice of austerities

From then onwards the prince led a religious life, and dili-
gently studied the various systems practised among ascetics
and yogins. After a time the sage, in search of a lonely retreat,
went to live on the bank of the river Nairañjana, the purity
of which appealed to that of his own valour. Five mendicants
had gone there before him to lead a life of austerity, in scrupu-
lous observance of their religious vows, and proud of their
control over the five senses. When the monks saw him there,
they waited upon him in their desire for liberation, just as the
objects of sense wait upon a lordly man to whom the merits

of his past lives have given wealth, and the health to enjoy
them. They greeted him reverently, bowed before him, followed his instructions, and placed themselves as pupils under
his control, just as the restless senses serve the mind. He, however, embarked on further austerities, and particularly on
starvation as the means which seemed most likely to put an
end to birth and death. In his desire for quietude he emaciated
his body for six years, and carried out a number of strict
methods of fasting, very hard for men to endure. At meal-
times he was content with a single jujube fruit, a single sesamum seed, and a single grain of rice – so intent he was on
winning the further, the unbounded, shore of Samsara. The
bulk of his body was greatly reduced by this self-torture, but
by way of compensation his psychic power grew correspond-
ingly more and more. Wasted away though he was, his glory
and majesty remained unimpaired, and his sight gladdened
the eyes of those who looked upon him. It was as welcome to
them as the full moon in autumn to the white lotuses that
bloom at night. His fat, flesh, and blood had all gone. Only
skin and bone remained. Exhausted though he was, his depth
seemed unexhausted like that of the ocean itself.

After a time, however, it became clear to him that this kind
of excessive self-torture merely wore out his body without
any useful result. Impelled both by his dread of becoming and
by his longing for Buddhahood, he reasoned as follows: 'This
is not the Dharma which leads to dispassion, to enlightenment,
to emancipation. That method which some time ago I found
under the rose-apple tree (see page 42), that was more certain
in its results. But those meditations cannot be carried out in
this weakened condition; therefore I must take steps to increase again the strength of this body. When that is worn
down and exhausted by hunger and thirst, the mind in its turn
must feel the strain, that mental organ which must reap the
fruit. No, inward calm is needed for success! Inward calm
cannot be maintained unless physical strength is constantly
and intelligently replenished. Only if the body is reasonably
nourished can undue strain on the mind be avoided. When the
mind is free from strain and is serene, then the faculty of Tran-

sic concentration can arise in it. When thought is joined to Transic concentration, then it can advance through the various stages of trance. We can then win the dharmas which finally allow us to gain that highest state, so hard to reach, which is tranquil, ageless, and deathless. And without proper nourishment this procedure is quite impossible.'

10. *Nandabala's gift*

His courage was unbroken, but his boundless intellect led him to the decision that from now on again he needed proper food. In preparation for his first meal he went into the Nairañjana river to bathe. Afterwards he slowly and painfully worked his way up the river bank, and the trees on the slope reverently bent low their branches to give him a helping hand. At the instigation of the deities, Nandabala, daughter of the overseer of the cowherds, happened to pass there, her heart bursting with joy. She looked like the foamy blue waters of the Yamuna river, with her blue dress, and her arms covered with blazing white shells. When she saw him, faith further increased her joy, her lotus eyes opened wide, she prostrated herself before him, and begged him to accept milk-rice from her. He did, and his meal marked the most fruitful moment of her life. For himself, however, he gained the strength to win enlightenment. Now that his body had been nourished, the Sage's bodily frame became fully rounded again. But the five mendicants left him, because they had formed the opinion that he had now quite turned away from the holy life – just as in the Samkhya system the five elements leave the thinking soul once it is liberated. Accompanied only by his resolution, he proceeded to the root of a sacred fig-tree, where the ground was carpeted with green grass. For he was definitely determined to win full enlightenment soon.

The incomparable sound of his footsteps woke Kala, a serpent of high rank, who was as strong as a king elephant. Aware that the great Sage had definitely determined on enlightenment, he uttered this eulogy: 'Your steps, O Sage, resound like thunder reverberating in the earth; the light that issues from your body shines like the sun: No doubt that you to-day will taste the fruit you so desire! The flocks of blue jays which are whirling round up in the sky show their respect by keeping their right sides towards you; the air is full of gentle breezes: It is quite certain that to-day you will become a Buddha.'

The Sage thereupon collected fresh grass from a grass cutter, and, on reaching the foot of the auspicious great tree, sat down and made a vow to win enlightenment. He then adopted the cross-legged posture, which is the best of all because so immovable, the limbs being massive like the coils of a sleeping serpent. And he said to himself: 'I shall not change this my position so long as I have not done what I set out to do!' Then the denizens of the heavens felt exceedingly joyous, the herds of beasts, as well as the birds, made no noise at all, and even the trees ceased to rustle when struck by the wind: for the Lord had seated himself with his spirit quite resolved.

11. *The defeat of Mara*

Because the great Sage, the scion of a line of royal seers, had made his vow to win emancipation, and had seated himself in the effort to carry it out, the whole world rejoiced – but Mara, the inveterate foe of the true Dharma, shook with fright. People address him gladly as the God of Love, the one who shoots with flower-arrows, and yet they dread this Mara as the one who rules events connected with a life of passion, as one who hates the very thought of freedom. He had with him his three sons – Flurry, Gaiety, and Sullen Pride – and his three daughters – Discontent, Delight, and Thirst. These asked him why he was so disconcerted in his mind. And he replied to them with these words: 'Look over there at that sage, clad in the armour of determination, with truth and spiritual virtue as his weapons, the arrows of his intellect drawn ready to shoot! He has sat down with the firm intention of conquering my realm. No wonder that my mind is plunged in deep despondency! If he should succeed in overcoming me, and could proclaim to the world the way to final beatitude, then my realm would be empty to-day, like that of the king of Videha of whom we hear in the Epics that he lost his kingdom because he misconducted himself by carrying off a Brahmin's daughter. But so far he has not yet won the eye of full knowledge. He is still within my sphere of influence. While there is time I therefore will attempt to break his solemn purpose, and throw myself against him like the rush of a swollen river breaking against the embankment!'

But Mara could achieve nothing against the Bodhisattva, and he and his army were defeated, and fled in all directions – their elation gone, their toil rendered fruitless, their rocks, logs, and trees scattered everywhere. They behaved like a hostile army whose commander had been slain in battle. So Mara, defeated, ran away together with his followers. The great seer, free from the dust of passion, victorious over darkness' gloom, had vanquished him. And the moon, like a maiden's gentle smile, lit up the heavens, while a rain of sweet-scented flowers, filled with moisture, fell down on the earth from above.

12. *The Enlightenment*

Now that he had defeated Mara's violence by his firmness and calm, the Bodhisattva, possessed of great skill in Transic meditation, put himself into trance, intent on discerning both the ultimate reality of things and the final goal of existence. After he had gained complete mastery over all the degrees and kinds of trance:

1. In the *first watch* of the night he recollected the successive series of his former births. 'There was I so and so; that was my name; deceased from there I came here' – in this way he remembered thousands of births, as though living them over again. When he had recalled his own births and deaths in all these various lives of his, the Sage, full of pity, turned his compassionate mind towards other living beings, and he thought to himself: 'Again and again they must leave the people they regard as their own, and must go on elsewhere, and that without ever stopping. Surely this world is unprotected and helpless, and like a wheel it turns round and round.' As he continued steadily to recollect the past thus, he came to the definite conviction that this world of Samsara is as unsubstantial as the pith of a plantain tree.

2. Second to none in valour, he then, in the *second watch* of the night, acquired the supreme heavenly eye, for he himself was the best of all those who have sight. Thereupon with the perfectly pure heavenly eye he looked upon the entire world, which appeared to him as though reflected in a spotless mirror. He saw that the decease and rebirth of beings depend on whether they have done superior or inferior deeds. And his compassionateness grew still further. It became clear to him that no security can be found in this flood of Samsaric existence, and that the threat of death is ever-present. Beset on all sides, creatures can find no resting place. In this way he surveyed the five places of rebirth with his heavenly eye. And he found nothing substantial in the world of becoming, just as no core of heartwood is found in a plantain tree when its layers are peeled off one by one.

3. Then, as the *third watch* of that night drew on, the supreme master of trance turned his meditation to the real and essential nature of this world: 'Alas, living beings wear themselves out in vain! Over and over again they are born, they age, die, pass on to a new life, and are reborn! What is more, greed and dark delusion obscure their sight, and they are blind from birth. Greatly apprehensive, they yet do not know how to get out of this great mass of ill.' He then surveyed the twelve links of conditioned co-production (see p. 187), and saw that, beginning with ignorance, they lead to old age and death, and, beginning with the cessation of ignorance, they lead to the cessation of birth, old age, death, and all kinds of ill.

When the great seer had comprehended that where there is no ignorance whatever, there also the karma-formations are stopped – then he had achieved a correct knowledge of all there is to be known, and he stood out in the world as a Buddha. He passed through the eight stages of Transic insight, and quickly reached their highest point. From the summit of the world downwards he could detect no self anywhere. Like the fire, when its fuel is burnt up, he became tranquil. He had reached perfection, and he thought to himself: 'This is the authentic Way on which in the past so many great seers, who also knew all higher and all lower things, have travelled on to ultimate and real truth. And now I have obtained it!'

4. At that moment, in the *fourth watch* of the night, when dawn broke and all the ghosts that move and those that move not went to rest, the great seer took up the position which knows no more alteration, and the leader of all reached the state of all-knowledge. When, through his Buddhahood, he had cognized this fact, the earth swayed like a woman drunken with wine, the sky shone bright with the Siddhas who appeared in crowds in all the directions, and the mighty drums of thunder resounded through the air. Pleasant breezes blew softly, rain fell from a cloudless sky, flowers and fruits dropped from the trees out of season – in an effort, as it were, to show reverence for him. Mandarava flowers and lotus blossoms, and also water lilies made of gold and beryl, fell from the sky on to the ground near the Shakya sage, so that it looked like a place in the world of the gods. At that moment no one anywhere was angry, ill, or sad; no one did evil, none was proud; the world became quite quiet, as though it had reached full perfection. Joy spread through the ranks of those gods who longed for salvation; joy also spread among those who lived in the regions below. Everywhere the virtuous were strengthened, the influence of Dharma increased, and the world rose from the dirt of the passions and the darkness of ignorance. Filled with joy and wonder at the Sage's work, the seers of the solar race who had been protectors of men, who had been royal seers, who had been great seers, stood in their mansions in the heavens and showed him their reverence. The great seers among the hosts of invisible beings could be heard widely proclaiming his fame. All living things rejoiced and sensed that things went well. Mara alone felt deep displeasure, as though subjected to a sudden fall.

For seven days He dwelt there – his body gave him no trouble, his eyes never closed, and he looked into his own mind. He thought: 'Here I have found freedom', and he knew that the longings of his heart had at last come to fulfilment. Now that he had grasped the principle of causation, and finally convinced himself of the lack of self in all that is, he roused himself again from his deep trance, and in his great compassion he surveyed the world with his Buddha-eye, intent on giving it peace. When, however, he saw on the one side the world lost in low views and confused efforts, thickly covered with the dirt of the passions, and saw on the other side the exceeding subtlety of the Dharma of emancipation, he felt inclined to take no action. But when he weighed up the significance of the pledge to enlighten all beings he had taken in the past, he became again more favourable to the idea of proclaiming the path to Peace. Reflecting in his mind on this question, he also considered that, while some people have a great deal of passion, others have but little. As soon as Indra and Brahma, the two chiefs of those who dwell in the heavens, had grasped the Sugata's intention to proclaim the path to Peace, they shone brightly and came up to him, the weal of the world their concern. He remained there on his seat, free from all evil and successful in his aim. The most excellent Dharma which he had seen was his most excellent companion. His two visitors gently and reverently spoke to him these words, which were meant for the weal of the world: 'Please do not condemn all those that live as unworthy of such treasure! Oh, please engender pity in your heart for beings in this world! So varied is their endowment, and while some have much passion, others have only very little. Now that you, O Sage, have yourself crossed the ocean of the world of becoming, please rescue also the other living beings who have sunk so deep into suffering! As a generous lord shares his wealth, so may also you bestow your own virtues on others! Most of those who know what for them is good in this world and the next, act only for their own advantage. In the world of men and in heaven it is hard to find anyone who is impelled by concern for the weal of the world.' Having made this request to the great seer, the two gods returned to their celestial abode by the way they had come. And the sage pondered over their words. In consequence he was confirmed in his decision to set the world free.

Then came the time for the alms-round, and the World-Guardians of the four quarters presented the seer with begging-bowls. Gautama accepted the four, but for the sake of his Dharma he turned them into one. At that time two merchants of a passing caravan came that way. Instigated by a friendly deity, they joyfully saluted the seer, and, elated in their hearts, gave him alms. They were the first to do so.

After that the sage saw that Arada and Udraka Ramaputra were the two people best equipped to grasp the Dharma. But then he saw that both had gone to live among the gods in heaven. His mind thereupon turned to the five mendicants. In order to proclaim the path to Peace, thereby dispelling the darkness of ignorance, just as the rising sun conquers the darkness of night, Gautama betook himself to the blessed city of Kashi, to which Bhimaratha gave his love, and which is adorned with the Varanasi river and with many splendid forests. Then, before he carried out his wish to go into the region of Kashi, the Sage, whose eyes were like those of a bull, and whose gait like that of an elephant in rut, once more fixed his steady gaze on the root of the Bodhi-tree, after he had turned his entire body like an elephant.

13. *The meeting with the mendicant*

He had fulfilled his task, and now, calm and majestic, went on alone, though it seemed that a large retinue accompanied him. A mendicant, intent on Dharma, saw him on the road, and in wonderment folded his hands and said to him: 'The senses of others are restless like horses, but yours have been tamed. Other beings are passionate, but your passions have ceased. Your form shines like the moon in the night-sky, and you appear to be refreshed by the sweet savour of a wisdom newly tasted. Your features shine with intellectual power, you have become master over your senses, and you have the eyes of a mighty bull. No doubt that you have achieved your aim. Who then is your teacher, who has taught you this supreme felicity?' But he replied: 'No teacher have I. None need I venerate, and none must I despise. Nirvana have I now obtained, and I am not the same as others are. Quite by myself, you see, have I the Dharma won. Completely have I understood what must be understood, though others failed to understand it. That is the reason why I am a Buddha. The hostile forces of defilement I have vanquished. That is the reason why I should be known as one whose self is calmed. And, having calmed myself, I now am on my way to Varanasi, to work the weal of fellow-beings still oppressed by many ills. There shall I beat the deathless Dharma's drum, unmoved by pride, not tempted by renown. Having myself crossed the ocean of suffering, I must help others to cross it. Freed myself, I must set others free. This is the vow which I made in the past when I saw all that lives in distress.' In reply the mendicant whispered to himself, 'Most remarkable, indeed!' and he decided that it would be better not to stay with the Buddha. He accordingly went his way, although repeatedly he looked back at Him with eyes full of wonderment, and not without some degree of longing desire.

14. *The meeting with the five mendicants*

In due course the Sage saw the city of Kashi, which resembled the interior of a treasury. It lies where the two rivers Bhagirathi and Varanasi meet, and, like a mistress, they hold it in their embrace. Resplendent with majestic power, shining like the sun, he reached the Deer Park. The clusters of trees resounded with the calls of the cuckoos and great seers frequented it. The five mendicants – he of the Kaundinya clan, Mahanaman, Vashpa, Ashvajit, and Bhadrajit – saw him from afar, and said to one another: 'There is our pleasure-loving friend, the mendicant Gautama, who gave up his austerities! When he comes to us, we must certainly not get up to meet him, and he is certainly not worth saluting. People who have broken their vows do not deserve any respect. Of course, if he should wish to talk to us, let us by all means converse with him. For it is unworthy of saintly people to act otherwise towards visitors, whoever they may be.' Although they had thus decided what to do, the mendicants, when the Buddha actually moved towards them, soon went back on their plans. The nearer he came, the weaker was their resistance. One of them took his robe, another with folded hands reached out for his alms-bowl, the third offered him a proper seat, and the two remaining ones presented him with water for his feet. By these manifold tokens of respect they all treated him as their teacher. But, as they did not cease calling him by his family name, the Lord, in his compassion, said to them: 'To an Arhat, worthy of reverence, you should not speak, O mendicants, in the same way as you did formerly, omitting the special veneration due to him! As for myself, praise and contempt are surely the same. But in your own interest you should be warned against behaving in a manner which will bring you harm. It is for the weal of the world that a Buddha has won enlightenment, and the welfare of all that lives has been his aim. But the Dharma is cut off for those who slight their teacher by addressing him with his family name, for that is like showing disrespect for one's parents.' So spoke the great seer, the best of all speakers, filled with compassion. But, led astray by delusion and a deficiency in spiritual solidity, they answered him with a slight smile on their faces: 'Gautama, so far the supreme and most excellent austerities have not led you to an understanding of true reality! Only by them can the goal be achieved, but you dwell in sensuous comfort! What is your ground for saying to us that you have seen the truth?'

15. *Turning the wheel of Dharma*

Since the mendicants thus refused to believe in the truth found by the Tathagata, He, who knew the path to enlightenment to be different from the practice of austerities, expounded to them the path from his direct knowledge of it: 'Those foolish people who torment themselves, as well as those who have become attached to the domains of the senses, both these should be viewed as faulty in their method, because they are not on the way to deathlessness. These so-called austerities but confuse the mind which is overpowered by the body's exhaustion. In the resulting stupor one can no longer understand the ordinary things of life, how much less the way to the Truth which lies beyond the senses. The minds of those, on the other hand, who are attached to the worthless sense-objects, are overwhelmed by passion and darkening delusion.

They lose even the ability to understand the doctrinal treatises, still less can they succeed with the method which by suppressing the passions leads to dispassion. So I have given up both these extremes, and have found another path, a middle way. It leads to the appeasing of all ill, and yet it is free from happiness and joy.'

The Buddha then expounded to the five mendicants the holy eightfold path, and the four holy truths (see pp. 186–7).

'And so I came to the conviction that suffering must be comprehended, its cause given up, its stopping mastered, and this path developed. Now that I have comprehended suffering, have given up its cause, have realized its stopping, and have developed this path – now I can say that my organ of spiritual vision has been opened. As long as I had not seen these four divisions of the holy real truth, so long did I not claim to be emancipated, so long did I not believe I had done what was to be done. But when I had penetrated the holy truths, and had thereby done all that had to be done: then I did claim to be emancipated, then I did see that I had reached my goal.' And when the great seer, full of compassion, had thus proclaimed the Dharma, he of the Kaundinya clan, and hundreds of gods with him, obtained the insight which is pure and free from dust.

16. *The meeting of father and son*

In due course the Buddha went to Kapilavastu, and preached the Dharma to his father. He also displayed to him his proficiency in wonderworking power, thereby making him more ready to receive his Dharma. His father was overjoyed by what he heard, folded his hands, and said to him: 'Wise and fruitful are your deeds, and you have released me from great suffering. Instead of rejoicing at the gift of the earth, which brings nothing but sorrow, I will now rejoice at having so fruitful a son. You were right to go away and give up your prosperous home. It was right of you to have toiled with such great labours. And now it is right of you that you should have compassion on us, your dear relations, who loved you so dearly, and whom you did leave. For the sake of the world in distress you have trodden the path to supreme reality, which could not be found even by those seers of olden times who were gods or kings. If you had chosen to become a universal monarch, that could have given me no more joy than I have now felt at the sight of your miraculous powers and of your holy Dharma. If you had chosen to remain bound up with the things of this world, you could as a universal monarch have protected mankind. Instead, having conquered the great ills of the Samsaric world, you have become a Sage who proclaims the Dharma for the weal of all. Your miraculous powers, your mature intellect, your definite escape from the countless perils of the Samsaric world – these have made you into the sovereign master of the world, even without the insignia of royalty. That you could not have done if you had remained among the things of this world, and you would have been truly powerless, how ever much you had thrived as a king.'

17. *Further conversions*

After that the Buddha visited Shravasti, accepted the gift of the Jetavana Grove, admonished king Prasenajit, and exhibited his miraculous powers to confute the disputants of other schools. His miracles caused the people of Shravasti greatly to honour and revere him. He, however, departed from them, and rose in glorious majesty miraculously above the Triple world, reached the heaven of the Thirty-three where his mother dwelt, and there preached the Dharma for her benefit. His cognition enabled the Sage to educate his mother. He passed the rainy season in that heaven, and accepted alms in due form from the king of the gods who inhabit the ether. Then, descending from the world of the Gods, he came down in the region of Samkashya. The Gods, who by his presence had gained spiritual calm, stood in their mansions and followed him with their eyes. And the kings on earth raised their faces to the sky, bowed low, and received him respectfully.

After in heaven he had instructed his mother and those gods who desired to be saved, the Sage travelled over the earth, converting those who were ripe for conversion.

18. *Devadatta*

Devadatta, his cousin, and a member of the order of monks, saw His greatness and success, and was offended in his pride. His mind, so proficient in the trances, whirled round in a kind of delirium, he became quite frenzied and did many despicable things. He created a schism in the Sage's community, and the resulting separation further increased his ill-will. It was through him that on Vulture Peak a huge rock rolled down on the Sage with great force, but, though aimed at Him, it did not hit Him, but broke into two pieces before it could reach Him. On the royal highway he let loose a king elephant who rushed towards the Tathagata, with a noise like the thundering of the black clouds at the end of the world, and with the force of the wind in the sky on a dark moonless night. So the elephant rushed towards the Lord, murder in his heart, and the people wept and held up their arms. But without hesitating the Lord went on, collected and unmoved, and without any feeling of ill-will. His friendliness made him compassionate towards all that lives, and in addition he was protected by the gods who with devoted love followed close behind him. So even that great elephant could not touch the Sage, who calmly advanced on his way. The monks who followed the Buddha fled in haste even while the elephant was a long way off. Ananda alone stayed with the Buddha. But when the elephant had come quite near, the Sage's spiritual power soon brought him to his senses, inducing him to lower his body and place his head on the ground, like a mountain, the sides of which have been shattered by a thunderbolt. With the well-formed webbed fingers of his hand, beautiful and soft as a lotus, the Sage stroked the elephant's head, as the moon touches a cloud with its rays. But Devadatta, after he had in his malice done many wicked and evil deeds, fell to the regions below, detested by all alike, whether they were kings or citizens, Brahmins or sages.

19. *The desire for death*

Years later, the Lord was at Vaisali, on the bank of Markata's pool. He sat there under a tree, in shining majesty. Mara appeared in the grove, and said to him: 'Formerly, on the bank of the Nairañjana river, when I spoke to you immediately after your enlightenment, I said to you, O Sage: "You have done what there was to be done. Now enter the final Nirvana!" But you replied: "I shall not enter the final Nirvana until I have given security to the afflicted and made them get rid of their defilements." Now, however, many have been saved, others desire to be saved, others again will be saved. It is right therefore that now you should enter the final Nirvana.' On hearing these words, the supreme Arhat replied: 'In three months' time I shall enter the final Nirvana. Do not be impatient, and wait a while!' This promise convinced Mara that his heart's desire would soon be fulfilled. Jubilant and exulting, he disappeared.

Tathagatas have the power to live on to the end of the aeon. But the great Seer now entered into a trance with such a force of Yoga, that he gave up the physical life which was still due to him, and after that he continued to live on in a unique way for a while by the might of his miraculous psychic power. And at the moment that he gave up his claim to live to the end of the aeon, the earth staggered like a drunken woman, and in all directions great firebrands fell from the sky. Indra's thunderbolts flashed unceasingly on all sides, pregnant with fire and accompanied by lightning. Everywhere flames blazed up, as if the end of the world with its universal conflagration had come. Mountain tops toppled down and shed heaps of broken trees. There was the terrible sound of the heavenly drums thundering in the sky, like that of a cavern filled to the brim with wind. During this commotion which affected alike the world of men, the heavens and the sky, the great Sage emerged from his deep trance, and uttered these words: 'Now that I have given up my claim to live up to the end of the aeon, my body must drag itself along by its own power, like a chariot when the axle has been taken out. Together with my future years I have been set free from the bonds of becoming, as a bird which, on hatching, has broken through its shell.'

When Ananda saw the commotion in the world, his hair

stood on end, he wondered what it might be, trembled and lost his habitual serenity. He asked the omniscient one, who is experienced in finding causes, for the cause of this event. The Sage replied: 'This earthquake indicates that I have given up the remaining years of life still due to me. For three months only, reckoned from to-day, will I sustain my life.' On hearing this Ananda was deeply moved, and his tears flowed, as gum flows from a sandal tree when a mighty elephant breaks it down.

20. *The leave-taking from Vaisali, the final couch, instructions to the Mallas*

Three months later the great Sage turned his entire body round like an elephant, looked at the town of Vaisali, and uttered these words: 'O Vaisali, this is the last time that I see you. For I am now departing for Nirvana!' He then went to Kusinagara, bathed in the river, and gave this order to Ananda: 'Arrange a couch for me between those twin Sal trees! In the course of this night the Tathagata will enter Nirvana!' When Ananda had heard these words, a film of tears spread over his eyes. He arranged the Sage's last resting place, and then amid laments informed him that he had done so. In measured steps the Best of Men walked to his final resting place – no more return in store for him, no further suffering. In full sight of his disciples he lay down on his right side, rested his head on his hand, and put one leg over the other. At that moment the birds uttered no sound, and, as if in trance, they sat with their bodies all relaxed. The winds ceased to move the leaves of the trees, and the trees shed wilted flowers, which came down like tears.

In his compassion the All-knowing, when he lay on his last resting place, said to Ananda, who was deeply disturbed and in tears: 'The time has come for me to enter Nirvana. Go, and tell the Mallas about it. For they will regret it later on if they do not now witness the Nirvana.' Nearly fainting with grief, Ananda obeyed the order, and told the Mallas that the Sage was lying on his final bed.

The Mallas, their faces covered with tears, came along to

see the Sage. They paid homage to Him, and then, anguish in their minds, stood around Him. And the Sage spoke to them as follows: 'In the hour of joy it is not proper to grieve. Your despair is quite inappropriate, and you should regain your composure! The goal, so hard to win, which for many aeons I have wished for, now at last it is no longer far away. When that is won – no earth, or water, fire, wind or ether present; unchanging bliss, beyond all objects of the senses, a peace which none can take away, the highest thing there is; and when you hear of that, and know that no becoming mars it, and nothing ever there can pass away – how is there room for grief then in your minds? At Gaya, at the time when I won enlightenment, I got rid of the causes of becoming, which are nothing but a gang of harmful vipers; now the hour comes near when I get rid also of this body, the dwelling place of the acts accumulated in the past. Now that at last this body, which harbours so much ill, is on its way out; now that at last the frightful dangers of becoming are about to be extinct; now that at last I emerge from the vast and endless suffering – is that the time for you to grieve?'

So spoke the Sage of the Shakya tribe, and the thunder of his voice contrasted strangely with the deep calm with which He faced his departure. All the Mallas felt the urge to reply, but it was left to the oldest among them to raise his voice, and to say: 'You all weep, but is there any real cause for grief? We should look upon the Sage as a man who has escaped from a house on fire! Even the gods on high see it like that, how much more so we men! But that this mighty man, that the Tathagata, once He has won Nirvana, will pass beyond our ken – that is what causes us grief! When those who travel in a dreadful wilderness lose their skilful guide, will they not be deeply disturbed? People look ridiculous when they come away poor from a goldmine; likewise those who have seen the great Teacher and Sage, the All-seeing himself, in his actual person, ought to have some distinctive spiritual achievement to carry away with them!' Folding their hands like sons in the presence of their father, the Mallas thus spoke much that was to the point. And the Best of Men, aiming at their welfare and tranquillity, addressed to them these meaningful words: 'It is indeed a fact that salvation cannot come from the mere sight of Me. It demands strenuous efforts in the practice of Yoga. But if someone has thoroughly understood this my Dharma, then he is released from the net of suffering, even though he never cast his eyes on Me. A man must take medicine to be cured; the mere sight of the physician is not enough. Likewise the mere sight of Me enables no one to conquer suffering; he will have to meditate for himself about the gnosis I have communicated. If self-controlled, a man may live away from Me as far as can be; but if he only sees my Dharma then indeed he sees Me also. But if he should neglect to strive in concentrated calm for higher things, then, though he live quite near Me, he is far away from Me. Therefore be energetic, persevere, and try to control your minds! Do good deeds, and try to win mindfulness! For life is continually shaken by many kinds of suffering, as the flame of a lamp by the wind.' In this way the Sage, the Best of All those who live, fortified their minds. But still the tears continued to pour from their eyes, and perturbed in their minds they went back to Kusinagara. Each one felt helpless and unprotected, as if crossing the middle of a river all on his own.

21. *Parinirvana*

Thereupon the Buddha turned to his Disciples, and said to them: 'Everything comes to an end, though it may last for an aeon. The hour of parting is bound to come in the end. Now I have done what I could do, both for myself and for others. To stay here would from now on be without any purpose. I have disciplined, in heaven and on earth, all those whom I could discipline, and I have set them in the stream. Hereafter this my Dharma, O monks, shall abide for generations and generations among living beings. Therefore, recognize the true nature of the living world, and do not be anxious; for separation cannot possibly be avoided. Recognize that all that lives is subject to this law; and strive from to-day onwards that it shall be thus no more! When the light of gnosis has dispelled the darkness of ignorance, when all existence has been seen as without substance, peace ensues when life draws to an end, which seems to cure a long sickness at last. Everything, whether stationary or movable, is bound to perish in the end. Be ye therefore mindful and vigilant! The time for my entry into Nirvana has now arrived! These are my last words!'

Thereupon, supreme in his mastery of the trances, He at that moment entered into the first trance, emerged from it and went on to the second, and so in due order he entered all of them without omitting one. And then, when he had ascended through all the nine stages of meditational attainment, the great Seer reversed the process, and returned again to the first trance. Again he emerged from that, and once more he ascended step by step to the fourth trance. When he emerged from the practice of that, he came face to face with everlasting Peace.

And when the Sage entered Nirvana, the earth quivered like a ship struck by a squall, and firebrands fell from the sky. The heavens were lit up by a preternatural fire, which burned without fuel, without smoke, without being fanned by the wind. Fearsome thunderbolts crashed down on the earth, and violent winds raged in the sky. The moon's light waned, and, in spite of a cloudless sky, an uncanny darkness spread everywhere. The rivers, as if overcome with grief, were filled with boiling water. Beautiful flowers grew out of season on the Sal trees above the Buddha's couch, and the trees bent down over him and showered his golden body with their flowers. Like as many gods the five-headed Nagas stood motionless in the sky, their eyes reddened with grief, their hoods closed and their bodies kept in restraint, and with deep devotion they gazed upon the body of the Sage. But, well-established in the practice of the supreme Dharma, the gathering of the gods round king Vaishravana was not grieved and shed no tears, so great was their attachment to the Dharma. The Gods of the Pure Abode, though they had great reverence for the Great Seer, remained composed, and their minds were unaffected; for they hold the things of this world in the utmost contempt. The kings of the Gandharvas and Nagas, as well as the Yakshas and the Devas who rejoice in the true Dharma – they all stood in the sky, mourning and absorbed in the utmost grief. But Mara's hosts felt that they had obtained their heart's desire. Overjoyed they uttered loud laughs, danced about, hissed like snakes, and triumphantly made a frightful din by beating drums, gongs and tom-toms. And the world, when the Prince of Seers had passed beyond, became like a mountain whose peak has been shattered by a thunderbolt; it became like the sky without the moon, like a pond whose lotuses the frost has withered, or like learning rendered ineffective by lack of wealth.

22. *The Relics*

Those who had not yet got rid of their passions shed tears. Most of the monks lost their composure and felt grief. Those only who had completed the cycle were not shaken out of their composure, for they knew well that it is the nature of things to pass away. In due course the Mallas heard the news. Like cranes pursued by a hawk they quickly streamed forth under the impact of this calamity, and cried in their distress, 'Alas, the Saviour!' In due course the weeping Mallas, with their powerful arms, placed the Seer on a priceless bier of ivory inlaid with gold. They then performed the ceremonies which befitted the occasion, and honoured Him with many kinds of charming garlands and with the finest perfumes. After that, with zeal and devotion they all took hold of the bier. Slender maidens, with tinkling anklets and copper-stained finger-nails, held a priceless canopy over it, which was like a cloud white with flashes of lightning. Some of the men held up parasols with white garlands, while others waved white yaks' tails set in gold. To the accompaniment of music the Mallas slowly bore along the bier, their eyes reddened like those of bulls. They left the city through the Naga Gate, crossed the Hiranyavati river, and then moved on to the Mukuta shrine, at the foot of which they raised a pyre. Sweet-scented barks and leaves, aloewood, sandalwood, and cassia they heaped on the pyre, sighing with grief all the time. Finally they placed the Sage's body on it. Three times they tried to light the pyre with a torch, but it refused to burn. This was due to Kashyapa the Great coming along the road, Kashyapa whose mind was meditating pure thoughts. He longed to see the remains of the holy body of the departed Hero, and it was his magical power which prevented the fire from flaring up. But now the monk approached with rapid steps, eager to see his Teacher once more, and immediately he had paid his homage to the Best of Sages the fire blazed up of its own. Soon it had burnt up the Sage's skin, flesh, hair and limbs. But although there was plenty of ghee, fuel, and wind, it could not consume His bones. These were in due time purified with the finest water, and placed in golden pitchers in the city of the Mallas. And the Mallas chanted hymns of praise over them: 'These jars now hold the relics great in virtue, as mountains hold their jewelled ore. No fire harms these relics great in virtue; like Brahma's realm when all else is burned up. These bones, His friendliness pervades their tissue; the fire of passion has no strength to burn them; the power of devotion has preserved them; cold though they are, how much they warm our hearts!'

For some days they worshipped the relics in due form and with the utmost devotion. Then, however, one by one, ambassadors from the seven neighbouring kings arrived in the town, asking for a share of the relics. But the Mallas, a proud people and also motivated by their esteem for the relics, refused to surrender any of them. Instead, they were willing to fight. The seven kings, like the seven winds, then came up with great violence against Kusinagara, and their forces were like the current of the flooded Ganges.

Wiser counsels prevailed, and the Mallas devotedly divided into eight parts the relics of Him who had understood Life. One part they kept for themselves. The seven others were handed over to the seven kings, one to each. And these rulers, thus honoured by the Mallas, returned to their own kingdoms, joyful at having achieved their purpose. There, with the appropriate ceremonies, they erected in their capital cities Stupas for the relics of the Seer.

23. *The Scriptures*

In due course the five hundred Arhats assembled in Raja-griha, on the slope of one of its five mountains, and there and then they collected the sayings of the great Sage, so that his Dharma might abide. Since it was Ananda who had heard Him speak more often than anyone else, they decided, with the agreement of the wider Buddhist community, to ask him to recite His utterances. The sage from Vaideha then sat down in their midst, and repeated the sermons as they had been spoken by the Best of All speakers. And each one he began with, 'Thus have I heard', and with a statement of the time, the place, the occasion, and the person addressed. It is in this way that he established in conjunction with the Arhats the Scriptures which contain the Dharma of the great Sage. They have in the past led to Nirvana those who have made the effort fully to master them. They still to-day help them to Nirvana, and they will continue to do so in the future.

Part Two

DOCTRINES

CHAPTER I

MORALITY

The spiritual training of a Buddhist is divided into three parts, known respectively as morality, meditation, and wisdom. A morally blameless or virtuous life is the basis of all other achievements.

(1) The *minimum moral obligations of laymen and monks are summed up in the* Five Precepts, *which I have given here together with the explanation of one of the Pali commentaries, which reached their present shape in Ceylon at the time of Buddhaghosa, about* A.D. 400. (2) The *monks, in their turn, were subject to some 250 rules of monastic restraint, known as the* Pratimoksha rules, *of which we possess about a dozen different recensions. My selection is taken from the Book of Discipline of the Sarvastivadins, who were the most influential and widespread of the Indian schools. In any case, the different recensions agree on all essentials.* (3) *A more poetical description of the conditions of the* monk's *life has been added from the* Sutta Nipata, *a Pali work of great antiquity. Here I have been content to print E. M. Hare's translation from his* Woven Cadences of Early Buddhists *(1944). This is one of the finest pieces of Buddhist translation in English, and I cannot hope to improve on it.*

(4) *Behind the respect for the moral rules lies the awareness of the inexorable law of Karma, which rewards good deeds and punishes evil-doing. Enlightened self-interest should therefore prompt us to lead good lives. I have illustrated this side of the Buddhist respect for morality by two chapters, comprising thirty-nine verses, from the* Dharmapada, *one of the most revered collections of sacred verses. My translation follows the recension of the Sarvastivadins which was found some forty years ago in the sands of Turkestan. Fourteen of the verses occur also in the Pali* Dhammapada, *in practically identical words. Twenty-five are not found in the much better known Pali work.* (5) *In a still more popular form, these same principles were re-stated for Tibetans by an unknown lama of the Kahgyutpa sect, who wrote, perhaps in the eighteenth century, a poem on 'The Buddha's Law among the Birds', which is a fine example of popular moral*

Buddhism. *His book relates how the Bodhisattva Avalokiteshvara, who represents the principle of compassion, expounded in the form of a cuckoo the doctrine of the Buddha to the assembled birds of Tibet, who in their turn gave expression to as much of the teaching as they were able to grasp.*

(6) Finally, the fundamental division of the community into laymen and monks, according to their respective attainments and tasks, *can be clarified from the 'Questions of King Milinda'. From the second of these extracts it becomes clear that faith and devotion, in addition to morality, are the layman's special province. Generally speaking, the monks alone can hope to advance from morality to higher things, first to meditation, and then to wisdom.*

I. THE FIVE PRECEPTS

'I UNDERTAKE to observe the rule
    to abstain from taking life;
    to abstain from taking what is not given;
    to abstain from sensuous misconduct;
    to abstain from false speech;
    to abstain from intoxicants as tending to cloud the mind.'

The first four precepts are explained by Buddhaghosa as follows:

(1) 'Taking life' means to murder anything that lives. It refers to the striking and killing of living beings. 'Anything that lives' – ordinary people speak here of a 'living being', but more philosophically we speak of 'anything that has the life-force'. 'Taking life' is then the will to kill anything that one perceives as having life, to act so as to terminate the life-force in it, in so far as the will finds expression in bodily action or in speech. With regard to animals it is worse to kill large ones than small. Because a more extensive effort is involved. Even where the effort is the same, the difference in substance must be considered. In the case of humans the killing is the more blameworthy the more virtuous they are. Apart from that, the extent of the offence is proportionate to the intensity of the

wish to kill. Five factors are involved: a living being, the perception of a living being, a thought of murder, the action of carrying it out, and death as a result of it. And six are the ways in which the offence may be carried out: with one's own hand, by instigation, by missiles, by slow poisoning, by sorcery, by psychic power.

(2) 'To take what is not given' means the appropriation of what is not given. It refers to the removing of someone else's property, to the stealing of it, to theft. 'What is not given' means that which belongs to someone else. 'Taking what is not given' is then the will to steal anything that one perceives as belonging to someone else, and to act so as to appropriate it. Its blameworthiness depends partly on the value of the property stolen, partly on the worth of its owner. Five factors are involved: someone else's belongings, the awareness that they are someone else's, the thought of theft, the action of carrying it out, the taking away as a result of it. This sin, too, may be carried out in six ways. One may also distinguish unlawful acquisition by way of theft, robbery, underhand dealings, stratagems, and the casting of lots.

(3) 'Sensuous misconduct' – here 'sensuous' means 'sexual', and 'misconduct' is extremely blameworthy bad behaviour. 'Sensuous misconduct' is the will to transgress against those whom one should not go into, and the carrying out of this intention by unlawful physical action. By 'those one should not go into', first of all men are meant. And then also twenty kinds of women. Ten of them are under some form of protection, by their mother, father, parents, brother, sister, family, clan, co-religionists, by having been claimed from birth onwards, or by the king's law. The other ten kinds are: women bought with money, concubines for the fun of it, kept women, women bought by the gift of a garment, concubines who have been acquired by the ceremony which consists in dipping their hands into water, concubines who once carried burdens on their heads, slave girls who are also concubines, servants who are also concubines, girls captured in war, temporary wives. The offence is the more serious, the more moral and virtuous the person transgressed against.

71

Four factors are involved: someone who should not be gone into, the thought of cohabiting with that one, the actions which lead to such cohabitation, and its actual performance. There is only one way of carrying it out: with one's own body.

(4) 'False' – this refers to actions of the voice, or actions of the body, which aim at deceiving others by obscuring the actual facts. 'False speech' is the will to deceive others by words or deeds. One can also explain: 'False' means something which is not real, not true. 'Speech' is the intimation that that is real or true. 'False speech' is then the volition which leads to the deliberate intimation to someone else that something is so when it is not so. The seriousness of the offence depends on the circumstances. If a householder, unwilling to give something, says that he has not got it, that is a small offence; but to represent something one has seen with one's own eyes as other than one has seen it, that is a serious offence. If a mendicant has on his rounds got very little oil or ghee, and if he then exclaims, 'What a magnificent river flows along here, my friends!', that is only a rather stale joke, and the offence is small; but to say that one has seen what one has not seen, that is a serious offence. Four factors are involved: something which is not so, the thought of deception, an effort to carry it out, the communication of the falsehood to someone else. There is only one way of doing it: with one's own body.

'To abstain from' – one crushes or forsakes sin. It means an abstention which is associated with wholesome thoughts. And it is threefold: (I) one feels obliged to abstain, (II) one formally undertakes to do so, (III) one has lost all temptation not to do so.

(I) Even those who have not formally undertaken to observe the precepts may have the conviction that it is not right to offend against them. So it was with Cakkana, a Ceylonese boy. His mother was ill, and the doctor prescribed fresh rabbit meat for her. His brother sent him into the field to catch a rabbit, and he went as he was bidden. Now a rabbit had run into a field to eat of the corn, but in its eagerness to get there had got entangled in a snare, and gave forth cries of distress. Cakkana followed the sound, and thought: 'This rabbit has got caught there, and it will make a fine medicine for my mother!' But then he thought again: 'It is not suitable for me that, in order to preserve my mother's life, I should deprive someone else of his life.' And so he released the rabbit, and said to it: 'Run off, play with the other rabbits in the wood, eat grass and drink water!' On his return he told the story to his brother, who scolded him. He then went to his mother, and said to her: 'Even without having been told, I know quite clearly that I should not deliberately deprive any living being of life.' He then fervently resolved that these truthful words of his might make his mother well again, and so it actually happened.

(II) The second kind of abstention refers to those who not only have formally undertaken not to offend against the precepts, but who in addition are willing to sacrifice their lives for that. This can be illustrated by a layman who lived near Uttaravarddhamana. He had received the precepts from Buddharakkhita, the Elder. He then went to plough his field, but found that his ox had got lost. In his search for the ox he climbed up the mountain, where a huge snake took hold of him. He thought of cutting off the snake's head with his sharp knife, but on further reflection he thought to himself: 'It is not suitable that I, who have received the Precepts from the venerable Guru, should break them again.' Three times he thought, 'My life I will give up, but not the precepts!' and then he threw his knife away. Thereafter the huge viper let him go, and went somewhere else.

(III) The last kind of abstention is associated with the holy Path. It does not even occur to the Holy Persons to kill any living being.

2. RULES OF MONASTIC RESTRAINT

'Here, Venerable Gentlemen, are the four rules about the offences which deserve expulsion. They should be recited every fortnight in the *Pratimokshasutra*:

1. If a monk should have sexual intercourse with anyone,

down to an animal, this monk has fallen into an offence which deserves expulsion, and he should no longer live in the community. This holds good for any monk who has entered on a life based on a monk's training, unless he has thereafter repudiated the training, and declared his weakness.

2. If a monk, whether he dwells in a village or in solitude, should take anything not given, he should no longer live in the community. This, however, only applies to thefts for which a king or his police would seize a thief, and kill, imprison, banish, fine, or reprove him.

3. If a monk should intentionally take the life of a human being or of one like a human being, with his own hand, or with a knife, or by having him assassinated, then he has fallen into an offence which deserves expulsion. And this applies also to a monk who incites others to self-destruction, and who speaks to them in praise of death, with such words as, 'O man, what is the use to you of this miserable life? It is better for you to die than be alive!'

4. Unless a monk be actuated by excessive self-conceit, he commits an offence which deserves expulsion if, vainly and without basis in fact, he falsely claims to have realized and perceived superhuman states or the fullness of the insight of the Saints; and if later on, whether questioned or not, in his desire to get rid of his fault and regain his purity, he admits that he had claimed to have realized, without having done so, that he had claimed to have perceived, without having done so, and that he had told a falsehood and lie.

Venerable Gentlemen, the four offences leading to expulsion have been recited. A monk who has committed any of them should no longer live in the community. – Now, I ask you, Venerable Ones, 'Are you quite pure in this matter?' A second and a third time I ask, 'Are you quite pure in this matter?' The Venerable Ones keep silence. They are therefore quite pure in this matter. So I do take it to be.

Here, Venerable Gentlemen, are the thirteen offences which deserve suspension, and which should every fortnight be recited in the *Pratimokshasutra*. These forbid a monk:

1. Intentionally to emit his semen, except in a dream.

2. With a mind excited and perverted by passion to come into bodily contact with a woman; he must not hold her hand or arm, touch her hair or any other part of her body, above or below, or rub or caress it.

3. With a mind excited and perverted by passion to persuade a woman to sexual intercourse, speaking wicked, evil, and vulgar words, as young men use to their girls.

4. With a mind excited and perverted by passion, in the presence of a woman to speak highly of the merit of the gift of her own body, saying: 'That is the supreme service or gift, dear sister, to offer intercourse to monks like us, who have been observing strict morality, have abstained from intercourse and lived lovely lives!'

5. To act as a go-between between women and men, arranging marriage, adultery, or even a brief meeting.

6. To build for himself, without the help of a layman, a temporary hut on a site which involves the destruction of living beings and has no open space round it, and that without showing the site to other monks, and without limiting its size to the prescribed measurements.

7. To build for himself, with the help of a layman, a more permanent living place on a dangerous and inaccessible site, which involves the destruction of living beings and has no open space round it, and that without showing the site to other monks.

8. From anger, malice, and dislike to accuse falsely a pure and faultless monk of an offence which deserves expulsion, intent on driving him out of the religious life. That becomes an offence which deserves suspension if on a later occasion he withdraws his accusation, and admits to having spoken from hatred; and likewise if –

9. He tries to base his false accusation on some trifling matter or other which is really quite irrelevant.

10. To persist, in spite of repeated admonitions, in trying to cause divisions in a community which lives in harmony, and in emphasizing those points which are calculated to cause division.

11. To side with a monk who strives to split the community.

12. To refuse to move into another district when reproved by the other monks for habitually doing evil deeds in a city or village where he resides, deeds which are seen, heard, and known, and which harm the families of the faithful. This becomes an offence deserving suspension when the erring monk persistently answers back, and says: 'You, Venerable Monks, are capricious, spiteful, deluded, and over-anxious. For you now want to send me away, though you did not send away other monks who have committed exactly the same offence.'

13. To refuse to be admonished by others about the non-observance of the Pratimoksha rules.

These, Venerable Gentlemen, are the thirteen offences which deserve suspension. The first nine become offences at once, the remaining four only after the third admonition. The offending monk will first be put on probation, then for six days and nights he must do penance, and thereafter he must undergo a special ceremony before he can be rehabilitated. But he can be reinstated only by a community which numbers at least twenty monks, not one less.

'Now, three times I ask the Venerable Ones, "Are you quite pure in this matter?" The Venerable Ones keep silent. They are therefore quite pure in this matter. And so I take it to be.'

The recitation then continues to enumerate two sexual offences which are 'punishable according to the circumstances', and then thirty offences which 'involve forfeiture' of the right to share in garments belonging to the Order, and which expose one to an unfavourable rebirth. I am content to give four of these:

'It is an offence of this kind for a monk: (18) to accept gold or silver with his own hand, or get someone else to accept or hold it in deposit for him; (19) to buy various articles with gold and silver; (20) to engage in any kind of buying or selling; (29) to divert to himself goods which he knows that the donor had intended for the community.'

Next we come to the ninety offences which, unless repented of and expiated, will be punished by an unfavourable rebirth. I give eighteen of these:

'It is an offence of this kind for a monk: (1) knowingly to

tell a lie; (2) to belittle other monks; (3) to slander them;
(4) to reopen a dispute which he knows has already been
settled by the community in accordance with the monastic
rules; (5) to preach Dharma in more than five or six words to
a woman, except in the presence of an intelligent man; (6) to
teach Dharma word by word to an unordained person; (7) to
announce his superhuman qualities to an unordained person,
even though he may actually possess them; (8) to inform,
except by permission of the community, an unordained person
of a fellow-monk's grave offence; (11) to destroy any kind of
vegetation; (29) to sit alone with a woman in the open; (40)
to ask, when in good health, householders for delicacies like
milk, curds, butter, ghee, oil, fish, cooked or dried meat;
(45) to go to look at an army drawn up in battle-array, except
for a valid reason; (54) to lie down with an unordained person
for more than two nights in the same room; (59) to omit dis-
colouring his new robe with either dark-blue, dirt-coloured,
or black paint; (61) deliberately to deprive an animal of life;
(73) to dig the earth with his own hands, or have it dug, or
hint at the desirability of it being dug; (79) to drink alcoholic
beverages; (85) to have a chair or bed made with legs higher
than eight inches.'

The *Pratimoksha* then gives four offences requiring con-
fession, 113 rules of decorum, 7 rules for the settling of
disputes, and it concludes with a few verses claiming the
authority of the Buddhas for this text.

3. THE MONK'S LIFE

3a. The Buddha's advice to Sariputra

The monk alert, rapt farer on the edge,
Should have no fear of these five fears:
Gadflies and stinging bees and things that creep,
Attacks of men and of four-footed beasts.

Nor should he be afraid of others' views,
When the great perils of them he hath seen;
So should the expert seeker overcome
All other troubles that may here befall.

When stricken by disease or hunger's pangs,
Cold and excessive heat should he endure;
When stricken sore by them, that homeless man
Must stir up energy and strive with strength.

Let him not steal nor let him tell a lie,
Let him show amity to weak and strong;
And when he knows disquiet of the mind,
Let him expel that as dark Mara's gloom.

Nor must he fall a prey to wrath and pride,
But digging up their roots, let him stay poised;
And, as he wrestles, let him overcome
All that is dear to him, all that repels.

With joy in what is lovely, wisdom-led,
Let him then put to flight these troubles here,
Conquer dislike for his lone lodging place,
Conquer the four that cause him discontent:

'Alack! what shall I eat, and where indeed?
How ill I've slept! Where shall I sleep to-day?'
Whosoe'er trains and leads the homeless life
Must oust these thoughts that lead to discontent.

With food and clothing timely gotten, he
Must therein measure know for his content;
He, faring thus, restrained and curbed, would speak
In village no harsh words, tho' vexed indeed.

Then let him loiter not, but eyes downcast,
Be ever bent on musing, much awake;
Then let him strive for poise, intent-of-self
Cut doubt and hankering and fretful ways.

Alert, let him rejoice, when urged by words,
Break fallowness in fellow-wayfarers,
Utter in season due the expert word,
Not ponder on the views and talk of folk.

Alert, then let him train to discipline
Those things which are the five dusts in the world:
To conquer lust for forms and sounds and tastes,
To conquer lust for scents and things of touch.

When he hath disciplined desire for these,
Alert, with mind released in full, that monk
As studies he the thing aright, in time
Alone, uplifted, may the darkness rend.

Thus spake the Master.

3b. The Rhinoceros

Put by the rod for all that lives,
Nor harm thou any one thereof;
Long not for son – how then for friend?
   Fare lonely as rhinoceros.

Love cometh from companionship;
In wake of love upsurges ill;
Seeing the bane that comes of love,
   Fare lonely as rhinoceros.

In ruth for all his bosom-friends,
A man, heart-chained, neglects the goal:
Seeing this fear in fellowship,
   Fare lonely as rhinoceros.

Tangled as crowding bamboo boughs
Is fond regard for sons and wife:
As the tall tops are tangle-free,
   Fare lonely as rhinoceros.

The deer untethered roams the wild
Whithersoe'er it lists for food:
Seeing the liberty, wise man,
   Fare lonely as rhinoceros.

Free everywhere, at odds with none,
And well content with this and that:
Enduring dangers undismayed,
   Fare lonely as rhinoceros.

If one find friend with whom to fare,
Rapt in the well-abiding, apt,
Surmounting dangers one and all,
With joy fare with him mindfully.

Finding none apt with whom to fare,
None in the well-abiding rapt,
As rajah quits the conquered realm,
   Fare lonely as rhinoceros.

Gay pleasures, honeyed, rapturous,
In divers forms churn up the mind:
Seeing the bane of pleasure's brood,
   Fare lonely as rhinoceros.

'They are a plague, a blain, a sore,
A barb, a fear, disease for me!'
Seeing this fear in pleasure's brood,
   Fare lonely as rhinoceros.

The heat and cold, and hunger, thirst,
Wind, sun-beat, string of gadfly, snake:
Surmounting one and all of these,
   Fare lonely as rhinoceros.

As large and full-grown elephant,
Shapely as lotus, leaves the herd
When as he lists for forest haunts,
   Fare lonely as rhinoceros.

'Tis not for him who loves the crowd
To reach to temporal release:
Word of Sun's kinsman heeding right,
   Fare lonely as rhinoceros.

Leaving the vanities of view,
Right method won, the way obtained:
'I know! No other is my guide!'
   Fare lonely as rhinoceros.

Morality

Gone greed, gone guile, gone thirst, gone grudge,
And winnowed all delusions, faults,
Wantless in all the world become.
   Fare lonely as rhinoceros.

Play, pleasures, mirth and worldly joys,
Be done with these and heed them not;
Aloof from pomp and speaking truth,
   Fare lonely as rhinoceros.

Son, wife and father, mother, wealth,
The things wealth brings, the ties of kin:
Leaving these pleasures one and all,
   Fare lonely as rhinoceros.

They are but bonds, and brief their joys,
And few their sweets, and more their ills,
Hooks in the throat! - this knowing, sure,
   Fare lonely as rhinoceros.

With downcast eyes, not loitering,
With guarded senses, warded thoughts,
With mind that festers not, nor burns,
   Fare lonely as rhinoceros.

Shed thou householders' finery,
As coral tree its leaves in fall:
And going forth in yellow clad,
   Fare lonely as rhinoceros.

Crave not for tastes, but free of greed,
Moving with measured step from house
To house, support of none, none's thrall,
   Fare lonely as rhinoceros.

Rid of the mind's five obstacles,
Void of all stains whate'er, thy trust
In none, with love and hate cut out,
   Fare lonely as rhinoceros.

And turn thy back on joys and pains,
Delights and sorrows known of old;
And gaining poise and calm, and cleansed,
   Fare lonely as rhinoceros.

Astir to win the yondmost goal,
Not lax in thought, no sloth in ways,
Strong in the onset, steadfast, firm.
   Fare lonely as rhinoceros.

Neglect thou not to muse apart,
'Mid things by Dharma faring aye,
Alive to all becomings' bane,
   Fare lonely as rhinoceros.

Earnest, resolved for craving's end,
Listener, alert, not hesitant,
Striver, assured, with Dharma summed,
   Fare lonely as rhinoceros.

Like lion fearful not of sounds,
Like wind not caught within a net,
Like lotus not by water soiled,
   Fare lonely as rhinoceros.

As lion, mighty-jawed and king
Of beasts, fares conquering, so thou;
Taking thy bed and seat remote,
   Fare lonely as rhinoceros.

Poise, amity, ruth, and release
Pursue, and timely sympathy;
At odds with none in all the world,
   Fare lonely as rhinoceros.

And rid of passion, error, hate,
The fetters having snapped in twain,
Fearless whenas life ebbs away,
   Fare lonely as rhinoceros.

Folk serve and follow with an aim:
Friends who seek naught are scarce to-day:
Men, wise in selfish aims, are foul:
   Fare lonely as rhinoceros!

4. VERSES FROM THE SANSKRIT DHARMAPADA

4a. The chapter on Karma

1. A single rule you set aside, or lying words you speak,
   The world beyond you ridicule – no evil you won't do!

2. Better for you to swallow a ball of iron red-hot and flaming with fire,
   Than on the alms of the people to live, while immoral, indulgent, intemperate.

3. If it's suffering you fear, if it's suffering you dislike,
   Just do no evil deeds at all – for all to see or secretly.

4. Even a flight in the air cannot free you from suffering,
   After the deed which is evil has once been committed.

5. Not in the sky nor in the ocean's middle,
   Nor if you were to hide in cracks in mountains,
   Can there be found on this wide earth a corner
   Where karma does not catch up with the culprit.

6. But if you see the evil others do, and if you feel you disapprove,
   Be careful not to do likewise, for people's deeds remain with them.

7. Those who cheat in business deals, those who act against the Dharma,
   Those who swindle, those who trick – not only harm their fellow-men,
   They hurl themselves into a gorge, for people's deeds remain with them.

8. Whatever deeds a man may do, be they delightful, be they bad,
   They make a heritage for him; deeds do not vanish without trace.

9. A man will steal while profit seems to lie that way.
   Then others steal from him, and so the thief by thieving is undone.

10. The fool, while sinning, thinks and hopes, 'This never will catch up with me'.
    Wait till you're in the other world, and there the fate of sinners learn!

11. The fool, while sinning, thinks and hopes, 'This never will catch up with me'.
    But later on there's bitterness, when punishment must be endured.

12. The fool does evil deeds while unaware of what they lead to.
    By his own deeds the stupid man is burnt, as though burnt up
      by fire.

13. The fools, unwise, behave as though they were their own worst
      enemies,
    Committing many evil deeds which issue then in bitter fruits.

14. Not is an action called 'well done', which makes us suffer after-
      wards,
    Of which we reap the fruit in tears, with weeping, wailing and
      lament.

15. That action only is 'well done', which brings no suffering in
      its train,
    Of which we reap the fruit quite glad, in happiness, with joyous
      heart.

16. In hot pursuit of their own joys they laugh when they do evil
      deeds.
    They'll weep with pain and misery, when they receive their
      punishment.

17. An evil deed need not at once cause trouble to the man who
      did it.
    It keeps up with the careless fool, just as a fire, smouldering
      under ashes.

18. Just like a new-forged blade the evil deed need not at once
      cause any wounds.
    Wait till you're in the other world, and there the fate of sinners
      learn!
    For later on there's bitterness, when punishment must be
      endured.

19. The iron itself createth the rust,
    Which slowly is bound to consume it.
    The evil-doer by his own deeds
    Is led to a life full of suffering.

4b. The chapter on Morality

1. If you want honour, wealth, or, after death, a blissful life among
     the gods,
   Then take good care that you observe the precepts of a moral
     life!

2. 3. The prudent man will lead a moral life
   When he considers it has four rewards:

A sense of virtue gives him peace,
His body is not over-taxed,
At night he sleeps a happy sleep,
And when he wakes, he wakes with joy.
A holy man, endowed with vision,
He thrives and prospers in this world.

4. How excellent a moral life pursued till death!
   How excellent a well-established faith!
   And wisdom is for men a treasure which brings merit,
   And which the thieves find very hard to steal.

5. The man of wisdom who did good,
   The man of morals who gave gifts,
   In this world and the next one too,
   They will advance to happiness.

6. 7. His moral habits planted firm, his senses well protected,
   In eating temperate, and to vigilance inclined,
   The monk who feels no weariness, and struggles day and night,
   His progress is assured, and he shall win Nirvana soon.

8. 9. His moral habits planted firm, his trance and wisdom first-rate,
   Unwearied, zealous, he shall gain, the end of ill for ever.
   Let him thus always moral be, preserve his meditation,
   And train his insight constantly, a man of thoughtful habits!

10. The wise, his fetters burst, the urge for further life exhausted,
    No more the prospect of rebirth for him at death, but full release.

11. The man whose moral habits, trances, wise reflections are full-grown,
    Secure for ever, pure and happy, he is then exempt from ever coming back again.

12. Free from his fetters, unattached, with perfect knowledge, without will to live,
    Raised high above the range of Mara's realms, he blazes radiant as the sun.

13. When a monk is full of himself, is heedless and given to things that are outside,
    He can never make progress in moral perfection, in trance or in wisdom.

14. Rain presses down on what is covered, but what is open lets it through;
    Uncover therefore what is covered, and so the rain will do no harm.

15. The wise will always carefully observe the moral rules,
    Thus clearing rapidly the path that to Nirvana leads them.

16. The scent of flowers travels with the wind,
    The scent of jasmine travels not against it.
    The odour of the good pervades in all directions,
    Their fragrance spreads, whatever be the wind.

17. Sandalwood or tagara scent, lotus flower or jasmine spray,
    Nobler than the perfume of all is the fragrance of virtuous lives.

18. Sandalwood or tagara shrubs, trifling the scent which they emit,
    Virtuous lives send their fragrance up high to the gods that are above.

19. If your morality is pure, if you are always wakeful and attentive,
    If you are freed by knowledge of the truth, then Mara cannot find you when you die.

20. This is the path which to safety leads,
    This is the path which brings purity.
    If you but tread it, and meditate,
    Then you'll escape from Mara's bonds!

5. POPULAR MORAL BUDDHISM

The Lord Buddha has said:

IN THE LANGUAGE OF ANGELS,

OF SERPENTS, OF FAIRIES,

IN THE SPEECH OF THE DEMONS,

THE TALK OF THE HUMANS,

IN THEM ALL I'VE EXPOUNDED

THE DHARMA'S DEEP TEACHINGS,

AND IN ANY TONGUE

THAT A BEING MAY GRASP THEM.

In order to teach the Dharma unto the feathered folk, the holy Lord Avalokita, who had transformed himself into a

Morality

Cuckoo, the great king of the birds, sat for many years day and night under a large sandalwood tree, immobile and in perfect trance.

One day Master Parrot came before the Great Bird, and addressed him, saying:

> Greetings, O great and noble bird!
> For one whole year, until to-day,
> You've sat there crouching, motionless,
> In the cool shade of a Santal tree.
> So silent, dumb and speechless;
> Does something anger or disturb your heart?
> When, O Great Bird, your trance has ended,
> Will you accept these seeds, the fine quintessence of all food?

And thus replied the Great Bird:

> Listen then, O parrot skilled in speech!
> I have surveyed this ocean of Samsara,
> And I have found nothing substantial in it.
> Down to the very last, I saw the generations die,
> They killed for food and drink – how pitiful!
> I saw the strongholds fall, even the newest,
> The work of earth and stones consumed – how pitiful!
> Foes will take away the hoarded spoils down to the very last,
> Oh to have avidly gathered this wealth, and hidden it – how
>   pitiful!
> Closest friends will be parted, down to the very last,
> Oh, to have formed those living thoughts of affection – how
>   pitiful!
> Sons will side with the enemy – even to the youngest,
> Oh to have given that care to those who were born of one's
>   body – how pitiful!
> Relatives united and intimate friends,
> Children reared, and riches stored,
> All are impermanent, like an illusion,
> And nothing substantial is found in them.
> My mind has now forsaken all activity.
> So that I may keep constant to my vows.
> Here, in the cool shade of a santal tree
> I dwell in solitude and silence,
> In trance I meditate, from all distractions far removed.

Go thou – repeat this speech of mine
To all large birds, and to all feathered creatures!

The Parrot, skilled in speech, then rose from the middle of
the ranks, and, swaying like a bamboo hurdle, saluted three
times and spoke as follows:

Greetings, you great and noble bird!
Though you are weary and disgusted with Samsara,
We beg you, give a little thought to us!
Ignorant and deluded creatures that we are;
The effects of many misdeeds in our past
Have tied us to this suffering, bound us, chained us.
We beg of you the good Dharma freeing us from suffering,
We beg the light dispelling all our ignorance,
We beg from you the Dharma – the cure of all defilements,
Birds of every kind assembled here,
We beg of you the good Dharma that we may ponder on it.

The Great Bird then spoke again as follows:

Smoke a sign of fire is,
The Southern cloud a sign of rain.
The little child will be a man,
The foal a stallion one day.

Deep thinking about death will lead to the unique and worthy
Dharma. The rejection of attachment to the wheel of Samsara, the
belief in the retribution of all deeds, mindfulness of the impermanence and mortality of this life – these are signs that we approach the
unique, worthy Dharma. O Birds assembled here, is there anything
of this nature in your minds? Tell me then your thoughts!

Thereupon the Golden Goose rose, shook his wings three
times, and said: *ṅaṅ stud ṅaṅ stud*, which means, *that prolongs
the bondage, that prolongs the bondage.*

To remain from birth to death without the Good Law – that
prolongs the bondage.
To desire emancipation, and still deserve a state of woe – that
prolongs the bondage.
To hope for miraculous blessings, and still have wrong opinions – that prolongs the bondage.

To neglect those things which turn the mind towards salvation – that prolongs the bondage.

To strive for purity of vision, and yet be blinded by a faulty judgement – that prolongs the bondage.

To give and yet be checked by meanness – that prolongs the bondage.

To aim at lasting achievements while still exposed to this world's distractions – that prolongs the bondage.

To try to understand one's inner mind while still chained to hopes and fears – that prolongs the bondage.

All you who thus prolong your bondage within this ocean of suffering,

Try to grasp the meaning of my words, for they will shorten your bondage.

Thereupon the Raven with his great wings rose, made a few sideways steps, and said: *grogs yoṅ grogs yoṅ*, which means, *help will come, help will come.*

When you have been true to your vows, help will come in the form of a happy life among men.

When you have given gifts, help will come in the form of future wealth.

When you have performed the acts of worship, help will come from the guardian angels.

When your solemn promises are made in all good faith, help will come from the love of the fairies.

When you are alert at the sacrificial festivals, help will come from the Guardians of the Dharma.

When in this life you learn to enter into higher meditation, help will come from the future Buddha.

Learn therefore to gain these virtues, for help comes through them.

Thereupon the Cock, the domestic bird, rose, flapped his wings three times, and said: *e go e go*, which means, *do you understand that? Do you understand that?*

Whilst you live in this samsaric world, no lasting happiness can be yours – do you understand that?

To the performance of worldly actions there is no end – do you understand that?

In flesh and blood there is no permanence – do you understand that?

The presence, at all times, of Mara, the Lord of Death – do you
understand that?

Even the rich man, when he is laid low, departs alone – do you
understand that?

He has no strength to take the wealth he gathered – do you
understand that?

Our bodies, so dear to us, will feed the birds and dogs – do
you understand that?

Wherever the mind may go, it cannot control its fate – do you
understand that?

We are bound to lose those we love and trust – do you understand that?

Punishment follows the evil we do – do you understand
that?

Wherever one looks, nothing is there substantial – do you
understand that?

Then from the centre of the ranks rose the Parrot, skilled
in speech, and said:

Listen, you beings of this samsaric world:
What you desire is happiness, what you find is grief.
While you inhabit a state of woe, salvation is not yet at hand.
Thinking on this must make me sad.
I now recall the good, the unique Law;
Hear it, you denizens of this samsaric world,
Perennial for time without beginning.
Because its benefits are so immense,
Let us here recall that unique Dharma:
'These ills in our state of woe are but the fruits of evil deeds,
The karmic outcome of your own accumulated acts;
For you and only you could make them.'
So now strip off the veil that clouds your thoughts:
This life, like dew on grass, is but impermanent,
And your remaining here for ever out of question.
So here and now, think on these things, and make your
effort!
'The pain from heat and cold in hell,
The hunger and the thirst which Pretas feel,
All are the fruits of evil deeds.' So has the Muni spoken.

Here, from within my heart, I make the vow
To shun all evil – to achieve the good.
From deep within my heart I seek my refuge
In the Three Treasures ever changeless,
Never failing, never fading,
Our precious ally through the whole of time.
In my mind, now free from doubt, is faith established.
Resolved to know the holy Dharma,
I now reject all things in this samsaric world.
And so, you great and noble bird,
We, this assembly, beg you grant us
Your esteemed instruction, teach us to understand the nature
    of all life!

So he spoke, and made three salutations.
Thereupon the Cuckoo, the Great Bird, spoke as follows:

Birds, large and small assembled here, well have you understood.
In all the speeches you have made not one has denied the truth.
Well have you spoken, well indeed! With undistracted mind keep
well these words within your hearts. And so, O birds assembled
here, the large birds and also the little youngsters lucky to be here,
hear me with reverence and attention!

    The things of this samsaric world are all illusion, like a
      dream.
    Where'er one looks, where is their substance?
    Palaces built of earth and stone and wood,
    Wealthy men endowed with food and dress and finery,
    Legions of retainers who throng round the mighty –
    These are like castles in the air, like rainbows in the sky.
    And how deluded those who think of this as truth!
    When uncles – nephews – brothers – sisters gather as kindred
      do,
    When couples and children gather as families do,
    When friends and neighbours gather in good fellowship –
    These are like meetings of dream friends, like travellers
      sharing food with strangers.
    And how deluded those who think of this as truth!
    This phantom body grown in uterine water from a union of
      seed and blood –
    Our habitual passions springing from the bad deeds of our
      past,

Our thoughts provoked by divers apparitions –
All are like flowers in autumn, clouds across the sky.
How deluded, O assembled birds, if you have thought of
    them as permanent.
The splendid plumage of the peacock with its many hues,
Our melodious words in which notes high and low are
    mingled,
The link of causes and effects which now have brought us
    here together –
They are like the sound of echoes, the sport of a game of
    illusion.
Meditate on this illusion, do not seize on them as truth!
Mists on a lake, clouds across a southern sky,
Spray blown by wind above the sea,
Lush fruits ripened by the summer sun –
In permanence they cannot last; in a trice they separate and
    fall away.
Meditate on their illusion, do not think of them as permanent!

When he finished speaking, the birds all rose with joy,
danced a while through the air, and sang their songs.

'*Happiness be yours and gladness too – may you prosper!*' said
the Great Bird, happy that he had come there. '*Cuckoo, cuckoo,*'
he sang, '*the light shed by the Dharma of the Birds brings me happiness. In joy and gladness leap and sway together in this graceful dance! Sing your songs and may you thrive!*'

'*May you prosper, may you prosper,*' he said, happy to be in
that plentiful land. '*Cuckoo, cuckoo,*' he sang, '*I am happy because the essence of the Dharma of the Birds has enriched you. In joy and gladness leap and sway together in this graceful dance! Sing your songs, and may you thrive!*'

'*Cu cu, ci ci,*' he said, glad that all these hosts of birds had
come together. '*Cuckoo, cuckoo,*' he sang, '*I am happy because I could give you the Dharma of the Birds. In joy and gladness leap and sway together in this graceful dance! Sing your songs, and may you thrive! Sing your happy songs which carry far! Dance your greatly joyful dance! Now you have won your hearts' desire.*'

All the birds sang happy songs, leapt up and danced with
gladness, and wished each other good fortune and abounding
joy. They then accompanied the Great Bird for one whole day,

and the Great Bird without mishap returned to India. On their way back, the birds of Tibet slept all together under a tree. The next day, when the sun of Jambudvipa rose, thrice they circled the tree where they had met, exchanged their hopes for another such joyful meeting, and each one, satisfied, returned on wings to his dwelling place.

6. LAYMEN AND MONKS

6a. Their respective attainments

King Milinda said: 'Venerable Nagasena, the Lord has said: "Right spiritual progress is praiseworthy for householders and homeless wanderers alike. Both householders and homeless wanderers, when progressing rightly, can accomplish, because of their right progress, the right method, the Dharma, that which is wholesome." If, Nagasena, a householder, dressed in white, enjoying the pleasures of the senses, inhabiting a house overcrowded with wife and family, using the sandalwood of Benares, as well as garlands, perfumes and unguents, owning gold and silver, wearing a turban ornamented with gold and jewels, can, if he progresses rightly, accomplish the right method, the Dharma, the wholesome; and if a homeless wanderer, bald-headed, clad in the saffron robe, dependent on begging for his livelihood, careful to fulfil correctly the four Sections of monastic morality, submitting to the 150 Patimokkha rules, and observing all the thirteen Austere Practices, without omitting any one, can also, if he progresses rightly, accomplish the right method, the Dharma, the wholesome; then, Venerable Sir, what is the difference between the householder and the homeless wanderer? Fruitless is your austerity, useless is the homeless life, barren is the observation of the Patimokkha rules, in vain do you observe the austere practices! What is the use of your inflicting pain upon yourself if you can thus while remaining at ease win the ease of Nirvana?'

Nagasena replied: 'You have quoted the Lord's words

correctly, your majesty. To make right progress is indeed the most excellent thing of all. And if the homeless wanderer, in the consciousness of being a homeless wanderer, should fail to progress rightly, then he would be far from the state of an ascetic, far from a holy life; and still more so would that apply to a householder dressed in white. But both the householder and the homeless wanderer are alike in that, when they progress rightly, they accomplish the right method, the Dharma, the wholesome. And nevertheless, your majesty, it is the homeless wanderer who is the lord and master of the ascetic life, and to be a homeless wanderer has many, has numerous, has infinite virtues. To measure the virtues of being a homeless wanderer is not at all possible. It is as with a jewel that fulfils all one's wishes; one cannot measure its value in terms of money, and say that it is worth so much. Or it is as with the waves in the great ocean, which one cannot measure and say that there are so many. All that the homeless wanderer still has to do, he succeeds in doing rapidly and without taking a long time over it. And why is that so? Because the homeless wanderer, your majesty, is content with little, easily pleased, secluded from the world, not addicted to society, energetic, independent, solitary, perfect in his conduct, austere in his practice, skilled in all that concerns purification and spiritual progress. He is like your javelin, your majesty. Because that is smooth, even, well polished, straight and shining clean, therefore, when well thrown, it will fly exactly as you want it to. In the same way, whatever the homeless wanderer still has to do, he succeeds in doing it all rapidly and without taking a long time over it.'

'Well spoken, Nagasena. So it is, and so I accept it.'

And Nagasena continued: 'But, in any case, your majesty, all those who as householders, living in a home and in the enjoyment of sensuous pleasures, realize the peace of Nirvana, the highest good, they have all been trained in their former lives in the thirteen Austere Practices peculiar to monks, and through them they have laid the foundations for their present sanctity. It is because then they had purified their conduct and behaviour by means of them, that now even as householders, living in a home and in the enjoyment of sense-pleasures, they can realize the peace of Nirvana, the highest good.

'But whosoever enters the Order of monks from bad motives, from covetousness, deceitfully, out of greed and gluttony, desirous of gain, fame, or reputation, unsuitably, unqualified, unfit, unworthy, unseemingly – he shall incur a twofold punishment, which will prove ruinous to all his good qualities: in this very life he shall be scorned, derided, reproached, ridiculed and mocked; he shall be shunned, expelled, ejected, removed, and banished. And in his next life, like foam which is tossed about, up and down and across, he shall cook for many hundreds of thousands of kotis of years in the great Avici hell, which is a hundred leagues big, and all ablaze with hot, scorching, fierce, and fiery flames. And when he has been released thence, his entire body will become emaciated, rough, and black, his head swollen, bloated and full of holes; hungry and thirsty, disagreeable and dreadful to look at, his ears all torn, his eyes constantly blinking, his whole body one putrid mass of sores and dense with maggots, his bowels all afire and blazing like a mass of fire fanned by a breeze, helpless and unprotected, weeping, crying, wailing, and lamenting, consumed by unsatisfied longings, he that once was a religious wanderer shall then, now a large Preta, roam about on the earth bewailing his fate.

'But if, on the other hand, a monk enters the Order suitably, qualified, fit, worthy and seemingly, content with little, easily pleased, secluded from the world, not addicted to society, energetic and resolute, without fraudulence and deceit, not gluttonous, not desirous of gain, fame, or reputation, devout and from faith, from a desire to free himself from old age and death and to uphold the Buddha's religion, then he deserves to be honoured in two ways by both gods and men. He is dear and pleasing to them, they love him and seek after him. He is to them as fine jasmine flowers are to a man bathed and anointed, or good food to the hungry, or a cool, clear, and fragrant drink to the thirsty, or an effective medicine to those who are poisoned, or a superb chariot drawn by thoroughbreds to those who want to travel fast, or a wishing jewel to those who want to enrich themselves, or a brilliantly white parasol, the emblem of royalty, to those who like to be kings, or as the supreme attainment of the fruit of Arhatship to those who wish for Dharma. In him the four applications of mindfulness reach their full development, the four right efforts, the four roads to psychic power, the five cardinal virtues, the five powers, the seven limbs of enlightenment, and the holy eightfold path; he attains to calm and insight, his progressive attainments continue to mature, and he becomes a repository of the four Fruits of the religious life, of the four Analytical knowledges, the three kinds of Knowledge, and the six Super-knowledges, in short, of the whole Dharma of the religious life, and he is consecrated with the brilliantly white parasol of emancipation.'

6b. *Their respective tasks, and the question of the adoration of relics*

King Milinda asked: 'The Tathagata has said: "Do not occupy yourselves, Ananda, with worshipping the bodily remains of the Tathagata!" And, on the other hand, we have been told:

> Worship the relics of Him who is worthy of worship!
> By doing so you'll go from here to paradise.

'Now if the first injunction were right, the second must be wrong, and if the second be right the first must be wrong. This is another dilemma, which I now put to you, and which you must solve.' Nagasena replied: 'The sentence, "Do not occupy yourselves, Ananda, with worshipping the bodily remains of the Tathagata!" was not addressed to everyone, but only to the Jina's sons, the monks. For worship is not their work. But the thorough understanding of all conditioned things, wise attention, the consideration of the applications of mindfulness, the seizing of the real essence of all objects of thought, the battle with the passions, and the pursuit of the highest good – that is what the Jina's sons have to do. Worship, however, is the task of the other gods and men. So, your majesty, it is the business of the princes of this earth to know all about elephants, horses, chariots, bows, swords, edicts, and seals, to be well versed in the textbooks of statecraft, in its tradition and customs, and to lead people into battle, whereas agriculture, trade, and the care of cattle are the tasks of other people, of ordinary traders, cultivators, and servants. The Tathagata therefore urged the monks to devote themselves to their own work, and not to that of others, when he said, "Do not occupy yourselves, Ananda, with worshipping the bodily remains of the Tathagata!" If the Tathagata had not said this, the monks might have taken his bowl and robe, and made it their business to worship the Buddha through them.'

'Very good, Nagasena. So it is, and so I accept it.'

CHAPTER 2

MEDITATION

In its insistence on morality, Buddhism is very much like most other religions. With Hindus, Taoists, Sufis, and Christian contemplatives the Buddhists share the belief that the higher spiritual life can be lived only in and through meditation.

(1) First of all I have given the twenty-eight advantages of meditation, *which Nagasena enumerates for King Menandros, so that the reader may get some idea of the benefits expected from this practice of quiet and abstracted musing, at first sight so barren and unprofitable. (2) Meditation differs from ordinary behaviour in that it implies a withdrawal from all outward activities and objects,* an extreme introversion, *which is held to open up a new world of reality beyond the ken of ordinary men. This attitude has been beautifully described by Shantideva, a Mahayana author of the seventh century, in his poem on the 'Practices of a Bodhisattva'. (3) The technical details of meditation do not fall within the scope of this book. The best textbook is Buddhaghosa's Path of Purification, of which a reliable translation by the Bhikkhu Nyanamoli has recently been published in Ceylon. On the other hand, it would be quite unthinkable to withhold all information about the practice of meditation, and I have again had recourse to a source intended for laymen. In Ashvaghosha's poem on 'Nanda the Fair' the Buddha explains to Nanda the more elementary stages of meditation in clear and easy terms. For the more advanced practices I must refer to Buddhaghosa, or to my own book on* Buddhist Meditation *(1956). (4) Not all kinds of meditation are equally salutary for everyone, and the psychological constitution of the disciple is important in his choice of a suitable subject. Recently there have been many attempts to divide people into types. It may be of interest to compare them with the division into* six types *which Buddhist tradition has adopted. I have followed here the 'Path to Purity' of Buddhaghosa, which has been my source also in the following extract (5), about the* five miraculous powers. *It is indeed a cherished belief among Buddhists that meditation not only widens the*

98

range of our spiritual awareness, but also adds one dimension or more to our actual existence, by awakening our psychic and supernatural gifts. These occult powers of the more advanced saints are a stock item of all Buddhist writing. In deference to the scepticism of the present age I have chosen a particularly sober and restrained account. Tibetan sources are more exuberant.

Finally, there is one development of meditation which has received so much attention in Europe that I cannot altogether pass it by. (6) It is the Zen, or Meditation, School. For the word 'Zen' (Chinese: Ch'an) comes from Sanskrit Dhyana, and simply means 'Meditation'. The two extracts I have given are Mr T. Leggett's translations of two essays by modern Japanese monks, the second being the Primate of the Soto sect. For Japanese Zen is divided into two main sects – Rinzai, which stresses the importance of wrestling with certain riddles, technically called koans, and Soto which does not. Soto, was introduced into Japan in 1127 by the Dogen mentioned on p. 138. The sentence on page 144, 'the practice is enlightenment' is one of the key phrases of the sect. The Buddha-nature is ever-present, not something to be attained or awaited, but only to be realized. The translations appeared first in Self-knowledge, *the quarterly journal of the Shanti Sadan, in 1957 (VIII, 1) and 1954 (V, 3). We will meet the Zen school twice again later on, once (II, 3, 5) in its formulation of wisdom, and then (II, 5, 4) in debate with other forms of wisdom-Buddhism.*

1. THE ADVANTAGES OF MEDITATION

SECLUDED meditation has many virtues. All the Tathagatas have won their all-knowledge in a state of secluded meditation, and, even after their enlightenment, they have continued to cultivate meditation in the recollection of the benefits it brought to them in the past. It is just as a man who has received some boon from a king, and who would, in recollection of the benefits he has had, remain also in the future in attendance on that king.

There are, in fact, twenty-eight advantages to be gained from secluded meditation, and they are the reason why the Tathagatas have devoted themselves to it. They are as follows:

secluded meditation guards him who meditates, lengthens his life, gives him strength, and shuts out faults; it removes ill-fame, and leads to good repute; it drives out discontent, and makes for contentment; it removes fear, and gives confidence; it removes sloth and generates vigour; it removes greed, hate, and delusion; it slays pride, breaks up preoccupations, makes thought one-pointed, softens the mind, generates gladness, makes one venerable, gives rise to much profit, makes one worthy of homage, brings exuberant joy, causes delight, shows the own-being of all conditioned things, abolishes rebirth in the world of becoming, and it bestows all the benefits of an ascetic life. These are the twenty-eight advantages of meditation which induce the Tathagatas to practise it.

And it is because the Tathagatas wish to experience the calm and easeful delight of meditational attainments that they practise meditation with this end in view. Four are the reasons why the Tathagatas tend meditation: so that they may dwell at ease; on account of the manifoldness of its faultless virtues; because it is the road to all holy states without exception; and because it has been praised, lauded, exalted, and commended by all the Buddhas.

2. THE PRACTICE OF INTROVERSION

With his vigour grown strong, his mind should be placed in
  samadhi;
For if thought be distracted we lie in the fangs of the passions.

No distractions can touch the man who's alone both in his body
  and mind.
Therefore renounce you the world, give up all thinking discursive!

Thirsting for gain, and loving the world, the people fail to renounce it.
But the wise can discard this love, reflecting as follows:

Through stillness joined to insight true,
His passions are annihilated.
Stillness must first of all be found.
That springs from disregarding worldly satisfactions.

Shortlived yourself, how can you think that others, quite as fleeting,
  are worthy of your love?
Thousands of births will pass without a sight of him you cherish so.

When unable to see your beloved, discontent disturbs your samadhi;
When you have seen, your longing, unsated as ever, returns as
  before.

Then you forfeit the truth of the Real; your fallen condition shocks
  you no longer;
Burning with grief you yearn for re-union with him whom you
  cherish.

Worries like these consume a brief life – over and over again to
  no purpose;
You stray from the Dharma eternal, for the sake of a transient
  friend.

To share in the life of the foolish will lead to the states of woe;
You share not, and they will hate you; what good comes from
  contact with fools?

Good friends at one time, of a sudden they dislike you,
You try to please them, quite in vain – the worldly are not easily
  contented!

Advice on their duties stirs anger; your own good deeds they
  impede;
When you ignore what they say they are angry, and head for a state
  of woe.

Of his betters he is envious, with his equals there is strife;
To inferiors he is haughty, mad for praise and wroth at blame;
Is there ever any goodness in these foolish common men?

Self-applause, belittling others, or encouragement to sin,
Some such evil's sure to happen where one fool another meets.

Two evils meet when fools consort together.
Alone I'll live, in peace and with unblemished mind.

Far should one flee from fools. When met, they should be won by
kindness,
Not in the hope of intimacy, but so as to preserve an even, holy,
mind.

Enough for Dharma's work I'll take from him, just as a bee takes
honey from a flower.
Hidden and unknown, like the new moon, I will live my life.

The fools are no one's friends, so have the Buddhas taught us;
They cannot love unless their interest in themselves impels them.

Trees do not show disdain, and they demand no toilsome wooing;
Fain would I now consort with them as my companions.

Fain would I dwell in a deserted sanctuary, beneath a tree, or in a
cave,
In noble disregard for all, and never looking back on what I left.

Fain would I dwell in spacious regions owned by no one,
And there, a homeless wanderer, follow my own mind,

A clay bowl as my only wealth, a robe that does not tempt the
robbers,
Dwelling exempt from fear, and careless of my body.

Alone a man is born, and quite alone he also meets his death;
This private anguish no one shares; and friends can only bar true
welfare.

Those who travel through Becoming should regard each incarna-
tion
As no more than a passing station on their journey through Samsara.

So will I ever tend delightful and untroubled solitude,
Bestowing bliss, and stilling all distractions.

And from all other cares released, the mind set on collecting my
own spirit,
To unify and discipline my spirit I will strive.

3. THE PROGRESSIVE STEPS OF MEDITATION

The restraint of the senses

By taking your stand on mindfulness you must hold back from the sense-objects your senses, unsteady by nature. Fire, snakes, and lightning are less inimical to us than our own senses, so much more dangerous. For they assail us all the time. Even the most vicious enemies can attack only some people at some times, and not at others, but everybody is always and everywhere weighed down by his senses. And people do not go to hell because some enemy has knocked them down and cast them into it; it is because they have been knocked down by their unsteady senses that they are helplessly dragged there. Those attacked by external enemies may, or may not, suffer injury to their souls; but those who are weighed down by the senses suffer in body and soul alike. For the five senses are rather like arrows which have been smeared with the poison of fancies, have cares for their feathers and happiness for their points, and fly about in the space provided by the range of the sense-objects; shot off by Kama, the God of Love, they hit men in their very hearts as a hunter hits a deer, and if men do not know how to ward off these arrows they will be their undoing; when they come near us we should stand firm in self-control, be agile and steadfast, and ward them off with the great armour of mindfulness. As a man who has subdued his enemies can everywhere live and sleep at ease and free from care, so can he who has pacified his senses. For the senses constantly ask for more by way of worldly objects, and normally behave like voracious dogs who can never have enough. This disorderly mob of the senses can never reach satiety, not by any amount of sense-objects; they are rather like the sea, which one can go on indefinitely replenishing with water.

In this world the senses cannot be prevented from being active, each in its own sphere. But they should not be allowed to grasp either the general features of an object, or its particularities. When you have beheld a sight-object with your eyes, you must merely determine the basic element (which it represents, e.g. it is a 'sight-object') and should not under any circumstances fancy it as, say, a woman or a man. But if now and then you have inadvertently grasped something as a 'woman' or a 'man', you should not follow that up by determining the hairs, teeth, etc., as lovely. Nothing should be subtracted from the datum, nothing added to it; it should be seen as it really is, as what it is like in real truth.

If you thus try to look continually for the true reality in that which the senses present to you, covetousness and aversion will soon be left without a foothold. Coveting ruins those living beings who are bent on sensuous enjoyment by means of pleasing forms, like an enemy with a friendly face who speaks loving words, but plans dark deeds. But what is called 'aversion' is a kind of anger directed towards certain objects, and anyone who is deluded enough to pursue it is bound to suffer for it either in this or a future life. Afflicted by their likes and dislikes, as by excessive heat or cold, men will never find either happiness or the highest good as long as they put their trust in the unsteady senses.

How the senses cause bondage

A sense-organ, although it may have begun to react to a sense-object, does not get caught up in it unless the mind conceives imaginary ideas about the object. Both fuel and air must be present for a fire to blaze up; so the fire of the passions is born from a combination of a sense-object with imaginations. For people are tied down by a sense-object when they cover it with unreal imaginations; likewise they are liberated from it when they see it as it really is. The sight of one and the same object may attract one person, repel another, and leave a third indifferent; a fourth may be moved to withdraw gently from it. Hence the sense-object itself is not the decisive cause of either bondage or emancipation. It is the presence or absence of imaginations which determines whether attachment takes place or not. Supreme exertions should therefore be made to bring about a restraint of the senses; for unguarded senses lead to suffering and continued becomings. In all circumstances you should therefore watch out for these enemies which cause so much evil, and you should always control them, i.e. your seeing, hearing, smelling, tasting, and touching. Do not be negligent in this matter even for a moment. The onrush of sense-experiences must be shut out with the sluice-gate of mindfulness.

Moderation in eating

Moreover you must learn to be moderate in eating, and eat only enough to remain healthy, and fit for trance. For excessive food obstructs the flow of the breath as it goes in and out, induces lassitude and sleepiness, and kills all valour. And as too much food has unfortunate consequences, so also starvation does not lead to efficiency. For starvation drains away the body's volume, lustre, firmness, performance, and strength. You should take food in accordance with your individual capacity, neither too much, nor, from pride, too little. As somebody with a running sore puts healing ointment on it, so the man who seeks liberation should use food only to remove his hunger. As the axle of a chariot must be lubricated so that it may work properly, so the wise man employs food only to maintain his life. He takes care of his body, and carries it along with him, not because he has any affection for it, but simply because it enables him to cross the flood of suffering. The spiritual man offers food to his body merely to dispel hunger, and not from greed, or from any love for it.

The avoidance of sleep

After he has passed his day in keeping his mind collected, the self-possessed man should shake off his sleepiness and spend also the night in the practice of Yoga. When threatened with sleepiness you should constantly mobilize in your mind the factors of exertion and fortitude, of stamina and courage. You should repeat long passages from the Scriptures which you know by heart, expound them to others and reflect on them yourself. In order to keep awake all the time, wet your face with water, look round in all directions and fix your eyes on the stars. With your senses turned inwards, unmoved and well-controlled, with your mind undistracted, you should walk about or sit down at night. Fear, zest, and grief keep sleepiness away; therefore cultivate these three when you feel drowsy. Fear is best fostered by the thought of death coming upon you, zest by thinking of the blessings of the Dharma, grief by dwelling on the boundless ills which result from birth. These, and similar steps, my friend, you should take to keep awake. For what wise man would not regret sleeping away his life uselessly? In fact a wise man, who wants to be saved from the great danger, would not want to go to sleep while ignoring his faults, which are like vicious snakes that have crept into a house. Who would think of lying down to sleep undisturbed when the whole living world is like a house on fire, blazing with the flames of death, disease, and old age? Therefore you should recognize sleep as a darkening of your mind, and it would be unworthy of you to become absorbed in it while your faults are still with you and threaten you like enemies with their swords. The first three of the nine hours of the night you should spend in strenuous activity; then only should you rest your body, and lie down to sleep, but without relaxing your self-control. With a tranquil mind you should lie on your right side, you should look forward to the time when you will wake up and when the sun will shine again. In the third watch you should get up, and, either walking or sitting, with a pure mind and well-guarded senses, continue your practice of Yoga.

Full awareness of the postures, etc.

You are further asked to apply mindfulness to your sitting, walking, standing, looking, speaking, and so on, and to remain fully conscious in all your activities. The man who has imposed strict mindfulness on all he does, and remains as watchful as a gatekeeper at a city-gate, is safe from injury by the passions, just as a well-guarded town is safe from its foes. No defilement can arise in him whose mindfulness is directed on all that concerns his body. On all occasions he guards his thought, as a nurse guards a child. Without the armour of mindfulness a man is an easy target for the defilements, just as on a battlefield someone who has lost his armour is easily shot by his enemies. A mind which is not protected by mindfulness is as helpless as a sightless man walking over uneven ground without a guide. Loss of mindfulness is the reason why people engage in useless pursuits, do not care for their own true interests, and remain unalarmed in the presence of things which actually menace their welfare. And, as a herdsman runs after his scattered cows, so mindfulness runs after all the virtues, such as morality, etc., wherever they can be found. The Deathless is beyond the reach of those who disperse their attention, but it is within the grasp of those who direct their mindfulness on all that concerns the body. Without mindfulness no one can have the correct holy method; and in the absence of the holy method he has lost the true Path. By losing the true Path he has lost the road to the Deathless; the Deathless being outside his reach, he cannot win freedom from suffering. Therefore you should superintend your walking by thinking 'I am walking', your standing by thinking 'I am standing', and so on; that is how you are asked to apply mindfulness to all such activities.

The advantages of solitary meditation

Then, my friend, you should find yourself a living-place which, to be suitable for Yoga, must be without noise and without people. First the body must be placed in seclusion; then detachment of the mind is easy to attain. But those who do not like to live in solitude, because their hearts are not at peace and because they are full of greed, they will hurt themselves there, like someone who walks on very thorny ground because he cannot find the proper road. It is no easier to deny the urges of a man who has not seen the real truth, and who finds himself standing in the fairground of the sensory world, fascinated by its brightness, than it is to deny those of a bull who is eating corn in the middle of a cornfield. A brightly shining fire, when not stirred by the wind, is soon appeased; so the unstimulated heart of those who live in seclusion wins peace without much effort. One who delights in solitude is content with his own company, eats wherever he may be, lodges anywhere, and wears just anything. To shun familiarity with others, as if they were a thorn in the flesh, shows a sound judgement, and helps to accomplish a useful purpose and to know the taste of a happy tranquillity. In a world which takes pleasure in worldly conditions and which is made unrestful by the sense-objects, he dwells in solitude indifferent to worldly conditions, as one who has attained his object, who is tranquil in his heart. The solitary man then drinks the nectar of the Deathless, he becomes content in his heart, and he grieves for the world made wretched by its attachment to sense-objects. If he is satisfied with living alone for a long time in an empty place, if he refrains from dallying with the agents of defilement, regarding them as bitter enemies, and if, content with his own company, he drinks the nectar of spiritual exultation, then he enjoys a happiness greater than that of paradise.

Concentration, and the forsaking of idle thoughts

Sitting cross-legged in some solitary spot, hold your body straight, and for a time keep your attention in front of you, either on the tip of the nose or the space on your forehead between the eyebrows. Then force your wandering mind to become wholly occupied with one object. If that mental fever, the preoccupation with sensuous desires, should dare to attack you, do not give your consent, but shake it off, as if it were dust on your clothes. Although, out of wise consideration, you may habitually eschew sense-desires, you can definitely rid yourself of them only through an antidote which acts on them like sunshine on darkness. There remains a latent tendency towards them, like a fire hidden under the ashes; this, like fire by water, must be put out by systematic meditation. As plants sprout forth from a seed, so sense-desires continue to come forth from that latent tendency; they will cease only when that seed is destroyed. When you consider what sufferings these sense-pleasures entail, by way of their acquisition, and so on, you will be prepared to cut them off at the root, for they are false friends. Sense-pleasures are impermanent, deceptive, trivial, ruinous, and largely in the power of others; avoid them as if they were poisonous vipers! The search for them involves suffering and they are enjoyed in constant disquiet; their loss leads to much grief, and their gain can never result in lasting satisfaction. A man is lost if he expect contentment from great possessions, the fulfilment of all his wishes from entry into heaven, or happiness from the sense-pleasures. These sense-pleasures are not worth paying any attention to, for they are unstable, unreal, hollow, and uncertain, and the happiness they can give is merely imaginary.

But if ill-will or the desire to hurt others should stir your mind, purify it again with its opposite, which will act on it like a wishing jewel on muddied water. Friendliness and compassionateness are, you should know, their antidotes; for they are forever as opposed to hatred as light is to darkness. A man who, although he has learned to abstain from overt immoral acts, still persists in nursing ill-will, harms himself by throwing dirt over himself, like an elephant after his bath. For a holy man forms a tender estimate of the true condition of mortal beings, and how should he want to inflict further suffering on them when they are already suffering enough from disease, death, old age, and so on? With his malevolent mind a man may cause damage to others, or he may not; in any case his own malevolent mind will be forthwith burned up. Therefore you should strive to think of all that lives with friendliness and compassion, and not with ill-will and a desire to hurt. For whatever a man thinks about continually, to that his mind becomes inclined by the force of habit. Abandoning what is unwholesome, you therefore ought to ponder what is wholesome; for that will bring you advantages in this world and help you to win the highest goal. For unwholesome thoughts will grow when nursed in the heart, and breed misfortunes for yourself and others alike. They not only bring calamities to oneself by obstructing the way to supreme beatitude, but they also ruin the affection of others, because one ceases to be worthy of it.

You must also learn to avoid confusion in your mental actions, and you should, my friend, never think even one single unwholesome thought. All the ideas in your mind which are tainted by greed, hate, and delusion deprive you of virtue and fashion your bondage. Delusion injures others, brings hardship to oneself, soils the mind, and may well lead to hell. It is better for you not to hurt yourself with such unwholesome thoughts! Just as an unintelligent person might burn precious aloe wood as if it were a piece of ordinary timber, so by not observing the correct method which leads to emancipation you would waste the rare opportunities offered by a human birth. To neglect the most excellent Dharma, and instead to think demeritorious thoughts, is like neglecting the jewels on a jewel-island and collecting lumps of earth instead. A person who has won existence as a human being, and who would pursue evil rather than good, is like a traveller to the Himalayas who would feed on deadly rather than on health-giving herbs. Having understood this, try to drive out disturbing thoughts by means of their appropriate antidotes, just as one pushes a wedge out of a cleft in a log with the help of a slender counter-wedge.

How to deal with thoughts concerning family and homeland

But if you start worrying about the prosperity or difficulties of your relatives, you should investigate the true nature of the world of the living, and these ideas will disappear again. Among beings whom their Karma drags along in the cycle of Samsara, who is a stranger, who a relation? Delusion alone ties one person to another. For in the past the person who is now one of your own people happened to be a stranger to you; in the future the stranger of to-day will be one of your own people. Over a number of lives a person is no more firmly associated with his own people than birds who flock together at the close of day, some here, some there. Relatives are no more closely united than travellers who for a while meet at an inn, and then part again, losing sight of each other. This world is by nature split up into disjointed parts; no one really belongs to anyone else; it is held together by cause and effect, as loose sand by a clenched fist. And yet, a mother will cherish her son because she expects that he will support her, and a son loves his mother because she bore him in her womb. As long as relatives agree with each other, they display affection; but disagreements turn them into enemies. We see relatives behave unkindly, while non-relatives may show us kindness. Men, indeed, make and break affections according to their interests. As an artist becomes enamoured of a woman he has himself painted, so the affection, which a person has for another with whom he feels at one, is entirely of his own making. As for him who in another life was bound to you by ties of kinship, and who was so dear to you then, what is he to you now or you to him? Therefore it is unworthy of you to allow your mind to become preoccupied with thoughts of your relatives. In the Samsaric world there is no fixed division between your own people and other people.

And if you should hit on the idea that this or that country is safe, prosperous, or fortunate, give it up, my friend, and do not entertain it in any way; for you ought to know that the world everywhere is ablaze with the fires of some faults or others. There is certain to be some suffering, either from the cycle of the seasons, or from hunger, thirst, or exhaustion, and a wholly fortunate country does not exist anywhere. Whether it be excessive cold or heat, sickness or danger, something always afflicts people everywhere; no safe refuge can thus be found in the world. And in all countries of the world people are greatly afraid of old age, disease, and death, and there is none where these fears do not arise. Wherever this body may go, there suffering must follow; there is no place in the world where it is not accompanied by afflictions. However delightful, prosperous, and safe a country may appear to be, it should be recognized as a bad country if consumed by the defilements. This world is smitten with countless ills, which affect both body and mind, and we cannot go to any country which is safe from them and where we can expect to live at ease.

Suffering is the lot of everyone, everywhere and all the time; therefore, my friend, do not hanker after the glittering objects of this world! And, once this hankering is extinct in you, then you will clearly see that this entire world of the living can be said to be on fire.

How to be mindful of death

But if you should make any plans that do not reckon with the inevitability of death, you must make an effort to lay them down again, as if they were an illness which attacks your own self. Not even for a moment should you rely on life going on, for Time, like a hidden tiger, lies in wait to slay the unsuspecting. There is no point in your feeling too strong or too young to die, for death strikes down people whatever their circumstances, and is no respecter of youthful vitality. The body we drag along with us is a fertile soil for all sorts of mishaps, and no sensible person would entertain any firm expectation of well-being or of life. Who could ever be free from cares as long as he has to bear with this body which, as a receptacle of the four great elements, resembles a pot full of snakes at war with each other? Consider how strange and wonderful it is that this man, on drawing in his breath, can immediately afterwards breathe out again; so little can life be trusted! And this is another strange and wonderful thing that, having slept, he wakes up again, and that, having got up, he goes to sleep again; for many are the adversities of those who have a body. How can we ever feel secure from death, when from the womb onwards it follows us like a murderer with his sword raised to kill us? No man born into this world, however pious or strong he be, ever gets the better of the King of Death, either now, or in the past or the future. For when Death in all its ferocity has arrived on the scene, no bargaining can ward him off, no gifts, no attempt at sowing dissension, no force of arms and no restraint. Our hold on life is so uncertain that it is not worth relying on. All the time Death constantly carries people away, and does not wait for them to reach the age of seventy! Who, unless he be quite mad, would make plans which do not reckon with death, when he sees the world so unsubstantial and frail, like a water bubble?

The four holy truths

Investigating the true nature of reality and directing his mind towards the complete destruction of the Outflows, the Yogin learns to understand correctly the four statements which express the four Truths, i.e. suffering, and the rest. First there is the ubiquitous fact of suffering, which can be defined as oppression; then the cause of suffering, which is the same as its origination; the extinction of suffering, which consists essentially in the definite escape from it; and finally the path which leads to tranquillity, and which has the essential function of saving. And those whose intellect has awakened to these four holy truths, and who have correctly penetrated to their meaning, their meditations shall overcome all the Outflows, they will gain the blessed calm, and no more will they be reborn. It is, on the other hand, through its failure to awaken to these four facts which summarize the essential nature of true reality, and through its inability to penetrate to their meaning, that the Samsaric world whirls round and round, that it goes from one becoming to another, and that it cannot win the blessed calm.

You should therefore, to explain it briefly, know with regard to the fact of ill, that birth is the basis of all the other misfortunes, like old age, and so on; for as all plants grow on the earth, so all calamities grow on the soil of birth. For the birth of a body endowed with sense-organs leads of necessity to manifold ills, and the production of a person's physical existence automatically implies that of death and sickness. As food, whether good or bad, far from sustaining us becomes merely destructive when mixed with poison, so all birth into this world, whether among animals, or above or below them, tends to ill and not to ease. The numerous afflictions of living beings, such as old age and so on, are unavoidably produced wherever there is Worldly Activity; but even the most frightful gales could not possibly shake trees that have never been planted. Where there is a body, there must also be such sufferings as disease, old age, and so on, and likewise hunger, thirst, wetness, heat, cold, etc. And the mind which is dependent on the body involves us in such ills as grief, discontent, anger, fear, etc. Wherever there is a psycho-physical organism, suffering is bound to take place; but for him who is liberated from it there can be no suffering, either now, or in the past, or the future.

And that suffering which we find bound up with Worldly Activity in this world is caused by the multitude of the defilements, such as craving, and the rest; but it is not due to a Creator, or Primordial Matter, or Time, or the Nature of things, or Fate, or Chance. And for that reason, i.e. because all Worldly Activity is a result of the defilements, we can be sure that the passionate and the dull will die, whereas those who are without passion and dullness will not be born again.

Therefore, once you have seen, my friend, that craving, etc., are the causes of the manifold ills which follow on birth, remove those causes if you want to be free from suffering; for an effect ceases when its cause has been stopped, and so also suffering becomes extinct when its cause has been quite exhausted. You must therefore come face to face with the holy, calm, and fortunate Dharma, which through dispassion has turned away from craving, which is the supreme place of rest, wherein all Worldly Activity is stopped, a shelter which abides eternally and which nothing can ever take away; that secure place which is final and imperishable, and where there is no birth, old age, death, or disease, no conjunction with unpleasant things, no disappointment over one's wishes, nor separation from what is dear. When the flame of a lamp comes to an end, it does not go anywhere down in the earth or up in the sky, nor into any of the directions of space, but because its oil is exhausted it simply ceases to burn. So, when an accomplished saint comes to the end, he does not go anywhere down in the earth or up in the sky, nor into any of the directions of space, but because his defilements have become extinct he simply ceases to be disturbed.

The wise man who wishes to carry out the sacred precepts of tradition should, as a means for the attainment of this Dharma, develop the eightfold Path – three of its steps, i.e. right speech, right bodily action, and right livelihood concern morality; three, i.e. right views, right intentions, and right effort concern wisdom; two again, i.e. right mindfulness and right concentration promote tranquillizing concentration. As a result of morality the defilements no longer proliferate, as seeds no longer germinate after the right season for them has passed; for when a man's morality is pure, the vices attack his mind but half-heartedly, as if they had become ashamed. Concentration, in its turn, blocks the defilements, as a rock blocks the torrent of a mighty river; for the faults are unable to attack a man who is absorbed in trance, as if they were spell-bound snakes immobilized by mantras. Wisdom, finally, completely destroys the defilements, as a river, which in the rainy season overflows its banks, sweeps away the trees that grow on them; consumed by wisdom, the faults cease to thrive and grow, like a tree burnt up by the fire which flares up after it has been struck by a thunderbolt. By entering on this eightfold path, which has morality, concentration, and wisdom for its three divisions, and which is holy, incorruptible, and straight, one forsakes those faults which are the causes of suffering, and one attains the state of absolute peace. Ten qualities are required of those who proceed along it: steadfastness, sincerity, self-respect, vigilance, seclusion from the world, contentment with little, simplicity of tastes, non-attachment, aversion to Worldly Activity, and patience. For he who discovers the true nature of ill, its origin and its cessation, can advance on the holy path, in the company of spiritual friends, towards Peace. It is like someone who correctly diagnoses a disease as a disease, and who correctly determines its cause and its cure; when treated by skilful friends he will soon be healthy again. You should therefore regard ill as a disease, the defilements as its cause, their cessation as the state of health, and the path as the remedy. What you must furthermore understand is that suffering is the same as Worldly Activity, and that it is kept going by the defilements; that their stopping is the same as inactivity, and that it is the path which leads to that. As though your turban or your clothes were on fire, so with a sense of urgency should you apply your intellect to the comprehension of the truths. It is because it fails to perceive the guidance given by these truths that the world of the living is being burnt alive. When therefore someone sees that his psycho-physical organism is something that ought to be extinguished, then he has the correct vision; in consequence of his correct insight he becomes disgusted with the things of the world; and as he is no longer drawn to them, his greed gradually exhausts itself. Solemnly I assure you that his mind is definitely liberated when passion and the hope of pleasure have become extinct; and that, once his mind is well freed of those two, there is nothing further that he has to do. For I proclaim it as a fact that the effective extinction of all the Outflows lies in seeing and discerning the own-being of the psycho-physical personality, its cause and its disappearance.

4. THE SIX TYPES OF PERSONS

Meditations should be appropriate to the character and temperament of those who undertake them. And six types of characteristic behaviour are here distinguished, due to:

Greed	Hate	Delusion
Faith	Intelligence	Discursiveness

Accordingly there are six kinds of persons: some dominated by greed, others by hate or delusion, others by faith, intelligence, or discursiveness.

Those who act from *faith* are akin to those who act from *greed*: for in people who are dominated by greed faith is bound to be strong at the time when they act in a wholesome way, because its qualities are similar to those of greed; as on the unwholesome plane greed clings, and takes no offence, so does faith on the wholesome plane. As greed seeks out the objects of sense-desire, so faith the virtues of morality, and so on. As greed does not let go that which is harmful, so faith that which is beneficial.

Those who act from *intelligence* are akin to those who act from *hate*: for in people who are dominated by hate wisdom is bound to be strong at the time when they act in wholesome ways, because its qualities are similar to those of hate; as on the unwholesome plane hatred does not cling, does not stick to its object, so wisdom on the wholesome plane. As hate seeks for faults, even though they do not exist, so wisdom seeks for the faults that do exist. As hate leads to the rejection of beings, so wisdom to that of all conditioned things.

Those who act from *discursiveness* are akin to those who act from *delusion*: for in people who are dominated by delusion, a great many obstructive thoughts usually arise whenever they strive to produce new wholesome states; this is because the characteristics of wholesome states, which have not yet arisen, are akin to delusion. As delusion is unsettled because of its complete confusion, so is reflection that is preoccupied with manifold topics. And as delusion is vacillating because unable to go deeply into anything, so is reflection that is due to facile surmise.

But how can it be known whether a given person is dominated by greed, or by hate, etc.? Here we have the rule that a person's disposition can be determined by (1) his postures; (2) his approach to what he has to do; (3) his attitude to food; (4) the way he looks at things; and (5) the kind of mental dharmas which are found in him.

1. As for the (four) *postures*: (a) The natural gait of someone who is dominated by greed is graceful; gently and evenly he puts down his foot, evenly he lifts it, and his step is springy. The hate-type walks as though digging up the ground with his toes; abruptly he puts down his foot, abruptly he lifts it up, and his step drags along. The delusion-type walks with a troubled gait; hesitantly he puts down his foot, hesitantly he lifts it, and the feet are pressed down rather hastily. (b) Now as to the way in which they stand – the greed-type looks pleasant and amiable, the hate-type stiff, the delusion-type bewildered. (c) The same applies to their sitting down. (d) The greed-type prepares his bed neatly and without haste, gently he lies down on it, curls himself up into a ball, and sleeps peacefully; when roused from his sleep he does not get up at once, and responds slowly, as though unwilling. The hate-type prepares his bed anyhow in great haste; he flings his body down on it to go to sleep with a furrowed brow; when roused from sleep he jumps up at once, and answers as though offended. The delusion-type spreads a badly shaped bed, and sleeps most of the time face downwards with his body sprawl-

ing; when roused he makes a grunting noise, and rises sluggishly.

2. As for their *approach to what they have to do*: when sweeping, the greed-type holds the broom just right, and makes a clean and even sweep, without hurrying or without strewing the sand all over the place; he behaves as if he were spreading out beautiful flowers from the Indus river. The hate-type energetically takes hold of the broom, and in great haste sweeps uncleanly and unevenly, making a harsh noise and piling up the sand on both sides. The delusion-type holds the broom loosely and sweeps uncleanly and unevenly, jumbling up the sand as it is turned over. As in sweeping, so in all his activities, such as washing and dyeing his robe, and so on, the greed-type is an elegant, graceful, even, and careful worker; the hate-type works roughly, stiffly, and unevenly; the delusion-type is a clumsy, confused, uneven, and inaccurate worker. They also differ in the manner in which they wear their robes: the greed-type wears it neither too tight nor too loose, he looks graceful in it, and covers the body all round; the hate-type wears it too tight, and without covering the body all round; the delusion-type wears it loosely and untidily.

3. Now about their *attitude to food*: the greed-type likes food fatty and sweet; when eating he rolls his food into lumps which are round and not too big, he eats slowly and pays attention to the taste of the food, and he is glad when he finds anything nice in his bowl. The hate-type likes rough and sour food; he eats hastily, stuffing his mouth full, and pays no attention to the taste of the food; when he finds anything unpleasant in his bowl, he feels annoyed. The delusion-type has no clear preference for any kind of food; when eating he rolls his food into small lumps which are not at all round, drops bits into his dish, and smears his mouth all over, his mind distractedly thinking of this and that.

4. Now about the *way they look at things*: when he sees something even moderately attractive, the greed-type looks at it for a long time, like one enchanted; he fastens on to its good points, however small they may be, and does not seize upon its faults, however real they may be; when walking on he

casts one last affectionate look upon it, as though he were loath to part from it. The hate-type, when he sees something even moderately unattractive, does not look at it for long, because of his general attitude of weariness; its faults, even though slight, strike him most forcibly, and he does not seize upon its good points, however real; when he walks on, he gives it no further consideration, as though glad to get away from it. In whatever the delusion-type sees, his reactions entirely depend on others: he finds fault when he hears them finding fault, he praises when he hears them praise; for he himself looks on with indifference, being deficient in intellectual power.

5. Finally, as to the kinds of *mental states* found in the various types. They are as follows:

Greed-type	*Hate-type*	*Delusion-type*
Deceit	Anger	Sloth
Craftiness	Grudges	Torpor
Conceit	Belittling the worth	Excitedness
Temptations	of others	Worry
Ostentatiousness	Imperiousness	Perplexity
Discontentedness	Envy	Obstinacy
Love of finery	Meanness	Tenacity
Fickleness		

Ruled by Faith	*Ruled by Intelligence*	*Ruled by Discursiveness*
Liberal generosity	Gentleness	Excessive talkativeness
Desire to see holy men	Capacity for friendship with wise men	Fondness for society
Desire to hear the true Dharma	Moderation in eating	Dislike for wholesome practices

Ruled by Faith	Ruled by Intelligence	Ruled by Discursiveness
Great cheerfulness	Mindful and fully conscious in all he does	Unsettled in all his doings
Straightforward-ness	Inclined to the practice of alert vigilance	By night he broods over what to do next day
Guilelessness	Agitation by things which should agitate	By day he carries out last night's plans
A serene confidence in things which deserve confidence	Wise efforts resulting from this agitation	Aimless rushing about

The suitability of the forty Subjects of Meditation for these six types can be seen from the following table:

Greed-type (11)	Ruled by Faith (6)	Hate-type (8)	Ruled by Intelligence (4)
Ten repulsive things (i.e. ten aspects of decomposing corpses) Recollection of what belongs to the body	Recollection of the Buddha the Dharma the Samgha Morality Liberality Devas	Friendliness Compassion Sympathetic joy Evenminded-ness Blue device Yellow device Red device White device	Recollection of death Recollection of Peace Analysis of the body into the four elements Perception of the disgusting aspects of food

Delusion-type (1)	*Ruled by Discursiveness* (1)	*All Types* (10)
Mindful respiration A large kasina-object is preferable	Mindful respiration A small kasina-object is preferable	Earth-device Water-device Fire-device Air-device Light-device Enclosed space-device The four formless trances

We must bear in mind, however, that this arrangement refers only to those exercises which directly counteract some given fault, or which are particularly beneficial to some given type. No meditational development of any kind can fail to impede the faults of those who are ruled by greed, hate, or delusion, nor can it fail to promote the faith, wisdom, or discursiveness of those who are ruled by them. And it has been said in the *Meghiyasutta:* 'Four dharmas should be further developed: the contemplation of the repulsiveness of decaying corpses so as to forsake greed, friendliness so as to forsake ill-will; mindful respiration so as to cut off discursive thoughts; attention to impermanence so as to uproot the pride that says: "I am".' Furthermore, in the *Rahulasutta* seven subjects of meditation are given to one single person, i.e. friendliness, compassion, sympathetic joy, and evenmindedness; meditation on the corrupt nature of the body and on the fleeting nature of things; and finally, mindfulness which comes from ordered breathing. One should therefore not rely on mere words, but everywhere search for the intention behind them.

5. THE FIVE MIRACULOUS POWERS

The Lord also wants to show to those sons of good family, who have achieved concentration on the fourth stage of trance, both the advantages and the increasingly sublime dharmas which flow from meditational development. With this in mind he has described the five Mundane Superknowledges, which are (1) the various magical powers; (2) the cognition by the heavenly ear; (3) the knowledge of others' thoughts; (4) the recollection of previous lives; and (5) the knowledge of the decease and rebirth of other beings.

I. *Various Magical Powers*

'*With his mind collected, perfectly pure and perfectly cleansed, unblemished and undefiled, quite supple and workable, firm and imperturbable, he directs and turns his thought to the various magical powers. And he experiences the various kinds of magical power as follows:* (1) (*The magical power of sustained resolution*), (1a) *having been one, he becomes many; having been many, he becomes one.*

As it has been said in the *Patisambhida*: 'One by nature, he turns his mind towards multiplication, hundredfold, thousandfold, or hundred-thousandfold; he then sustains this act of attention with his cognition, and resolves to become manifold. And thereupon he becomes manifold. Like the Venerable Panthaka, the Younger.' The last sentence refers to an actual instance of multiplication. And this is the story: There were two brothers, named Panthaka ('Way-man'), because they were born by the wayside. The elder brother went out into the homeless life, and won Arhatship together with the four kinds of Analytical Knowledge. He then received his brother into the Order, and gave him the following verse to learn:

> Lo! like a fragrant lotus at the dawn
> Of day, full blown, with virgin wealth of scent,
> Behold the Buddha's glory shining forth,
> As in the vaulted heaven beams the sun!

But even after four months the younger brother had not yet succeeded in learning this verse by heart. Thereupon the Elder expelled him from the monastery as unfit for the religious life.

At that time Panthaka the Elder was the superintendent of meals, and one day the layman Jivaka came to him and invited the Lord together with 500 monks for the following day to his house. The Elder agreed, but stipulated that his younger brother should be excluded from the invitation. And Panthaka the Younger stood weeping at the gate. The Lord saw him with his heavenly eye, went to him, asked him why he wept, and listened to his story.

The Lord then said to him: 'No one is unfit for the religious life in my Order just because he cannot learn by heart. Do not worry, my monk!' – took him by the arm and led him into the monastery. There he magically conjured up a piece of white cloth, and gave it to him with the words: 'Here, monk, rub that between your hands and repeat, "Dirt be removed! dirt be removed!" over and over again.' After Panthaka had done this for some time, the piece of cloth looked quite dark. And he thought to himself: 'This cloth was by itself quite clean; in it the fault does not lie, but surely it lies in my own body!' His cognition then plunged into the five Skandhas, and his insight grew so rapidly that he soon became ripe for Arhatship. To enlighten him still further, the Lord spoke to him these verses:

> Greed is the real dirt, not dust;
> Greed is the term for real dirt.
> The wise have shaken off this dirt,
> And in the dirt-free man's religion live.

And so with 'hate' and 'delusion' in place of 'greed'. By the time the Lord had spoken these verses, Panthaka the Younger had passed through the eight stages of the Supramundane Path, and had won Nirvana together with the four Analytical knowledges and the six Superknowledges.

On the following day the Teacher went to Jivaka's house accompanied by his monks. When they had washed their hands, the time came round for dishing out the rice-gruel. But the Lord covered his bowl with his hand. Jivaka asked why he did so. He answered: 'One monk has been left behind at the monastery!' So Jivaka sent a man to fetch him. But when the Lord had left the monastery,

'a thousand doubles of himself young Panthaka had con-
    jured up,
while waiting in the pleasant Mango grove to be invited'.

So when the man came to the monastery, he found the ground
one blaze of light from all the yellow robes. He went back,
and said to the Lord: 'The monastery, O Lord, is crammed
full of monks! I do not know which one the gentleman is.'
But the Lord replied: 'Just go, and the first one you see you
hold by the hem of his robe, tell him that the Teacher calls
him, and bring him here!' So he went back, and caught hold
of the hem of the Elder's robe. All these magical creations
thereupon vanished at once. The Elder sent the man off,
prepared himself for a meal by washing his mouth, and so on,
arrived at Jivaka's house even before the man had got there,
and sat down on the seat prepared for him.

(1b) *He becomes visible or invisible.* This means that he causes
visibility or invisibility. As it has been said in the *Patisambhida*:
' "To be visible" means not to be covered or hidden by anything, it means to be open to view and manifest. "To be
invisible" means to be covered up or hidden by something,
it means to be concealed and enclosed.'

Someone proficient in magical power, who wants to produce visibility, will therefore have to light up that which is
dark, to uncover that which is covered up, to bring within the
range of vision that which was outside it. And how does he
manage to do that? Suppose he wants to make a person,
either himself or someone else, visible to those who could not
normally see him, either because of their distance or because
of an obstruction in the field of vision – emerging from the
basic fourth Dhyana, he should prepare the miracle by intently
thinking: 'May this dark place be lit up!' or 'May this object,
now covered up, be uncovered!' or 'May this object, now
outside the field of vision, get inside it!' And he should sustain this thought with a firm resolution. As soon as he has
formed his resolution, it is realized: others can see the object
even from a remote distance, and he himself also can see it if
he wants to. There are many instances of this. For example,

in Ceylon, in Talangara, the Elder Dhammadinna used this power when he recited a Sutra from the *Anguttara Nikaya* in the open space round the shrine of the Great Tissa Monastery. He pointed his fan downwards, and all the way down to the Avici Hell there was nothing but open space; he pointed it upwards, and all the way to the Brahma-world there was nothing but open space. So the Elder backed up his explanation of the Dharma, for he could convincingly threaten his audience with the terrors of hell and entice them with the bliss of heaven. Some in consequence became Streamwinners, others Once-returners, others Never-returners, others Arhats.

When he wants to produce invisibility, he must use the reverse procedure to that employed for producing visibility. And who then has ever accomplished this miracle? The Lord. For the Lord brought it about that Yasa's father could not see his son, although he sat beside him. Likewise, the Lord once went for 120 miles to meet king Maha-Kappina. He established him in the fruit of a Never-returner, and his thousand ministers in the fruit of a Streamwinner. When queen Anoja, with her retinue of a thousand women, arrived on the scene and sat down quite close to the king, the Lord brought it about that she could see neither the king nor his retinue. When she asked the Lord whether he had seen the king, he replied: 'What then is better, to seek your king or to seek your own self?' 'To seek one's self' was her answer. And as she sat there he explained to her the Dharma in such a manner that she, with her thousand women, was established in the fruit of a Streamwinner, whereas the ministers advanced to that of a Never-returner, and the king himself to Arhatship.

(1c) *Right through a wall, a rampart, or a hill he glides unimpeded, as though through empty space.* If he wants to move along in this manner, he should enter into the concentration on the space-device, which begins with a contemplation of a hole in a wall, or a key-hole, or an open window. On emerging from this, he should turn his mind on any wall, rampart or mountain, and then prepare the miracle by the sustained resolve, 'may there be empty space!'; and there is only empty space! Whether he wants to go down or up, there are everywhere holes for him to go through. And if he wants to penetrate through a solid body, he will find an aperture through which to move. It is in this way that he glides unimpeded.

(1d) *He dives into the earth and out of it.* In order to achieve this, he should enter into concentration on the water-device, which begins with a contemplation of water in a bowl. On emerging from this he should mark off as much of the ground as he wishes to turn into water, and then prepare the miracle by the sustained resolve that this transformation should take place. Immediately the ground which he has marked off becomes water. And he can dive into it and out of it.

(1e) *He walks on water without sinking into it.* This is done with the help of the earth-device, which begins with a contemplation of a disk of clay, and which allows him to transform into hard earth as much of the water as he has marked off.

(1f) *Cross-legged he floats along like a bird on the wing.* In order to do that, he must first concentrate on the earth-device, and then emerge from his concentration. If he wishes to travel seated, he should mark off a place in the air which is big enough for him to sit on; if he wishes to travel lying down, he should mark off a place the size of a bed, and if he wants to walk, he should mark off as much space as is necessary for a path. In each case he should make the sustained resolve that so and so much of the air should change into earth; and immediately the air turns into earth. But the monk who wishes to float through the air should possess the heavenly eye. What for? So as to enable him to see the mountains, trees, and so on, which he meets on his way, and which are due either to physical causes, or to the magic of dragons, fairy-birds and other creatures who are envious of him. And what should he do when he sees them? He should enter into the basic fourth Jhana, emerge from it, and by his sustained resolve he can then change those mountains, etc., into empty space.

(1g) *Even the sun and the moon, powerful and mighty though they be, he touches and strokes with his hands.* If he wants to go to them and touch them, he can do so. But if he wants to touch them while sitting or lying down here on earth, he resolves that they should come to the palms of his hands. And in virtue of his sustained resolve they come along, like palm-fruits severed from their stalks, and when they have got to the palms of his hands he can touch them. Alternatively he can also make his hand grow, until it reaches up to the sun and the moon.

(1h) *Even as far as the world of Brahma he has power over his body*. The explanation of this can be found in the *Patisambhida*: 'If someone, mighty in his psychic power and in full control over his will, wishes to go to the Brahma-world, he resolves that the distant may become near, and it becomes near; he resolves that what is near should become distant, and it becomes distant; he resolves that what is much should become little, and it becomes little; he resolves that what is little should become much, and it becomes much. With his heavenly eye he sees the shape of Brahma, with his heavenly ear he hears his voice, with his cognition of the thoughts of others he reads that Brahma's mind. If that man, mighty in his psychic power and in full control over his will, wishes to go to Brahma's world with a visible body, then he alters his mind to accord with his body, determines his mind to accord with his body. A sensation of ease and lightness then comes over him, and he can travel with his visible body to Brahma's world. But if he wants to go there with an invisible body, he alters his body to accord with his mind, resolves his body to accord with his mind, with the result that a sensation of ease and lightness comes over him, and he can travel with an invisible body to Brahma's world. In front of that Brahma he conjures up a mind-made body, complete with all its limbs, in full possession of all its organs. If the magician walks up and down, his magical creation likewise walks up and down. If the magician stands, or sits down, or lies down, his magical creation always does likewise. If the magician emits smoke or fire; or if he demonstrates the Dharma, asks questions or answers them, his magical creation always does likewise. And if the magician stays for a while with that Brahma, talks and converses with him, then his magical creation will do likewise. For whatever that magician may do, that his magical creation will also do.'

The Lord once made 'what is little into much', as we know from the story of Kakavaliya. We are told there that Maha-kassapa, the Elder, after spending seven days absorbed in trance, decided to do a favour to Kakavaliya, a poor man, by waiting for alms at the door of his house. When Kakavaliya's wife saw the Elder, she poured into his bowl the saltless, sour gruel she had cooked for her husband. The Elder took it and handed it to the Lord, who resolved that it should suffice for the large assembly of monks. And that which had been brought in one single bowl proved sufficient for all. Kakavaliya, however, seven days later became a rich merchant.

And psychic power enables people not only to change what is little into what is much, but also to make sweet things not sweet, or unsweet things sweet, and whatever else they may wish to accomplish. One day Maha-Anula, the Elder, saw numerous monks sitting down on the banks of the Ganges, and eating their meal, just dry rice, which was all they had received on their alms-rounds. He thereupon resolved that the water of the Ganges should be turned into butter-cream. He gave a sign to the novices, and they fetched the butter-cream in small cups and brought it to the monks. And they all ate of the sweet butter-cream.

'A sensation of ease and lightness comes over him': the 'sensation of ease' is the sensation connected with evenmind-edness; for evenmindedness has been called the 'calm ease'. And the sensation should be regarded as one of 'lightness', because it is free from the (five) Hindrances, and from other states hostile to trance, such as discursive thinking, and so on. As soon as this sensation has come over the monk, his physical body becomes as light as a tuft of cotton wool. And so he goes to the Brahma-world with his visible body as light as a tuft of cotton-down blown along by the wind. If he wishes to, he can conjure up in space with the help of the earth-device a firm road, and along it he can walk on foot. Or, if he prefers, he can by his magical resolution raise a wind, and like cotton-down he then drifts along with it. But the desire to move along is the decisive factor. For where that exists, as soon as he has made a sustained resolve in his mind, he visibly hurries along, driven by the impact of his resolve, like an arrow shot by an archer.

'A mind-made body' – because it has been conjured up by a mind filled with sustained resolve. 'In full possession of all its organs' – this refers to the presence of organs in the shape of eyes, ears, and so on; but in magically created bodies these have no sensitivity. 'If the magician walks up and down, his magical creation likewise walks up and down', etc.: all this only refers to the magical creations conjured up by Disciples. The Buddha's magical creations also do whatever the Lord does, but they can also do something else, if the Lord so desires.

(2) *The power of miraculous transformation.* Here 'he first gives up his normal appearance, and then shows himself in the guise of a boy, or a dragon, a fairy-bird, or Asura, of Indra, a god, or Brahma; or in the form of the sea or a rock, of a lion, tiger, or leopard, of an elephant, horse, chariot, or foot-soldier; or of various army-formations'. He should, however, never resolve, 'May I become an elephant!', etc., but always, 'Let there be an elephant!', etc.

(3) *The power of producing mind-made bodies.* In order to achieve this, one must emerge from the basic fourth Jhana, turn one's attention to one's body, and resolve that there should be a hollow space there. In consequence there is a hollow space there. He then thinks attentively of a second body in the hollow space within his own body, makes the necessary preparations, produces a sustained resolve, and in consequence there is now within his own body still another body. That second he then pulls out, as one pulls a reed from its sheath, a sword from its scabbard, a snake from its slough. Hence it was said: 'Here the monk conjures up from his body another body, which has form, is mind-made, complete with all its limbs, in full possession of its organs. Just as if a man were to pull out a reed from its sheath, and say to himself: "This is the sheath, this the reed; the sheath is one thing, the reed another. But it is from the sheath that the reed has been pulled out."' And just as the reed is similar in shape to the sheath, and the sword to the scabbard, so also is the mind-made body similar to that of the body of the magician.

II. *The Heavenly Ear*

He further directs his mind to the heavenly ear. With the heavenly ear, perfectly pure and surpassing that of men, he hears sounds, celestial as well as human, far as well as near.

The capacity for hearing in this way is called 'heavenly' because it resembles that of the gods. For the gods have a heavenly organ of hearing, which can perceive objects even from a long distance, because it results from the good deeds they have done, suffers no obstruction from bile, phlegm, blood, etc., and is free from all imperfections. Similar to that is the hearing capacity which this cognition confers on a monk, and which results from the might which he has gained by the prolonged development of his vigour.

III. *The Knowledge of Others' Thoughts*

With his own mind he encompasses the minds of other beings, other persons, and he wisely knows the greedy mind as greedy, the greedless as greedless; he knows the hating mind as with hate, the hateless mind as without hate; he knows the deluded mind as deluded, the undeluded as undeluded. He knows the mind which is contracted (by sloth and torpor) *as contracted, and the mind which is distracted* (by excitedness) *as distracted. The lofty mind* (which reaches up to the worlds revealed by the trances) *he knows as lofty, the unlofty as unlofty. He knows the surpassable mind as surpassable, the unsurpassable* (or supramundane) *as unsurpassable. The collected mind he knows as collected, the uncollected as uncollected. He finally knows the emancipated mind as emancipated, the unemancipated as unemancipated.*

And how should this cognition be produced? Success here depends on the preliminary development of the heavenly eye. A monk should therefore spread the supernatural light which enables the heavenly eye to function (see page 133), look with his heavenly eyesight at the colour of another person's blood, which is conditioned by the state of his heart, and infer his thoughts from that. For when a person has glad thoughts, his heart-blood is red like a ripe banyan fruit, when sad thoughts, it is black like a ripe rose-apple, when neutral

thoughts, it is like clear sesamum oil. A monk should therefore build up his capacity for encompassing the thoughts of
others by repeatedly looking at the colour of their heart-blood,
and inferring their thoughts from it. First of all the feeling
tone of their thoughts should be inferred, i.e. whether they
are glad, sad, or neutral, and beginning with that he will
gradually come to know all their thoughts, whichever realm
they may belong to. After a time he will no longer have to
begin with a survey of the heart-blood, but will be able
directly to pass over from his own thoughts to those of
others.

IV. *The Recollection of Former Lives*

*He recalls his manifold former lives – one birth, or two births, or
up to 100,000 births or more, and many world cycles and aeons:
'There I was, that was my name, that was my family, that was my
caste, such was my food, this was the happiness, this the suffering
which I experienced, this was the duration of my life-span. Deceased
there I was reborn elsewhere, and there had this name, etc. It is thus
that he recalls his manifold previous lives, with all their modes, in all
their details.*

Six kinds of people can remember their former lives: Non-
Buddhists, ordinary disciples, great disciples, chief disciples,
Pratyekabuddhas, and Buddhas. The non-Buddhists can remember up to forty aeons, but no more, because they are weak
in wisdom, being unacquainted with the correct classification
of mental and physical phenomena. The ordinary disciples can
recall up to a hundred or a thousand aeons, because their
wisdom is strong. The eighty great disciples can remember
100,000 aeons, the two chief disciples one incalculable aeon
plus 100,000 aeons, and the Pratyekabuddhas two incalculable
aeons plus 100,000 aeons. For they aspire no further than that.
As for the Buddhas, there is no limit to their memory.

A monk who is still a beginner, and who wants to learn
how to remember his previous lives, should in the afternoon,
after he has finished his meal, go to a solitary and secluded
spot, and enter successively into the four trances. He should
then emerge from the fourth trance, which is the basis of the

Superknowledges, and think of the last thing he did before his meditation, which was the act of sitting down. After that he should, in reverse order, think of everything he did during the day and night, i.e. how he spread the seat on which he sat down, how he entered his lodging, got ready his robe and alms bowl, the time when he ate, when he came back from the village, when he went to the village for his alms, when he entered the village for his alms round, when he departed from the monastery, when he saluted the shrine, the time when he washed his alms bowl, when he took hold of his alms bowl, and from there whatever he did after the washing of the mouth, everything he did early in the day, everything he did in the last and everything he did in the first watch of the night.

All this becomes manifest to the ordinary mind already, but to the mind which is prepared by trance it stands out most distinctly. But if anything should not be obvious to him, he should once more enter into the basic fourth trance, and, on emerging from it, should direct his mind unto it. In that way these things become as clear to him as if lit up by a lamp. He should furthermore think back in reverse order on what he did two days ago, three, four, and five days ago, ten days ago, half a month ago, one month ago, up to one year ago. In this manner he goes on for ten years, twenty years, and so on, until he comes to the time of his birth in this becoming, and then he should also direct his mind on the mental and physical processes which took place at the moment of his decease in his immediately preceding existence.

A clever monk can manage already on his first attempt to penetrate beyond the moment of rebirth to a perception of the mental and physical processes at the time of his decease. But for those who are not very wise the passage from one existence to another is hard to see, and must seem impassable and very obscure, for the reason that the psycho-physical organism of the previous existence has wholly ceased and another one has arisen in its stead.

V. *The Knowledge of the Decease and Rebirth of Beings*

He directs his mind to the knowledge of the decease and rebirth of beings. With the heavenly eye, perfectly pure and surpassing that of men, he sees beings, as they are about to die or find a new rebirth – the low and the high, the beautiful and the ugly, the privileged and the unprivileged – and he sees that whatever happens to them happens in accordance with their deeds.

The 'heavenly eye' is called 'heavenly' for the same reason as the 'heavenly ear'. In addition it is considered as 'heavenly' because it spreads a brilliant supernatural light, and also because it has a great power of penetration and can discern objects which are hidden behind walls or other obstructions.

The monk who spreads this light downwards, in the direction of the hells, sees with the heavenly eye the beings in the hells suffering much pain. He then asks himself what deeds these beings must have done to suffer so much. And when he understands that it is because they have done this or that, then there arises in him the cognition which has their deeds for its object. Moreover, when he spreads the light upwards, to the world of the gods, he sees with the heavenly eye the beings in the celestial regions enjoying great bliss. He then asks himself what deeds these beings must have done to have so much bliss. And when he understands that it is because they have done this or that, then there arises in him the cognition which has their deeds for its object.

But the practice of the heavenly eye is not without its dangers for the ordinary person who has not yet won the Path. Light appears wherever he resolves it to appear, and so he may find himself surrounded by one huge blaze of light which pervades earth, sea, and mountains. And he will then see the terrifying shapes of ogres and demons, and fear will rise up in him, so that he will fall into mental confusion, and stray away from his trance. It is therefore better not to be over-ambitious in this matter of seeing shapes.

6. ZEN

6a. Sessan Amakuki. Zen Meditation

> Those who perform meditation for even one session
> Destroy innumerable accumulated sins;
> How should there be wrong paths for them?
> The Paradise of Amida Buddha is not far.

A verse from Hakuni's The Song of Meditation

These four lines speak of the effects of sitting in meditation (Za-zen) especially in regard to repentance and destruction of sins. The Sixth Patriarch, defining the word Zazen, says: 'Outwardly to be in the world of good and evil yet with no thought arising in the heart, this is Sitting (Za): inwardly to see one's own nature and not move from it, this is Meditation (Zen).' The 'wrong paths' of the verse are those which lead ultimately to reincarnation as a dweller in hell, as a ghost, or as an animal. If the meditation practice is really done, then the merits are as great as declared in the song. The important thing in practising Zen, rather than the question of the length or shortness of the time, is that the mind should be in a state where the meditation is steady and continuous. When the song teaches us that those who perform meditation for even one session destroy innumerable accumulated sins, it means that if this meditation goes into the real *Samadhi*, then even the one session has this great power. One session means a single sitting, as when we set up a stick of incense and do not leave our meditation till after it has burnt down.

Directions are given for our practice. In a place, which must be quiet, spread a thick cushion and sit yourself on it in an upright posture. Now first swell out the abdomen and put your strength there. Let the shoulders be in a straight line below the ears, and navel below the nose. Make the spine straight. The mouth should be shut, but you may have the eyes slightly opened. Making the breath flow gently will help to secure a correct posture. Then meditate on the text you have been given, or in the case of beginners there is a method in which they count their breaths and so remove dull and distracted thoughts. So entering the Samadhi of undisturbed purity, remain in the meditation. Those who are really determined to enter upon meditation should read some small classic on the subject.

Of course it may be that there are those whose insight and whose inner nature are so advanced that they would not necessarily require to practise in the way given. But I believe there are many advantages in beginning in the prescribed manner. If the practice is truly carried out, then one session of meditation is one session of being Buddha, a day of meditation is a day of being Buddha. Or as an Ancient has said: 'One inch of meditation, one inch of Buddha; so inch by inch, make the six-foot form of Buddha.'

If we do our meditation practice properly, then the thoughts which arise, though they be due to the sins and impediments accumulated for aeons past, will be extinguished of themselves, and then where should the wrong paths be? 'The Paradise of Amida is not far.' We shall enter the state where this very body is the Buddha. The thing to be kept in mind in meditation is to have the great conviction that this is the path that can save me, and it is only this path that can save me. The attitude of trying just to see what it is like, or as an experiment, is not appropriate in such a serious business. Underneath the great Faith you will come upon the great Inquiry, and then if you whip up your efforts with great determination and rush on ahead, below the great Inquiry there is the great Enlightenment, and without any doubt know that you will have it.

Without claiming that the practice of meditation will always lead at once to the removal of ignorance and the opening of enlightenment, yet to be able to sit quiet for a time and turn one's attention within oneself is a great advantage in ordinary life, and this is the beginning of meditation. People these days have their heads boiling with thought and are ever turned outwards as if searching for something. They have forgotten how to still the heart and turn within for the inward vision. In fact they know the way of going forward, but not how to withdraw. In controlling the traffic at cross-roads, we have the traffic lights, Go! and Stop! If there were only the Go! and not the Stop! accidents would be inevitable. The Stop! is essential. Modern people only strive to rush on, as if they were all in a horse-race, and they have lost the power of withdrawing and reflecting. They go ahead and go ahead, but in the end there is a deadlock, a jam, and they finish up pathetic victims of a spiritual disaster. By paying attention to how to withdraw, by turning within and reflecting, one can reach the inexhaustible treasure there, can experience directly the spiritual Paradise of Amida.

One has sometimes heard that to practise meditation it is necessary to retire to a mountain away from society, or perhaps to bury oneself in some old temple, to discard humanity and become a so-called hermit. Of course, it may be that for the final training in seeing one's own nature and attaining enlightenment it would in some cases be necessary for a time, but this is not one's objective. Zen must be to use that power which grips the Zen meditation and to bring it directly to bear upon and vivify our present daily life. Withdrawing into meditation, and then advancing and handling affairs – this advancing and withdrawing, movement and rest, together, must be Zen.

The Taoist book *Saikondan* says: 'The rest in rest is not the real rest; there can be rest even in movement.' An ancient worthy says: 'Meditation in movement is a hundred, a thousand, a million times superior to meditation at rest.' In this way he teaches the importance of meditation in activity.

The Sutra teaches that by the practice of meditation the lake of the heart becomes pure and calm, and when the lake of the ordinary man's heart becomes pure, it is the reflection of a Bodhisattva which appears within it. When the wellspring of the heart is purified, the wrong paths which otherwise appear as a result of his wrong actions, to that man become as if nonexistent. How should there be wrong paths for him? 'The Paradise of Amida Buddha is not far.' As the phrase goes: 'This heart becomes one's meditation room.' The world of light, of virtue, appears, and now our daily life has a changed meaning. In fact, for the first time our ordinary life becomes radiant with real meaning.

Many people have heard of the great painter Tanyu, whose work exists even to-day at the Myoshin Temple. This is the story of the time when he painted the great dragon on the ceiling of the main hall of the Temple, the dragon which was his masterpiece and to-day is one of the art treasures of the world. At that time the Master at the Myoshin Temple was the celebrated Zen Master Gudo, famous as the teacher of the Emperor. He had heard that the dragons painted by Tanyo were so realistic that when a ceiling on which one had been painted fell down by chance, some said it had been caused by the movement of the dragon's tail. When the painting of the dragon at Myoshin was mooted, Gudo went to the painter's house and told him: 'For this special occasion I particularly want to have the painting of a *living* dragon.' Naturally the painter was taken aback, and saying: 'This is most unexpected. As a matter of fact, I am ashamed to say that I have never seen a living dragon' – would have refused the commission. The Zen teacher, however, agreed that it would be unreasonable to expect a painting of a living dragon from one who had never seen one, but told him to try to have a look at one as soon as he could. The painter asked wonderingly: 'Where can one see a living dragon? Where do they dwell?' 'Oh, that's nothing. At my place there are any number – come and see them and paint one.' Tanyu joyfully went with the teacher, and when they arrived at once asked: 'Well, here I am to see the dragons. Where are they?' The Teacher, letting his gaze go round the room, replied: 'Plenty of them here; can't you see them? What a pity!' The painter, too, felt overcome with a feeling of regret, and in the event spent the next two years with Gudo, practising Zen assiduously.

One day something happened, and he rushed excitedly to the Teacher saying: 'Thanks to you I have to-day seen the form of a live dragon!' 'Oh, have you? Good. But tell me, what did his roar sound like?' At this query again the painter was at a loss, and for one further year laboured on at his spiritual practices. What he painted at the end of that year was the dragon of the Myoshin Temple, a supreme masterpiece in the history of art, remarkable for its technique but far more for the life which the artist has infused into it. It seems as if it contains the great Life which embraces heaven and earth, the universe and man also. It was to pierce through to this reality that the master-painter Tanyo poured out his heart's blood for three years. But when he had one experience of reality, he had no need to seek any farther.

When one hears a story like this it is indeed wonderful. But it is no easy thing, and we must not allow ourselves to be discouraged. It takes time before we can have a taste of the experience of Reality. The Sutra says: 'Heroes become Buddhas with one thought, but the lazy people are given the three collections of scriptures to traverse.'

6b. Rosen Takashina. *Controlling the Mind*

What was it that Buddha wished to teach? Was it sagacity, was it brilliant academic understanding? Was his aim to encourage the reading of the scriptures, or asceticism, or austerities? In reality it was none of these. He simply wished to show all living beings how to set in order body and mind. The method of doing this is given in the classic on meditation called *Zazengi*: 'Think of not thinking of anything at all. How is one to think of not thinking of anything at all? Be without thoughts – this is the secret of meditation.' Being without thoughts is the object of Zen meditation; the control of body and mind is only a method of reaching it. When body and mind have been controlled, then from the ensuing absence of thoughts are born naturally and rightly brilliant understanding, perfect Buddha-wisdom, reading of the scriptures and devotion, asceticism, and austerities. There are some who have too hastily assumed that holy reading, devotion, or austerities have a value in themselves, but this is not the traditional Zen, as handed down through the great master Do-gen.

What is meant by absence of thoughts?

The living *Samadhi* of all the Buddhas is no other than that state of absolute absence of thoughts. Taking the words literally, one might think it meant to be like a tree or a stone, but it is not that at all. It cannot be understood by our ordinary consciousness, but neither shall we get it by unconsciousness. We can only grasp it by experiencing it in ourselves.

Beginners, when they first hear that the secret of Zen is to be without thoughts but that it cannot be got by consciousness or by unconsciousness, cannot understand at all what it can be and are bewildered. Now instead of wondering how to get it, or trying to understand it or to analyse it, the essential thing is resolutely to take a leap into death, to give up one's body and life itself. It means to cut off at the root and source, all our discriminating fancies. If we really cut them off at the root, then of itself the freedom from thought will come, which means that our own true nature appears, and this is called enlightenment. An ancient says: 'In Zen the important thing is to stop the course of the heart.' It means to stop the workings of our empirical consciousness, the mass of thoughts, ideas, and perceptions. A great master said: 'Try to cut off thought. By this alone eight or nine out of ten people will attain the Way.' Attaining the Way is realizing the Buddha heart which is our own true nature. The radiance of the Buddha heart breaks forth from ourselves, the compassion of the Buddha flows out of the Buddha heart within us. We come to know that the majesty of Buddha is our own majesty also.

The doctrine of *Karma* is one aspect of Buddhism. In this doctrine, the whole phenomenal universe as perceived by us is understood to be an effect, corresponding to previous thoughts, speech, and physical actions of the individual and of all living beings, which are the cause. In fact the whole phenomenal universe is experienced according to our *Karma*. The three forms of *Karma*, namely action of body, speech, and thought, can all be embraced under the heading of actions of the mind or heart. Whether this heart is the Buddha heart or not is the cause which determines good or evil for us. And if we only stress our ego and do not cut off the thoughts, the Buddha heart does not appear.

The real difficulty of Zen meditation is how to stop the course of the mind, how to cut off thought. Some two and a half thousand years ago at Kusinara in India, the World-honoured One, Shakyamuni Buddha, was about to die. In the final teachings to his disciples, the last phrase of the warnings about mind and senses is: 'You must subjugate the mind.' This does not mean the Buddha mind or Buddha heart, but it means the egoistic heart of the ordinary man who employs his mind actively all the time. Was there ever any chameleon comparable to the human heart? Just now it was happy and laughing, but all at once it is sad, then in a rage about something or other; or it wants to eat, or to sleep, to praise or to slander. In so-called women's gossip the confusions of the mind become noisily apparent as speech. And so far it may be all right, but then there also spring up terrible things, robbery and murder – all transformations of the egoistic heart. This is why in the Consciousness Only school of Buddhism, all changes are called transformations of consciousness.

As to whether the heart in itself is good or bad, some say good and some say bad, and there was also a view among the ancients that it is neither. However that may be, what is clear is that our hearts from morning to evening in their ceaseless activity undergo thousands and millions of changes and transformations, good or bad. Reason and morality tell us to take every possible care that we do not slip into a wrong path, but instead strive to pull the carriage of our life on the right road. An old poet sings: 'When you feel it pulling, do not loose the reins of the colt of the heart, which would enter the evil paths' – and again – 'In the cooking-pot of the world, cook well and not badly; the human heart is the free-moving ladle'. According to how much the free ladle is lifted and lowered, the things are cooked well or badly. The human heart is likewise fundamentally free. Some say that it is important all the time to give attention to doing the right thing. But Zen does not speak in this way. It is just a question of the Buddha heart which tells us to take a step beyond, to end the coursing of the heart, to cut off the thought. Once and for all we have to cut off the working of the mind, which is the inner ego from which evil emerges. Buddhism teaches that the human heart has two aspects. They are, the pure heart and the impure heart. But the heart in itself is not two; it is only classified in these two ways according to its workings. The pure heart is the pure heart of our own nature, our natural heart which is not a whit different from the Buddha heart.

Opposed to this is the impure heart which gives us no peace from morning till night, the egoistic heart of illusions, the passion-ridden heart. Because the selfish passionate heart is not natural, we are always afflicted with sufferings; endlessly this heart, absolutely careless, leads men astray.

Fundamentally our true heart, our true nature, is pure and infinite, like the moon clear in the blue sky. At some distant time past our knowing, it was tainted by passion and became the impure heart, something not our real selves but which came afterwards. But this which came afterwards becomes predominant and sets at naught the true heart, just as the concubine sets at naught the real wife. How often one has read in the papers that the steward of some large estate, or the manager of a great firm perhaps, has set at naught his masters and using the money for himself has brought ruin all round. Just in this way we entrust ourselves to the operations of the deluded and passion-ridden heart, so that the real master, the Buddha heart, cannot even show its face. The thoughts of the impure heart are topsy-turvy, for it sees reality as upside-down. The villains who act as chief contributors to the delusion are what the World-honoured One called 'the brigands of the five senses'. These five—eye, ear, nose, tongue, and body – receive all the tempting objects and convey them to the impure heart in order to satisfy it. For this reason they are technically called 'roots', because just so the roots of a tree convey the sap to the branches and leaves to satisfy them. Of course the mischievous operation of the senses is not natural; their true working is not wrong. But the impure heart misuses them, and only lets them work in wrong directions. As it is said in the Buddha's last teachings: 'These five take the heart as their master.' So the wicked nature of the impure heart is compared to a venomous serpent or a wild beast. It bears off the life which should develop into the Buddha who is our true nature. In our breast is coiled the poisonous serpent which is always breathing out the fire of the three poisons, bringing on us agonies and sufferings.

To drive out the devilish impure heart and to enable the pure radiance to shine from the pure heart within us, the five senses have to be cut off. And hence it is said that we should cut off thought. How are we to do it? There are several methods, but the Zen method is to sit in the meditation posture and swell with our breath and vitality the abdomen below the navel. In this way the whole frame is invigorated. Then we meditate, discarding body and mind. Now the delusions which are the impure heart come up without ceasing. We should make these fancies, coming one after another, the *Koan* (theme) of our meditation. What, after all, is this thought? Where did it come from? We penetrate with the spear-point of our meditation to the source of the successive fancies.

When we practise sitting in this way repeatedly and make progress in meditation, then of itself the meditation becomes deeper and fuller until there is no room for the fancies to show their heads. The practice is quite unrestricted, and the entry into the experience of truth is also unrestricted; in the end the wonderful vision appears of one's true nature, the experience of the absolute. This is called seeing one's real face, and it is said that eight or nine out of ten people can achieve it (in this very life). The practice as described has nothing artificial about it, but though it seems easy it is not easy, and the old masters all had a hard time with it. There are many famous sayings about this, such as: 'After winning a hundred battles, now I grow old in great peace', or 'How many times for your sake do I enter the green dragon's cave where the jewel is hidden!'

There is another method. First in the same way filling the whole body with vigour, we wrestle with a *Koan* which the teacher gives us. The 'not' of Master Jo-Shu, the 'tree in the fore-court', the 'true face', the 'sound of one hand' – any of them will do. It is a question of using the *Koan* to practise our meditation with all the force of our will, one-pointedly and without distraction. If there is the least little bit of discriminating in this meditation, it will fail completely. Suppose for instance we are meditating on the 'Sound of One Hand', though we try to understand this with the discriminating intellect, it will never be understood. We may think that we have understood it, but this is no more than the understanding of the discriminating impure heart, which thinks 'I' and 'my' and 'I do it'. Zen meditation means to cut off at the root the mind which thinks 'I understand it', and to enter the state where there is no impure discrimination, and that one who rests satisfied at the stage of intellectual understanding is far from the goal of Zen. We are told to hear the sound of one hand, which alone cannot make a sound, and discrimination or analysis obviously cannot understand it. The essential thing is that the whole body and mind should be taken up with the *Koan* and no other thought should be able to arise, so that not only at the time of meditation but standing and walking and sitting and lying the meditation must continue without a break. Then all unknown the power of the meditation becomes ripe. Abbot Rei-Un, seeing the peach flowers, became enlightened, and Zen Master Kyo-Gen at hearing the crack of a bamboo. It happens at the moment our *Karma* may direct. Heaven and earth are split apart in an instant; as if a sluice had been opened, suddenly we attain bliss and life infinite.

Such was the enlightenment of the old masters, and of this the *Zazengi* classic says: 'Loosing and dropping off body and mind, see before you your true nature.' But there must not be any relaxation of attention; if there is even a slight wavering, then the *karma* does not ripen into the psychological moment, any more than in the case of a dead man.

Once one has penetrated completely into one of the *Koans*, it is sufficient. The great Enlightenment is once for all; if there had to be a repetition, it would not have been complete Enlightenment. Of course there is nothing against a man examining all the seventeen hundred *Koans* which exist in order to try the power of his vision of the true self, but it does not mean that one has to solve several of them in order to be enlightened. If in the way described one presses on with burning faith, throwing one's whole power into the meditation, then it is absolutely certain that the time will come when he enters the living *Samadhi* of all the Buddhas. To adopt the method of *Koan* is called the Zen of 'Awaiting Enlightenment'. But in Soto Zen the practice *is* enlightenment. It is just meditating earnestly in the realization of the Absolute, as the Buddha himself did, and it is not a question of wrestling with the *Koan* and waiting for Enlightenment. We should be grateful for this practice of earnest sitting in meditation which is the most important thing in the mental training leading to our real good, the bringing out of the Buddha light from our humanity. If it is done, then naturally through the Buddha heart our human nature is elevated. There is no distinction here of sharp or dull or clever or stupid. It is a fact that any one, if he devotes himself wholeheartedly to spiritual meditation without wavering, reaches the supreme state.

CHAPTER 3

WISDOM

Now to wisdom (prajña), the crown of all Buddhist endeavour. It is an attempt to penetrate to the actual reality of things as they are in themselves. (1) For a non-technical introduction to this vast subject I have once more relied on the Questions of King Milinda. *In the course of his discussions with the monk Nagasena all the basic problems of Buddhist wisdom are touched upon, as the reader can see for himself.*

In the Mahayana, wisdom then developed into 'Perfect Wisdom' (prajña-paramita), the 'wisdom which has gone beyond', or 'transcendental wisdom'. From the enormous literature devoted to this topic I have chosen three fairly short texts. (2) The Heart Sutra *(c. 350) is an epitome of the whole doctrine, which is so condensed that I have added seven headings in order at least slightly to clarify the progress of the argument. (3) Equally famous is the* Diamond Sutra *(c. 350), from which I have selected some of the more intelligible passages. They have here been arranged first in the order of the stages which a Bodhisattva has to go through, and then of the attributes of a Buddha which are considered in the Sutra. Again the headings are my own. (4) Finally there is Rahulabhadra's (c. 150) Hymn to Perfect Wisdom, a well-known poem often copied out at the beginning of manuscripts containing texts on the Perfection of Wisdom.*

(5) The teaching on Perfect Wisdom determined the further course of Mahayana thought. In China, in the so-called Ch'an school, it underwent a fusion with Taoist ideas. In Chapter 2 we illustrated the meditation-aspect of Zen. Now we show its wisdom-aspect by D. T. Suzuki's translation of Seng-ts'an's (c. 600) poem on 'Believing in Mind'. Arthur Waley, who has translated it under the title 'On Trusting in the Heart' in my 'Buddhist Texts' (No. 211) testifies to 'its extreme celebrity in China and Japan'. He adds that 'it would be possible, of course, to furnish it with an enormous commentary', but that he feels 'that it gains, for the ordinary reader, by remaining slightly mysterious'. This is indeed the long and the short of it.

(6) Finally, from the fifth century onwards, the thinking on 'Perfect Wisdom' combined in Northern India with age-old magical practices to form the Tantra. As just one document from the vast literature of the Buddhist Tantra I give an extract from the full translation of Saraha's (c. 850) Poems, which Dr Snellgrove has contributed to my 'Buddhist Texts' (No. 188). This must suffice here, because the bulk of this literature is couched in a deliberately mysterious language which would convey nothing to the average reader.

I. THE QUESTIONS OF KING MILINDA

1. *Introduction*

IN the land of the Bactrian Greeks there was a city called Sagala, a great centre of trade. Rivers and hills beautified it, delightful landscapes surrounded it, and it possessed many parks, gardens, woods, lakes and lotus-ponds. Its king was Milinda, a man who was learned, experienced, intelligent and competent, and who at the proper times carefully observed all the appropriate Brahminic rites, with regard to things past, future and present. As a disputant he was hard to assail, hard to overcome, and he was recognized as a prominent sectarian teacher.

One day a numerous company of Arhats, who lived in a well-protected spot in the Himalayas, sent a messenger to the Venerable Nagasena, then at the Asoka Park in Patna, asking him to come, as they wished to see him. Nagasena immediately complied by vanishing from where he was and miraculously appearing before them. And the Arhats said to him: 'That king Milinda, Nagasena, constantly harasses the order of monks with questions and counter-questions, with arguments and counter-arguments. Please go, Nagasena, and subdue him!' But Nagasena replied: 'Never mind just this one king Milinda! If all the kings of India would come to me with their questions, I could well dispose of them, and they would give no more trouble after that! You may go to Sagala without any fear whatever!' And the Elders went to Sagala, lighting up the city with their yellow robes which shone like lamps, and bringing with them the fresh breeze of the holy mountains.

The Venerable Nagasena stayed at the Sankheyya hermitage together with 80,000 monks. King Milinda, accompanied by a retinue of 500 Greeks, went up to where he was, gave him a friendly and courteous greeting, and sat on one side. Nagasena returned his greetings, and his courtesy pleased the king's heart.

2. THE DOCTRINE OF NOT-SELF

2a. *The chariot*

And King Milinda asked him: 'How is your Reverence known, and what is your name, Sir?' 'As Nagasena I am known, O great king, and as Nagasena do my fellow religious habitually address me. But although parents give such names as Nagasena, or Surasena, or Virasena, or Sihasena, nevertheless this word "Nagasena" is just a denomination, a designation, a conceptual term, a current appellation, a mere name. For no real person can here be apprehended.' But King Milinda explained: 'Now listen, you 500 Greeks and 80,000 monks, this Nagasena tells me that he is not a real person! How can I be expected to agree with that!' And to Nagasena he said: 'If, most reverend Nagasena, no person can be apprehended in reality, who then, I ask you, gives you what you require by way of robes, food, lodging, and medicines? Who is it that consumes them? Who is it that guards morality, practises meditation, and realizes the [four] Paths and their Fruits, and thereafter Nirvana? Who is it that kills living beings, takes what is not given, commits sexual misconduct, tells lies, drinks intoxicants? Who is it that commits the five Deadly Sins? For, if there were no person, there could be no merit and no demerit; no doer of meritorious or demeritorious deeds, and no agent behind them; no fruit of good and evil deeds, and no reward or punishment for them. If someone should kill you, O Venerable Nagasena, he would not commit any murder. And you yourself, Venerable Nagasena, would not be a real teacher, or instructor, or ordained monk! You just told me that your fellow religious habitually address you as "Nagasena". What then is this "Nagasena"? Are perhaps the hairs of the head "Nagasena"?' – 'No, great king!' 'Or perhaps the hairs of the body?' – 'No, great king!' 'Or perhaps the nails, teeth, skin, muscles, sinews, bones, marrow, kidneys, heart, liver, serous membranes, spleen, lungs, intestines, mesentery, stomach, excrement, the bile, phlegm, pus, blood, grease, fat, tears, sweat, spittle, snot, fluid of the joints, urine, or the brain in the skull – are they this "Nagasena"?' – 'No, great king!' – 'Or is form this "Nagasena", or feeling, or perceptions, or impulses, or consciousness?' – 'No, great king!' – 'Then is it the combination of form, feelings, perceptions, impulses, and consciousness?' – 'No, great king!' – 'Then is it outside the combination of form, feelings, perceptions, impulses, and consciousness?' – 'No, great king!' – 'Then, ask as I may, I can discover no Nagasena at all. Just a mere sound is this "Nagasena", but who is the real Nagasena? Your Reverence has told a lie, has spoken a falsehood! There really is no Nagasena!'

Thereupon the Venerable Nagasena said to King Milinda: 'As a king you have been brought up in great refinement and you avoid roughness of any kind. If you would walk at midday on this hot, burning, and sandy ground, then your feet would have to tread on the rough and gritty gravel and pebbles, and they would hurt you, your body would get tired, your mind impaired, and your awareness of your body would be associated with pain. How then did you come – on foot, or on a mount?'

'I did not come, Sir, on foot, but on a chariot.' – 'If you have come on a chariot, then please explain to me what a chariot is. Is the pole the chariot?' – 'No, reverend Sir!' – 'Is then the axle the chariot?' – 'No, reverend Sir!' – 'Is it then the wheels, or the framework, or the flag-staff, or the yoke, or the reins, or the goad-stick?' – 'No, reverend Sir!' – 'Then is it the combination of pole, axle, wheels, framework, flagstaff, yoke, reins, and goad which is the "chariot"?' – 'No, reverend Sir!' – 'Then is this "chariot" outside the combination of pole, axle, wheels, framework, flag-staff, yoke, reins, and goad?' – 'No, reverend Sir!' – 'Then, ask as I may, I can discover no chariot at all. Just a mere sound is this "chariot". But what is the real chariot? Your Majesty has told a lie, has spoken a falsehood! There really is no chariot! Your Majesty is the greatest king in the whole of India. Of whom then are you afraid, that you do not speak the truth?' And he exclaimed: 'Now listen, you 500 Greeks and 80,000 monks, this king Milinda tells me that he has come on a chariot. But when asked to explain to me what a chariot is, he cannot establish its existence. How can one possibly approve of that?'

The five hundred Greeks thereupon applauded the Venerable Nagasena and said to king Milinda: 'Now let your Majesty get out of that if you can!'

But king Milinda said to Nagasena: 'I have not, Nagasena, spoken a falsehood. For it is in dependence on the pole, the axle, the wheels, the framework, the flagstaff, etc., that there takes place this denomination "chariot", this designation, this conceptual term, a current appellation and a mere name'. – 'Your Majesty has spoken well about the chariot. It is just so with me. In dependence on the thirty-two parts of the body and the five Skandhas there takes place this denomination "Nagasena", this designation, this conceptual term, a current appellation and a mere name. In ultimate reality, however, this person cannot be apprehended. And this has been said by our Sister Vajira when she was face to face with the Lord:

> "Where all constituent parts are present,
> The word 'a chariot' is applied.
> So likewise where the skandhas are,
> The term a 'being' commonly is used." '

'It is wonderful, Nagasena, it is astonishing, Nagasena! Most brilliantly have these questions been answered! Were the Buddha himself here, he would approve what you have said. Well spoken, Nagasena, well spoken!'

2b. *Personal identity and rebirth*

The king asked: 'When someone is reborn, Venerable Nagasena, is he the same as the one who just died, or is he another?' – The Elder replied: 'He is neither the same nor another'. – 'Give me an illustration!' – 'What do you think, great king: when you were a tiny infant, newly born and quite soft, were you then the same as the one who is now grown up?' – 'No, that infant was one, I, now grown up, am another'. – 'If that is so, then, great king, you have had no mother, no father, no teaching, and no schooling! Do we then take it that there is one mother for the embryo in the first stage, another for the second stage, another for the third, another for the fourth, another for the baby, another for the grown-up man? Is the schoolboy one person, and the one who has finished school another? Does one commit a crime, but the hands and feet of another are cut off?' – 'Certainly not! But what would you say, Reverend Sir, to all that?' – The Elder replied: 'I was neither the tiny infant, newly born and quite soft, nor am I now the grown-up man; but all these are comprised in one unit depending on this very body.' – 'Give me a simile!' – 'If a man were to light a lamp, could it give light throughout the whole night?' – 'Yes, it could.' – 'Is now the flame which burns in the first watch of the night the same as the one which burns in the second?' – 'It is not the same.' – 'Or is the flame which burns in the second watch the same as the one which burns in the last one?' – 'It is not the same.' – 'Do we then take it that there is one lamp in the first watch of the night, another in the second, and another again in the third?' – 'No, it is because of just that one lamp that the light shines throughout the night.' – 'Even so must we understand the collocation of a series of successive dharmas. At rebirth one dharma arises, while another stops; but the two processes take place almost simultaneously (i.e. they are continuous). Therefore the first act of consciousness in the new existence is neither the same as the last act of consciousness in the previous existence, nor is it another.' – 'Give me another simile!' – 'Milk, once the milking is done, turns after some time into curds; from curds it turns into fresh butter, and from fresh butter into ghee. Would it now be correct to say that the milk is the same thing as the curds, or the fresh butter, or the ghee?' – 'No, it would not. But they have been produced because of it.' – 'Just so must be understood the collocation of a series of successive dharmas.'

2c. Personal identity and Karma

The king asked: 'Is there, Nagasena, any being which passes on from this body to another body?' – 'No, your majesty!' – 'If there were no passing on from this body to another, would not one then in one's next life be freed from the evil deeds committed in the past?' – 'Yes, that would be so if one were not linked once again with a new organism. But since, your majesty, one is linked once again with a new organism, therefore one is not freed from one's evil deeds.' – 'Give me a simile!' – 'If a man should steal another man's mangoes, would he deserve a thrashing for that?' – 'Yes, of course!' – 'But he would not have stolen the very same mangoes as the other one had planted. Why then should he deserve a thrashing?' – 'For the reason that the stolen mangoes had grown because of those that were planted.' – 'Just so, your majesty, it is because of the deeds one does, whether pure or impure, by means of this psycho-physical organism, that one is once again linked with another psycho-physical organism, and is not freed from one's evil deeds.' – 'Very good, Nagasena!'

3. THE FIVE CARDINAL VIRTUES

The king said: 'Is it through wise attention that people become exempt from further rebirth?' – 'Yes, that is due to wise attention, and also to wisdom, and the other wholesome dharmas.' – 'But is not wise attention the same as wisdom?' – 'No, your majesty! Attention is one thing, and wisdom another. Sheep and goats, oxen and buffaloes, camels and asses have attention, but wisdom they have not.' – 'Well put, Nagasena!'

The king said: 'What is the mark of attention, and what is the mark of wisdom?' – 'Consideration is the mark of attention, cutting off that of wisdom.' – 'How is that? Give me a simile!' – 'You know barley-reapers, I suppose?' – 'Yes, I do.' – 'How then do they reap the barley?' – 'With the left hand they seize a bunch of barley, in the right hand they hold a sickle, and they cut the barley off with that sickle.' – 'Just so, your majesty, the Yogin seizes his mental processes with his attention, and by his wisdom he cuts off the defilements.' – 'Well put, Venerable Nagasena!'

The king said: 'When you just spoke of "the other wholesome dharmas", which ones did you mean?' – 'I meant morality, faith, vigour, mindfulness, and concentration.' – 'And what is the mark of morality?' – 'Morality has the mark of providing a basis for all wholesome dharmas, whatever they may be. When based on morality, all the wholesome dharmas will not dwindle away.' – 'Give me an illustration!' – 'As all plants and animals which increase, grow, and prosper, do so with the earth as their support, with the earth as their basis, just so the Yogin, with morality as his support, with morality as his basis, develops the five cardinal virtues, i.e. the cardinal virtues of faith, vigour, mindfulness, concentration, and wisdom.'

'Give me a further illustration!'

'As the builder of a city when constructing a town first of all clears the site, removes all stumps and thorns, and levels it; and only after that he lays out and marks off the roads and cross-roads, and so builds the city. Even so the Yogin develops the five cardinal virtues with morality as his support, with morality as his basis.'

The king said: 'What is the mark of *faith*?' – 'Faith makes serene, and it leaps forward.' – 'And how does faith make serene?' – 'When faith arises it arrests the [five] Hindrances, and the heart becomes free from them, clear, serene and undisturbed.' – 'Give me an illustration!' – 'A universal monarch might on his way, together with his fourfold army, cross over a small stream. Stirred up by the elephants and horses, by the chariots and infantry, the water would become disturbed, agitated and muddy. Having crossed over, the universal monarch would order his men to bring some water for him to drink. But the king would possess a miraculous water-clearing gem, and his men, in obedience to his command, would throw it into the stream. Then at once all fragments of vegetation would float away, the mud would settle at the bottom, the stream would become clear, serene and undisturbed, and fit to be drunk by the universal monarch. Here the stream corresponds to the heart, the monarch's men to the Yogin, the fragments of vegetation and the mud to the defilements, and the miraculous water-clearing gem to faith.'

'And how does faith leap forward?' – 'When the Yogin sees that the hearts of others have been set free, he leaps forward, by way of aspiration, to the various Fruits of a holy life, and he makes efforts to attain the yet unattained, to find the yet unfound, to realize the yet unrealized.' – 'Give me an illustration!' – 'Suppose that a great cloud were to burst over a hill-slope. The water then would flow down the slope, would first fill all the hill's clefts, fissures, and gullies, and would then run into the river below, making its banks overflow on both sides. Now suppose further that a great crowd of people had come along, and unable to size up either the width or the depth of the river, should stand frightened and hesitating on the bank. But then some man would come along, who, conscious of his own strength and power, would firmly tie on his loin-cloth and jump across the river. And the great crowd of people, seeing him on the other side, would cross likewise. Even so the Yogin, when he has seen that the hearts of others have been set free, leaps forward, by aspiration, to the various Fruits of the holy life, and he makes efforts to attain the yet unattained, to find the yet unfound, to realize the yet unrealized. And this is what the Lord has said in the *Samyutta Nikaya*:

> "By faith the flood is crossed,
>   By wakefulness the sea;
>   By vigour ill is passed;
>   By wisdom cleansed is he." '

'Well put, Nagasena!'

The king asked: 'And what is the mark of *vigour*?' – 'Vigour props up, and, when propped up by vigour, all the wholesome dharmas do not dwindle away.' – 'Give me a

simile!' – 'If a man's house were falling down, he would prop
it up with a new piece of wood, and, so supported, that house
would not collapse.'

The king asked: 'And what is the mark of *mindfulness*?' –
'Calling to mind and taking up.'

'How is calling to mind a mark of mindfulness?' – 'When
mindfulness arises, one calls to mind the dharmas which
participate in what is wholesome and unwholesome, blameable
and blameless, inferior and sublime, dark and light, i.e. these
are the four applications of mindfulness, these the four right
efforts, these the four roads to psychic power, these the five
cardinal virtues, these the five powers, these the seven limbs
of enlightenment, this is the holy eightfold path; this is calm,
this insight, this knowledge and this emancipation. Thereafter
the Yogin tends those dharmas which should be tended, and
he does not tend those which should not be tended; he par-
takes of those dharmas which should be followed, and he does
not partake of those which should not be followed. It is in
this sense that calling to mind is a mark of mindfulness.' –
'Give me a simile!' – 'It is like the treasurer of a universal
monarch, who each morning and evening reminds his royal
master of his magnificent assets: "So many elephants you have,
so many horses, so many chariots, so much infantry, so many
gold coins, so much bullion, so much property; may your
majesty bear this in mind!" In this way he calls to mind his
master's wealth.'

'And how does mindfulness take up?' – 'When mindfulness
arises, the outcome of beneficial and harmful dharmas is
examined in this way: "These dharmas are beneficial, these
harmful; these dharmas are helpful, these unhelpful." Thereafter the Yogin removes the harmful dharmas, and takes up
the beneficial ones; he removes the unhelpful dharmas, and
takes up the helpful ones. It is in this sense that mindfulness
takes up.' – 'Give me a comparison!' – 'It is like the invaluable
adviser of a universal monarch who knows what is beneficial
and what harmful to his royal master, what is helpful and what
unhelpful. Thereafter what is harmful and unhelpful can be
removed, what is beneficial and helpful can be taken up.'

The king asked: 'And what is the mark of *concentration*?' – 'It stands at the head. Whatever wholesome dharmas there may be, they all are headed by concentration, they bend towards concentration, lead to concentration, incline to concentration.' – 'Give me a comparison!' – 'It is as with a building with a pointed roof: whatever rafters there are, they all converge on the top, bend towards the top, meet at the top, and the top occupies the most prominent place. So with concentration in relation to the other wholesome dharmas.' – 'Give me a further comparison!' – 'If a king were to enter battle with his fourfold army, then all his troops – the elephants, cavalry, chariots, and infantry – would be headed by him, and would be ranged around him. Such is the position of concentration in relation to the other wholesome dharmas.'

The king then asked: 'What then is the mark of *wisdom*?' – 'Cutting off is, as I said before, one mark of wisdom. In addition it illuminates.' – 'And how does wisdom illuminate?' – 'When wisdom arises, it dispels the darkness of ignorance, generates the illumination of knowledge, sheds the light of cognition, and makes the holy truths stand out clearly. Thereafter the Yogin, with his correct wisdom, can see impermanence, ill, and not-self.' – 'Give me a comparison!' – 'It is like a lamp which a man would take into a dark house. It would dispel the darkness, would illuminate, shed light, and make the forms in the house stand out clearly.' – 'Well put, Nagasena!'

4. EMANCIPATION AND NIRVANA

4a. *Problems of Nirvana*

The king asked: 'Is cessation Nirvana?' – 'Yes, your majesty!' – 'How is that, Nagasena?' – 'All the foolish common people take delight in the senses and their objects, are impressed by them, are attached to them. In that way they are carried away by the flood, and are not set free from birth, old age, and death, from grief, lamentation, pain, sadness, and despair – they are, I say, not set free from suffering. But the well-informed holy disciples do not take delight in the senses and their objects, are not impressed by them, are not attached to them, and in consequence their craving ceases; the cessation of craving leads successively to that of grasping, of becoming, of birth, of old age and death, of grief, lamentation, pain, sadness, and despair – that is to say to the cessation of all this mass of ill. It is thus that cessation is Nirvana.' – 'Very good, Nagasena!'

The king asked: 'Do all win Nirvana?' – 'No, they do not. Only those win Nirvana who, progressing correctly, know by their superknowledge those dharmas which should be known by superknowledge, comprehend those dharmas which should be comprehended, forsake those dharmas which should be forsaken, develop those dharmas which should be developed, and realize those dharmas which should be realized.' – 'Very good, Nagasena!'

The king asked: 'Do those who have not won Nirvana know how happy a state it is?' – 'Yes, they do.' – 'But how can one know this about Nirvana without having attained it?' – 'Now what do you think, your majesty? Do those who have not had their hands and feet cut off know how bad it is to have them cut off?' – 'Yes, they do.' – 'And how do they know it?' – 'From hearing the sound of the lamentations of those whose hands and feet have been cut off.' – 'So it is by hearing the words of those who have seen Nirvana that one knows it to be a happy state.' – 'Very good, Nagasena!'

4b. *The nature of Nirvana*

King Milinda said: 'I will grant you, Nagasena, that Nirvana is absolute Ease, and that nevertheless one cannot point to its form or shape, its duration or size, either by simile or explanation, by reason or by argument. But is there perhaps some quality of Nirvana which it shares with other things, and which lends itself to a metaphorical explanation?' – 'Its form, O king, cannot be elucidated by similes, but its qualities can.' – 'How good to hear that, Nagasena! Speak then, quickly, so that I may have an explanation of even one of the aspects of Nirvana! Appease the fever of my heart! Allay it with the cool sweet breezes of your words!'

'Nirvana shares one quality with the lotus, two with water, three with medicine, ten with space, three with the wishing jewel, and five with a mountain peak. As the lotus is unstained by water, so is Nirvana unstained by all the defilements. – As cool water allays feverish heat, so also Nirvana is cool and allays the fever of all the passions. Moreover, as water removes the thirst of men and beasts who are exhausted, parched, thirsty, and overpowered by heat, so also Nirvana removes the craving for sensuous enjoyments, the craving for further becoming, the craving for the cessation of becoming. – As medicine protects from the torments of poison, so Nirvana from the torments of the poisonous passions. Moreover, as medicine puts an end to sickness, so Nirvana to all sufferings. Finally, Nirvana and medicine both give security. – And these are the ten qualities which Nirvana shares with space. Neither is born, grows old, dies, passes away, or is reborn; both are unconquerable, cannot be stolen, are unsupported, are roads respectively for birds and Arhats to journey on, are unobstructed and infinite. – Like the wishing jewel, Nirvana grants all one can desire, brings joy, and sheds light. – As a mountain peak is lofty and exalted, so is Nirvana. As a mountain peak is unshakeable, so is Nirvana. As a mountain peak is inaccessible, so is Nirvana inaccessible to all the passions. As no seeds can grow on a mountain peak, so the seeds of all the passions cannot grow in Nirvana. And finally, as a mountain peak is free from all desire to please or displease, so is Nirvana.' – 'Well said, Nagasena! So it is, and as such I accept it.'

4c. *The realization of Nirvana*

King Milinda said: 'In the world one can see things produced of karma, things produced from a cause, things produced by nature. Tell me, what in the world is not born of karma, or a cause, or of nature?' – 'There are two such things, space and Nirvana.' – 'Do not, Nagasena, corrupt the Jina's words, do not answer the question ignorantly!' – 'What did I say, your majesty, that you speak thus to me?' – 'What you said about space not being born of karma, or from a cause, or from nature, that was correct. But with many hundreds of arguments has the Lord proclaimed to his disciples the way to the realization of Nirvana – and then you say that Nirvana is not born of a cause!' – 'It is true that the Lord has with many hundreds of arguments proclaimed to his disciples the way to the realization of Nirvana; but that does not mean that he has spoken of a cause for the production of Nirvana.'

'Here, Nagasena, we do indeed enter from darkness into greater darkness, from a jungle into a deeper jungle, from a thicket into a denser thicket, inasmuch as we are given a cause for the realization of Nirvana, but no cause for the production of that same dharma (i.e. Nirvana). If there is a cause for the realization of Nirvana, we would also expect one for its production. If there is a son's father, one would for that reason also expect the father to have had a father; if there is a pupil's teacher, one would for that reason also expect the teacher to have had a teacher; if there is a seed for a sprout, one would for that reason also expect the seed to have had a seed. Just so, if there is cause for the realization of Nirvana, one would for that reason also expect a cause for its production. If a tree or creeper has a top, then for that reason it must also have a middle and a root. Just so, if there is a cause for the realization of Nirvana, one would for that reason also expect a cause for its production.' – 'Nirvana, O king, is not something that should be produced. That is why no cause for its production has been proclaimed.' – 'Please, Nagasena, give me a reason, convince me by an argument, so that I can understand this point!'

'Well then, O king, attend carefully, listen closely, and I will tell you the reason for this. Could a man with his natural strength go up from here to the Himalaya mountains?' – 'Yes, he could.' – 'But could that man with his natural strength bring the Himalaya mountains here?' – 'No, he could not.' – 'Just so it is possible to point out the way to the realization of Nirvana, but impossible to show a cause for its production. Could a man, who with his natural strength has crossed in a boat over the great ocean, get to the farther shore?' – 'Yes, he could.' – 'But could that man with his natural strength bring the farther shore of the great ocean here?' – 'No, he could not.' – 'Just so one can point out the way to the realization of Nirvana, but one cannot show a cause for its production. And what is the reason for that? Because that dharma, Nirvana, is unconditioned.' – 'Is then, Nagasena, Nirvana unconditioned?' – 'So it is, O king, unconditioned is Nirvana, not made by anything. Of Nirvana one cannot say that it is produced, or unproduced, or that it should be produced; that it is past, or future, or present; or that one can become aware of it by the eye, or the ear, or the nose, or the tongue, or the body.' – 'In that case, Nagasena, you indicate Nirvana as a dharma which is not, and Nirvana does not exist.' – 'Nirvana is something which is. It is cognizable by the mind. A holy disciple, who has followed the right road, sees Nirvana with a mind which is pure, sublime, straight, unimpeded and disinterested.' – 'But what then is that Nirvana like? Give me a simile, and convince me by arguments. For a dharma which exists can surely be illustrated by a simile!'

'Is there, great king, something called "wind"?' – 'Yes, there is such a thing.' – 'Please, will your majesty show me the wind, its colour and shape, and whether it is thin or thick, long or short.' – 'One cannot point to the wind like that. For the wind does not lend itself to being grasped with the hands, or to being touched. But nevertheless there is such a thing as "wind".' – 'If one cannot point to the wind, one might conclude that there is no wind at all.' – 'But I know, Nagasena, that there is wind, I am quite convinced of it, in spite of the fact that I cannot point it out.' – 'Just so, your majesty, there is Nirvana, but one cannot point to Nirvana, either by its colour or its shape.' – 'Very good, Nagasena. Clear is the simile, convincing is the argument. So it is, and so I accept it: there is a Nirvana.'

4d. The saints and their bodies

The king asked: 'Does someone who is no more reborn feel any unpleasant feelings?' – The Elder replied: 'Some he feels, and others not.' – 'Which ones does he feel, and which ones not?' – 'He feels physical, but not mental pain.' – 'How is that?' – 'The causes and conditions which produce feelings of physical pain have not ceased to operate, whereas those which produce feelings of mental pain have. And so it has been said by the Lord: "Only one kind of feelings he feels, physical, and not mental." ' – 'And when he feels a physical pain, why does he not escape into final Nirvana, by dying quickly?' – 'An Arhat has no more likes or dislikes. Arhats do not shake down the unripe fruit, the wise wait for it to mature. And so it has been said by the Elder Sariputra, the Dharma's general:

> "It is not death, it is not life I cherish.
> I bide my time, a servant waiting for his wage.
> It is not death, it is not life I cherish.
> I bide my time, in mindfulness and wisdom steeped." '

'Well put, Nagasena!'

The king asked: 'Is the body dear to you recluses?' – 'No, it is not.' – 'But why then do you look after it, and cherish it so?' – 'Has your majesty somewhere and at some time in the course of a battle been wounded by an arrow?' – 'Yes, that has happened.' – 'In such cases, is not the wound anointed with salve, smeared with oil, and bandaged with fine linen?' – 'Yes, so it is.' – 'Is then this treatment a sign that the wound is dear to your majesty?' – 'No, it is not dear to me, but all this is done to it so that the flesh may grow again.' – 'Just so the body is not dear to the recluses. Without being attached to the body they take care of it for the purpose of making a holy life possible. The Lord has compared the body to a wound, and so the recluses take care for the body as for a wound, without being attached to it. For the Lord has said:

> "A damp skin hides it, but it is a wound, large, with nine
>   openings,
> All around it oozes impure and evil-smelling matter." '

'Well answered, Nagasena!'

The king asked: 'What is the difference between someone

with greed and someone without greed?' – 'The one is attached, the other unattached.' – 'What does that mean?' – 'The one covets, the other does not.' – 'As I see it, the greedy person and the one who is free from greed both wish for agreeable food, and neither of them wishes for bad food.' – 'But the one who is not free from greed eats his food while experiencing both its taste and some greed for tastes; the one who is free from greed eats his food while experiencing its taste, but without having any greed for it.' – 'Very good, Nagasena!'

The king asked: 'For what reason does the common worldling suffer both physical and mental pain?' – 'Because his thought is so undeveloped. He is like a hungry and excited ox, who has been tied up with a weak, fragile and short piece of straw or creeper, and who, when agitated, rushes off, taking his tether with him. So, someone whose thought is undeveloped, gets agitated in his mind when a pain arises in him, and his agitated mind bends and contorts his body, and makes it writhe. Undeveloped in his mind he trembles, shrieks, and cries with terror. This is the reason why the common worldling suffers both physical and mental pain.' – 'And what is the reason why Arhats feel only one kind of feelings, physical and not mental?' – 'The thought of the Arhats is developed, well developed, it is tamed, well tamed, it is obedient and disciplined. When invaded by a painful feeling, the Arhat firmly grasps at the idea of its impermanence, and ties his thought to the post of contemplation. And his thought, tied to the post of contemplation, does not tremble or shake, remains steadfast and undisturbed. But the disturbing influence of the pain, nevertheless, makes his body bend, contorts it, makes it writhe.

'That, Nagasena, is indeed a most wonderful thing in this world, that someone's mind should remain unshaken when his body is shaken. Tell me the reason for that!' – 'Suppose, your majesty, that there is a gigantic tree, with trunk, branches, and leaves. If it were hit by the force of the wind, its branches would shake, but would the trunk also shake?' – 'No, Venerable Sir!' – 'Just so the thought of the Arhat does not tremble or shake, like the trunk of the gigantic tree.' – 'Wonderful, Nagasena, most admirable, Nagasena!'

5. *Conclusion*

The king, as a result of his discussions with the Venerable Nagasena, was overjoyed and humbled; he saw the value in the Buddha's religion, gained confidence in the Triple Jewel, lost his spikiness and obstinacy, gained faith in the qualities of the Elder – in his observation of the monastic rules, his spiritual progress and his general demeanour – became trusting and resigned, free from conceit and arrogance. Like a cobra whose fangs have been drawn, he said: 'Well said, well said, Nagasena! You have answered my questions, which would have given scope to a Buddha, you have answered them well! Apart from the Elder Sariputra, the supreme general of the Dharma, there is no one in this religion of the Buddha who can deal with questions as well as you do. Forgive my transgressions, Nagasena! May the Venerable Nagasena accept me as a lay-follower, as one who takes his refuge with the Triple Jewel, from to-day onwards, as long as I shall live!'

2. THE HEART SUTRA

I. *The invocation*

Homage to the Perfection of Wisdom, the lovely, the holy!

II. *The prologue*

Avalokita, the holy Lord and Bodhisattva, was moving in the deep course of the wisdom which has gone beyond. He looked down from on high, he beheld but five heaps, and he saw that in their own-being they were empty.

III. *The dialectics of emptiness. First stage*

Here, O Sariputra, form is emptiness, and the very emptiness is form; emptiness does not differ from form, form does not differ from emptiness; whatever is form, that is emptiness, whatever is emptiness, that is form. The same is true of feelings, perceptions, impulses, and consciousness.

IV. *The dialectics of emptiness. Second stage*

Here, O Sariputra, all dharmas are marked with emptiness; they are not produced or stopped, not defiled or immaculate, not deficient or complete.

V. *The dialectics of emptiness. Third stage*

Therefore, O Sariputra, in emptiness there is no form, nor feeling, nor perception, nor impulse, nor consciousness; no eye, ear, nose, tongue, body, mind; no forms, sounds, smells, tastes, touchables or objects of mind; no sight-organ-element, and so forth, until we come to: no mind-consciousness-element; there is no ignorance, no extinction of ignorance, and so forth, until we come to: there is no decay and death, no extinction of decay and death; there is no suffering, no origination, no stopping, no path; there is no cognition, no attainment, and no non-attainment.

VI. *The concrete embodiment and practical basis of emptiness*

Therefore, O Sariputra, it is because of his indifference to any kind of personal attainment that a Bodhisattva, through having relied on the perfection of wisdom, dwells without thought-coverings. In the absence of thought-coverings he has not been made to tremble, he has overcome what can upset, and in the end he attains to Nirvana.

VII. *Full emptiness is the basis also of Buddhahood*

All those who appear as Buddhas in the three periods of time fully awake to the utmost, right and perfect enlightenment because they have relied on the perfection of wisdom.

VIII. *The teaching brought within reach of the comparatively unenlightened*

Therefore one should know the Prajñaparamita as the great spell, the spell of great knowledge, the utmost spell, the unequalled spell, allayer of all suffering, in truth – for what could go wrong? By the Prajñaparamita has this spell been delivered. It runs like this: Gone, Gone, Gone beyond, Gone altogether beyond, O what an awakening, All Hail!

This completes the Heart of Perfect Wisdom.

3. FROM THE 'DIAMOND SUTRA'

The Bodhisattva and Dipankara

The Lord asked Subhuti: What do you think, was there any dharma which awoke the Tathagata, when he was with the Tathagata Dipankara (see page 20) to the utmost, right, and perfect enlightenment? – Subhuti replied: As I understand the meaning of the Lord's teaching, this was not due to any dharma. – The Lord said: So it is, Subhuti, so it is. If again, Subhuti, the Tathagata had fully known any dharma, then the Tathagata would not have predicted of me: 'You, young Brahmin, will in a future period be a Tathagata, Arhat, Fully Enlightened, by the name of Shakyamuni!' But he made this prediction because it is not through any dharma that the Tathagata, the Arhat, the Fully Enlightened One has fully known the utmost, right, and perfect enlightenment.

The initial vow of a Bodhisattva

The Lord said: Here, Subhuti, someone who has set out in the vehicle of a Bodhisattva should think in this manner: 'As many beings as there are in the universe of beings, comprehended under the term "beings" – egg-born, born from a womb, moisture-born, or miraculously born; with or without form; with perception, without perception, or with neither perception nor no-perception – as far as any conceivable form of beings is conceived: all these I must lead to Nirvana, into that Realm of Nirvana which leaves nothing behind. And yet, although innumerable beings have thus been led to Nirvana, in fact no being at all has been led to Nirvana.' And why? If in a Bodhisattva the notion of a 'being' should take place, he could not be called a 'Bodhi-being'. And why? He is not to be called a Bodhi-being, in whom the notion of a self or of a being should take place, or the notion of a living soul or a person.

The practice of perfect giving

Moreover, Subhuti, a Bodhisattva who gives gifts should not lean on anything, or anywhere. When he gives gifts he should not be supported by sight-objects, sounds, smells, tastes, touchables, or mind-objects. For, Subhuti, the Bodhisattva, the great being should give gifts in such a way that he is not supported by the notion of a sign. And why? Because the heap of merit of that Bodhi-being, who unsupported gives a gift, is not easy to measure.

The practice of perfect patience

Moreover, Subhuti, the Tathagata's perfection of patience is really a non-perfection. And why? Because, Subhuti, when the king of Kali cut my flesh from every limb, at that time I had no notion of a self, a being, a soul, or a person. In fact I had no notion or non-notion at all. And why? If, Subhuti, at that time I had had a notion of self, I would also have conceived ill-will at that time. And likewise if I had had a notion of a being, a soul, or a person. And why? By my supernatural knowledge I know the past, and that five hundred births ago I was the Rishi 'Preacher of Patience', and furthermore that then also I had no notion of a self, a being, a soul, or a person.

The Bodhisattva's final Nirvana

Therefore then, Subhuti, the Bodhisattva should produce an unsupported thought, i.e. a thought which is nowhere supported, a thought unsupported by sights, sounds, smells, tastes, touchables, or mind-objects.

The Bodhisattva as a fully enlightened Buddha

The Lord asked: What do you think, Subhuti, is there any dharma which the Tathagata has fully known as the utmost, right, and perfect enlightenment, or is there any dharma which the Tathagata has demonstrated? – Subhuti replied: No, not as I understand what the Lord has said. And why? This dharma which the Tathagata has fully known or demonstrated – it cannot be grasped, it cannot be talked about, it is neither a dharma nor a non-dharma. And why? Because an Absolute exalts the Holy Persons.

The Buddha's physical body

The Lord asked: What do you think, Subhuti, can the Tathagata be seen by means of his possession of marks? – Subhuti replied: No indeed, O Lord, not as I understand what the Lord has taught. – The Lord said: Well said, well said, Subhuti. So it is, Subhuti, so it is, as you say. For if the Tathagata were one who could be seen by his possession of the thirty-two Marks, then also the universal monarch would be a Tathagata. Therefore the Tathagata is not to be seen by means of his possession of Marks. – And further the Lord taught on that occasion the following stanza:

> Those who by my form did see me,
> And those who followed me by voice,
> Wrong the efforts they engaged in,
> Me those people will not see.

The Buddha as the Tathagata

Whosoever says that the Tathagata goes or comes, stands, sits, or lies down, he does not understand the meaning of my teaching. And why? 'Tathagata' is called one who has not gone to anywhere, and who has not come from anywhere. Therefore is he called 'the Tathagata, the Arhat, the Fully Enlightened One'.

The Buddha as a teacher

The Lord asked: What do you think, Subhuti, does it occur to the Tathagata that he has demonstrated dharma? – Subhuti replied: No indeed, O Lord, it does not. – The Lord said: Whosoever should say that 'the Tathagata has demonstrated dharma', he would speak falsely, he would misrepresent me by seizing on what is not there. And why? One speaks of 'demonstration of dharma', Subhuti, but there is not any dharma which could be apprehended as demonstration of dharma.

The Buddha as a saviour

What do you think, Subhuti, does it occur to a Tathagata that he has set beings free? Not so should one see it, Subhuti. And why? There is not any being whom the Tathagata has set free. For if there had been any being to be set free by the Tathagata, then surely there would have been on the part of the Tathagata a seizing on a self, a being, a soul, a person. One speaks of 'seizing on a self', but as a no-seizing, Subhuti, has that been taught by the Tathagata. And yet it has been seized upon by foolish common people. One speaks of 'foolish common people', but as really no people have they been taught by the Tathagata. Therefore are they called 'foolish common people'.

The application to the present day

Subhuti asked: Will there be any beings in the future period, in the last time, in the last epoch, in the last five hundred years, at the time of the collapse of the good doctrine, who, when these words of the Sutra are being taught, will understand their truth? – The Lord replied: Do not speak thus, Subhuti! Yes, even then there will be such beings. For even at that time, Subhuti, there will be Bodhisattvas who are gifted with good conduct, gifted with virtuous qualities, gifted with wisdom, and who, when these words of the Sutra are being taught, will understand their truth. And these Bodhisattvas, Subhuti, will not be such as have honoured only one single Buddha, nor such as have planted their roots of merit under one single Buddha only. On the contrary, Subhuti, those Bodhisattvas who, when these words of the Sutra are being taught, will find even one single thought of serene faith, they will be such as have honoured many hundreds of thousands of Buddhas, such as have planted their roots of merit under many hundreds of thousands of Buddhas. Known they are, Subhuti, to the Tathagata through his Buddha-cognition, seen they are, Subhuti, by the Tathagata with his Buddha-eye, fully known they are, Subhuti, to the Tathagata. And they all, Subhuti, will beget and acquire an immeasurable and incalculable heap of merit. And why? Because, Subhuti, in these Bodhisattvas no perception of a self takes place, no perception of a being, of a soul, of a person. Nor do they have a perception of a dharma, or a no-dharma. No perception or non-perception takes place in them. And why? If, Subhuti, these Bodhisattvas should have a perception of either a dharma or a no-dharma, they would thereby seize on a self, a being, a soul, or a person. And why? Because a Bodhisattva should not seize on either a dharma or a no-dharma. Therefore this saying has been taught by the Tathagata with a hidden meaning: 'Those who know the discourse on dharma as like unto a raft, should forsake dharmas, still more so no-dharmas'.

4. RAHULABHADRA.
'HYMN TO PERFECT WISDOM'

1. Homage to Thee, Perfect Wisdom,
   Boundless, and transcending thought!
   All Thy limbs are without blemish,
   Faultless those who Thee discern.

2. Spotless, unobstructed, silent,
   Like the vast expanse of space;
   Who in truth does really see Thee
   The Tathagata perceives.

3. As the moonlight does not differ
   From the moon, so also Thou
   Who abound'st in holy virtues,
   And the Teacher of the world.

4. Those, all pity, who came to Thee,
   Buddhadharmas heralding,
   They will win with ease, O Gracious!
   Majesty beyond compare.

5. Pure in heart, when once they duly
   Look upon Thee, surely then
   Their complete success is certain —
   O, Thou fruitful to behold!

6. To all heroes who of others
   Have the welfare close at heart,
   Thou a mother, who doest nourish,
   Givest birth, and givest love.

7. Teachers of the world, the Buddhas,
   Are Thine own compassionate sons;
   Then art Thou, O Blessed Lady,
   Grandam thus of beings all.

8. All th' immaculate perfections
   At all times encircle Thee,
   As the stars surround the crescent,
   O Thou blameless holy one!

9. Those in need of light considering,
   The Tathagatas extol
   Thee, the Single One, as many,
   Multiformed and many-named.

10. As the drops of dew in contact
    With the sun's rays disappear,
    So all theorizings vanish,
    Once one has obtainèd Thee.

11. When as fearful Thou appearest
    Thou engender'st fear in fools;
    When benignly Thou appearest
    Comes assurance to the wise.

12. How will one who no affection
    Has for Thee, though yet you saved him,
    Have, O Mother, greed and loathing
    For the many other things?

13. Not from anywhere Thou comest,
    And to nowhere dost Thou go;
    In no dwelling place have sages
    Ever apprehended Thee.

14. Not to see Thee in this manner
    Is to have attained to Thee,
    Gaining thus the final freedom —
    O how wonderful is this!

15. One indeed is bound who sees Thee;
    One who sees not is bound too.
    One again is freed who sees Thee;
    One who sees not freed is too.

16. Wonderful, profound, illustrious,
    Hard Thou art to recognize.
    Like a mock show Thou art seen, and
    Yet Thou art not seen at all.

17. By all Buddhas, Single Buddhas,
    By Disciples courted, too,
    Thou the one path to salvation,
    There's no other verily.

18. Saviours of the world, from pity,
    So that men might understand,
    Speak of Thee, observing custom,
    Yet of Thee they do not speak.

19. Who is able here to praise Thee,
    Lacking signs and featureless?
    Thou the range of speech transcending,
    Not supported anywhere.

20. In such words of current language
    Constantly we laud Thee, whom
    None of our acclaim concerneth;
    So we reach beatitude.

21. By my praise of Perfect Wisdom
    All the merit I may rear,
    Let that make the world devoted
    To this wisdom without peer.

5. SENG-TS'AN, 'ON BELIEVING IN MIND'

1. The perfect way knows no difficulties
   Except that it refuses to make preferences;
   Only when freed from hate and love
   It reveals itself fully and without disguise;
   A tenth of an inch's difference,
   And heaven and earth are set apart.
   If you wish to see it before your own eyes
   Have no fixed thoughts either for or against it.

2. To set up what you like against what you dislike –
   That is the disease of the mind:
   When the deep meaning (of the Way) is not understood,
   Peace of mind is disturbed to no purpose.

3. (The Way) is perfect like unto vast space,
   With nothing wanting, nothing superfluous.
   It is indeed due to making choice
   That its Suchness is lost sight of.

4. Pursue not the outer entanglements,
   Dwell not in the inner Void;
   Be serene in the oneness of things,
   And dualism vanishes by itself.

5. When you strive to gain quiescence by stopping motion,
   The quiescence thus gained is ever in motion;
   As long as you tarry in the dualism,
   How can you realize oneness?

6. And when oneness is not thoroughly understood,
   In two ways loss is sustained:
   The denying of reality is the asserting of it,
   And the asserting of emptiness is the denying of it.

7. Wordiness and intellection –
   The more with them, the further astray we go;
   Away therefore with wordiness and intellection,
   And there is no place where we cannot pass freely.

8. When we return to the root, we gain the meaning;
   When we pursue external objects we lose the reason.
   The moment we are enlightened within,
   We go beyond the voidness of a world confronting us.

9. Transformations going on in an empty world which confronts
   us
   Appear real all because of ignorance:
   Try not to seek after the true,
   Only cease to cherish opinions.

10. Abide not with dualism,
    Carefully avoid pursuing it;
    As soon as you have right and wrong,
    Confusion ensues, and Mind is lost.

11. The two exist because of the One,
    But hold not even to this One;
    When a mind is not disturbed,
    The ten thousand things offer no offence.

12. No offence offered, and no ten thousand things;
    No disturbance going, and no mind set up to work;
    The subject is quieted when the object ceases,
    The object ceases when the subject is quieted.

13. The object is an object for the subject,
    The subject is a subject for the object;
    Know that the relativity of the two
    Rests ultimately on one emptiness.

14. In one emptiness the two are not distinguished,
    And each contains in itself all the ten thousand things;
    When no discrimination is made between this and that,
    How can a one-sided and prejudiced view arise?

15. The Great Way is calm and large-hearted,
    For it nothing is easy, nothing hard;
    Small views are irresolute, the more in haste, the tardier they go.

16. Clinging is never kept within bounds,
    It is sure to go the wrong way;
    Quit it, and things follow their own courses,
    While the essence neither departs nor abides.

17. Obey the nature of things, and you are in concord with
    The Way, calm, and easy, and free from annoyance;
    But when your thoughts are tied, you turn away from the truth,
    They grow heavier and duller, and are not at all sound.

18. When they are not sound, the spirit is troubled;
    What is the use of being partial and one-sided then?
    If you want to walk the course of the One Vehicle,
    Be not prejudiced against the six sense objects.

19. When you are not prejudiced against the six sense objects,
    You are then one with the enlightenment.
    The wise are non-active,
    While the ignorant bind themselves up;
    While in the Dharma itself there is no individuation.
    They ignorantly attach themselves to particular objects.
    It is their own mind that creates illusions,
    Is this not the greatest of all self-contradictions?

20. The ignorant cherish the idea of rest and unrest,
    The enlightened have no likes and dislikes;
    All forms of dualism
    Are contrived by the ignorant themselves.
    They are like unto visions and flowers in the air:
    Why should we trouble ourselves to take hold of them?
    Gain and loss, right and wrong –
    Away with them once for all!

21. If an eye never falls asleep,
    All dreams will by themselves cease;
    If the Mind retains its absoluteness,
    The ten thousand things are of one Suchness.

22. When the deep mystery of one Suchness is fathomed,
    All of a sudden we forget the external entanglements;

When the ten thousand things are viewed in their oneness,
We return to the origin and remain where we ever have been.

23. Forget the wherefore of things,
And we attain to a state beyond analogy;
Movement stopped and there is no movement,
Rest set in motion and there is no rest;
When dualism does no more obtain,
Oneness itself abides not.

24. The ultimate end of things where they cannot go any further,
Is not bound by rules and measures;
In the Mind harmonious (with the Way) we have the principle
Of identity, in which we find all strivings quieted;
Doubts and irresolutions are completely done away with,
And the right faith is straightened;
There is nothing left behind,
There is nothing retained,
All is void, lucid, and self-illuminating,
There is no exertion, no waste of energy —
This is where thinking never attains,
This is where the imagination fails to measure.

25. In the higher realm of true Suchness
There is neither 'self' nor 'other':
When direct identification is sought,
We can only say 'not two'.

26. In being 'not two', all is the same,
All that is is comprehended in it;
The wise in the ten quarters,
They all enter into this Absolute Reason.

27. This Absolute Reason is beyond quickening (time) and extend-
ing (space),
For it one instant is ten thousand years;
Whether we see it or not,
It is manifest everywhere in all the ten quarters.

28. Infinitely small things are as large as large things can be,
For here no external conditions obtain;
Infinitely large things are as small as small things can be,
For objective limits are here of no consideration.

29. What is is the same as what is not,
    What is not is the same as what is:
    Where this state of things fails to obtain,
    Indeed, no tarrying there.

30. One in All,
    All in One –
    If only this is realized,
    No more worry about your not being perfect.

31. When Mind and each believing mind are not divided,
    And undivided are each believing mind and Mind,
    This is where words fail;
    For it is not of the past, present, and future.

6. FROM SARAHA'S 'TREASURY OF SONGS'

He who does not enjoy the senses purified,
And practises only the Void,
Is like a bird that flies up from a ship
And then wheels round and lands back there again.

But do not be caught by attachment to the senses, Saraha says.
Consider the fish, the butterfly, the elephant, the bee, and the deer.

Whatever pours forth from the mind,
Possesses the nature of the owner.
Are waves different from the water?
Their nature like that of space is one and the same.

Who speaks, who listens, and what is confided?
Like the dust in a dusty tunnel,
That which arises in the heart goes to rest in the heart.

Even as water entering water
Has an identical savour,
So faults and virtues are accounted the same
As there's no opposition between them.

Do not cling to the notion of voidness,
But consider all things alike.
Indeed even the husk of a sesame-seed
Causes pain like that of an arrow.

One thing is so, another is not so.
The action is like that of a wish-granting gem.
Strange how these pandits go to grief through their own errors,
For in self-experience consists this great bliss.

In it all forms are endowed with the sameness of space,
And the mind is held steady with the nature of this same same-
    ness.
When the mind ceases thus to be mind,
The true nature of the Innate shines forth.

In this house and that the matter is discussed,
But the basis of the great bliss is unknown.
The world is enslaved by thought, Saraha says,
And no one has known this non-thought.

There is one Lord revealed in many scriptures,
Who becomes clearly manifest at your wish.

Oneself is the Lord, and another is the enemy.
This is the notion they have in their houses.
In eating the one, he consumes all the other,
But she goes outside and looks for her master.

He is not seen to come,
Nor known to stay or go;
As signless and motionless the supreme Lord is known.

If you do not abandon coming and going,
How may you gain this rare one, this splendour?

Thought is pure when consigned to the forehead.
Do not then conceive differences in yourself.
When there is no distinction between Body, Speech, and Mind,
Then the true nature of the Innate shines forth.

There how should another arise,
Where the wife without hesitation consumes the householder?
This yogini's action is peerless.

She consumes the householder and the Innate shines forth.
There is neither passion nor absence of passion.
Seated beside her own, her mind destroyed, thus I have seen the
    yogini.

One eats and drinks and thinks what occurs to the thought.
It is beyond the mind and inconceivable, this wonder of the
    yogini.

Here Sun and Moon lose their distinction,
In her the triple world is formed.
O know this yogini, perfecter of thought and unity of the Innate.

The whole world is tormented by words
And there is no one who does without words.
But in so far as one is free from words
Does one really understand words.

The same without as within,
Firmly established at the fourteenth stage,
The bodiless form is concealed in the body.
He who knows this is therein released.

I used to recite (the text-book, which begins with the words),
    'Let there be success'.
But I drank the elixir and forgot it.
There is but one word that I know now,
And of that, my friend, I know not the name.

At the moment of the embrace does he then win the great bliss,
Who does not comprehend that everything is of his own nature?
He is like a thirsty deer that runs for water which is but a mirage.
It dies of thirst, and how should he obtain the divine waters?

The five skandhas, the five material elements, the twelve sense-
    fields, the six faculties of sense and their spheres, these with
    their various modifications are the water. In these doha-
    verses which are altogether new nothing is anywhere con-
    cealed.

So pandits, please have patience with me,
For here there is no hesitating.
That which I have heard by the word of my master,
Why should I speak of it secretly?

That blissful delight that consists between lotus and vajra,
Who does not rejoice there?
In the triple world whose hopes does it fail to fulfil?

This moment may be the bliss of Means or of both (Wisdom
     and Means),
And by the favour of their master and by merit it is known by
     a few.

It is profound, it is vast.
It is neither self nor other.
O know this self-experience
Of the Innate in the Fourth Moment!

Even as the moon makes light in black darkness,
So in one moment the supreme bliss removes all defilement.

When the sun of suffering has set,
Then arises this bliss, this lord of the stars.
It creates with continuous creativity,
And of this comes the mandala-circle.

See thought as thought, O fool, and leave all false views,
Gain purification in bliss supreme,
For here lies final perfection.

Question not with hesitation.
Release this elephant which is your mind,
That he may drink the river-waters
And stay on the bank at his pleasure.

Held in the trunk of the elephant that now represents the senses,
One may appear as lifeless,
But the yogin like a nimble rider slips away and goes.

As is Nirvana, so is Samsara.
Do not think there is any distinction.
Yet it possesses no single nature,
For I know it as quite pure.

Do not sit at home, do not go to the forest,
But recognize mind wherever you are.
When one abides in complete and perfect enlightenment,
Where is Samsara and where is Nirvana?

O know this truth,
That neither at home nor in the forest does enlightenment dwell.
Be free from prevarication
In the self-nature of immaculate thought!

'This is myself and this is another.'
Be free of this bond which encompasses you about,
And your own self is thereby released.

Do not err in this matter of self and other.
Everything is Buddha without exception.
Here is that immaculate and final stage,
Where thought is pure in its true nature.

The fair tree of thought that knows no duality,
Spreads through the triple world.
It bears the flower and fruit of compassion,
And its name is service of others.

The fair tree of the Void abounds with flowers,
Acts of compassion of many kinds,
And fruit for others appearing spontaneously,
For this joy has no actual thought of another.

So the fair tree of the Void also lacks compassion,
Without shoots or flowers or foliage,
And whoever imagines them there, falls down,
For branches there are none.

The two trees spring from one seed,
And for that reason there is but one fruit.
He who thinks of them thus indistinguishable,
Is released from Nirvana and Samsara.

If a man in need approaches and goes away hopes unfulfilled,
It is better he should abandon that house
Than take the bowl that has been thrown from the door.

Not to be helpful to others,
Not to give to those in need,
This is the fruit of Samsara.
Better than this is to renounce the idea of a self.

He who clings to the Void
And neglects Compassion,
Does not reach the highest stage.
But he who practises only Compassion
Does not gain release from toils of existence.
He, however, who is strong in practice of both,
Remains neither in Samsara nor in Nirvana.

CHAPTER 4

DOCTRINAL FORMULAS

An Anthology of Christian thought would have to pay special attention to the numerous creeds in which the doctrine from time to time found dogmatic formulation. So essential indeed is creed-making to Christians that, as I see from my copy of Denzinger's Enchiridion, these statements of dogma go back to the Apostles themselves. For various reasons Buddhists never felt the need to define their doctrinal position briefly and precisely. We had to wait 2,500 years for Mr Christmas Humphreys, an English lawyer, to bestow his 'Twelve Points' upon us. The Buddhists have doctrinal formulations of their own, which do not, however, aim at terminating controversy but are designed to act as a rallying point for meditation. The Scriptures contain a number of stereotyped formulas which are repeated over and over again with obvious relish. Their function is not so much to be read and listened to, but to be learnt by heart and meditated upon. They form a kind of bony structure within the system which gives it some firmness and consistency. Their letter is accepted as holy writ by all Buddhist schools, though there is some disagreement on their interpretation. It would be unreasonable to expect their full import to be understood at the first reading, but they cannot possibly be omitted, especially because they provide the indispensable definitions of many terms used elsewhere. They have been arranged under the five cardinal virtues – faith, vigour, mindfulness, concentration, and wisdom – which, in that order, make up the spiritual life. For reasons of space I have had to cut down on 'Mindfulness', as experts in these things will easily perceive. By way of compensation for this omission I have interspersed the dry formulas here and there with an edifying sentence, on the principle that

> Better than one thousand verses
> Where no profit wings the word,
> Is one solitary stanza
> Bringing peace of mind when heard.

I. FAITH

The Triple Refuge

To the Buddha for refuge I go; to the Dharma for refuge I go; to the Samgha for refuge I go.

For the second time to the Buddha for refuge I go; for the second time to the Dharma for refuge I go; for the second time to the Samgha for refuge I go.

For the third time to the Buddha for refuge I go; for the third time to the Dharma for refuge I go; for the third time to the Samgha for refuge I go.

The Buddha

This Lord is truly the Arhat, fully enlightened, perfect in his knowledge and conduct, well-gone, world-knower, unsurpassed, leader of men to be tamed, teacher of gods and men, the Buddha, the Lord.

> What had to be fully known, that I have fully known;
> What had to be developed, that I have developed;
> What was to be forsaken, that I have forsaken.
> Therefore, O Brahmin, I am the Buddha.

The Dharma

Well taught has the Lord the Dharma, it is verifiable, not a matter of time, inviting all to come and see, leading to Nirvana, to be known by the wise, each one for himself.

Enough, Vakkali, what is there to be seen in this putrid body of mine? Who sees Dharma, he sees me. Who sees me, he sees Dharma. Because it is by seeing Dharma that he sees me, it is by seeing me that he sees Dharma.

> The Dharma, incomparably profound and exquisite,
> Is rarely met with, even in hundreds of thousands of millions of kalpas.
> We are now permitted to see it, to listen to it, to accept and to hold it.
> May we truly understand the meaning of the Tathagata's words!

The Samgha

Well-behaved is the Community of the Lord's disciples, straight in their behaviour, upright and correct. The four pairs of men, the eight persons – these are the Community of the Lord's disciples. Worthy they are of offerings, worthy of hospitality, worthy of gifts, worthy of respectful salutation, they, the world's peerless field of merit.

And for a disciple, rightly delivered, whose thought is calm, there is nothing to be added to what has been done, and naught more remains for him to do. Just as a rock of one solid mass remains unshaken by the wind, even so, neither forms, nor sounds, nor smells, nor tastes, nor contacts of any kind, neither desired nor undesired dharmas, can agitate such a one. Steadfast is his thought, gained is deliverance.

> Who understand the skandhas five,
> In the good doctrine live their life,
> Worthy of praises, righteous men,
> These are the Buddha's genuine sons.

2. VIGOUR

The four right efforts

Here a disciple rouses his will, makes an effort, puts forth vigour, makes his thoughts tense, exerts himself (I) to bring about the (future) non-arising of evil and unwholesome dharmas, which have not (yet) arisen, (II) to effect the forsaking of evil and unwholesome dharmas which have arisen, (III) to effect the arising of wholesome dharmas which have not yet arisen, and (IV) to effect the stability, the non-disappearance, the increase, the extension, the development of the wholesome dharmas which have arisen.

The Bodhisattva's Vow

However innumerable sentient beings are, I vow to save them.

However inexhaustible the defilements are, I vow to extinguish them.

However immeasurable the dharmas are, I vow to master them.

However incomparable enlightenment is, I vow to attain it.

3. MINDFULNESS

On guarding the senses

Here someone (1), having seen a form with his eye, does not seize on its general appearance, or the (accessory) details of it. That which might, so long as he dwells unrestrained as to the (controlling) force of his eyes, give occasion for covetous, sad, evil, and unwholesome dharmas to flood him, that he sets himself to restrain; he guards the controlling force of his eye, and brings about its restraint. And likewise (2) when he has heard sounds with the ear, (3) smelled smells with the nose, (4) tasted tastes with the tongue, (5) touched touchables with the body, (6) cognized mind-objects with the mind. That is the guarding, defence, protection and restraint of these six dominants.

4. CONCENTRATION

The four trances

Detached from sense-desires, detached also from other unwholesome states, he dwells in the attainment of the first Dhyana, which is accompanied by applied and discursive thinking, born of detachment, rapturous and joyful. From the appeasing of applied and discursive thinking, he dwells in the attainment of the second Dhyana, where the inward heart is serene and uniquely exalted, and which is devoid of applied and discursive thinking, born of concentration, rapturous and joyful. Through distaste for rapture, he dwells evenmindedly, mindful and clearly conscious; he experiences with his body that joy of which the Aryans declare, 'Joyful lives he who is evenminded and mindful'. It is thus that he dwells in the attainment of the third Dhyana. From the forsaking of joy, from the forsaking of pain, from the going to rest of his former gladness and sadness, he dwells in the attainment of the fourth Dhyana, which is neither painful nor pleasurable – in utter purity of evenmindedness and mindfulness.

The four formless trances

By passing quite beyond all perceptions of form, by the going to rest of the perceptions of impact, by not attending to the perception of manifoldness, on thinking 'Endless Space', he dwells in the attainment of the station of endless space. By passing quite beyond the station of endless space, on thinking 'endless consciousness', he dwells in the attainment of the station of unlimited consciousness. By passing quite beyond the station of unlimited consciousness, on thinking 'There is not anything', he dwells in the attainment of the station of nothing whatever. By passing quite beyond the field of nothing whatever, he dwells in the attainment of the station of neither perception nor non-perception.

The four Unlimited

Here the disciple dwells suffusing one direction of space with a heart linked to friendliness, then a second, then a third, then a fourth, then above, below, around, and everywhere. And so he dwells, recognizing himself in all, suffusing the entire world with a heart linked to friendliness, far-reaching, wide-spread, unlimited, free from enmity and malice.

And as for friendliness, so with compassion, sympathetic joy, and evenmindedness.

Unlimited Friendliness

This is what should be done by the man who is wise, who seeks the good, and who knows the meaning of the place of peace.

Let him be strenuous, upright, and truly straight, without conceit of self, easily contented and joyous, free of cares; let him not be submerged by the things of the world; let him not take upon himself the burden of worldly goods; let his senses be controlled; let him be wise but not puffed up, and let him not desire great possessions even for his family. Let him do nothing that is mean or that the wise would reprove.

May all beings be happy and at their ease! May they be joyous and live in safety!

All beings, whether weak or strong – omitting none – in high, middle, or low realms of existence, small or great, visible or invisible, near or far away, born or to be born – may all beings be happy and at their ease!

Let none deceive another, or despise any being in any state! Let none by anger or ill-will wish harm to another!

Even as a mother watches over and protects her child, her only child, so with a boundless mind should one cherish all living beings, radiating friendliness over the entire world, above, below, and all around without limit. So let him cultivate a boundless good will towards the entire world, uncramped, free from ill-will or enmity.

Standing or walking, sitting or lying down, during all his waking hours, let him establish this mindfulness of good will, which men call the highest state!

Abandoning vain discussions, having a clear vision, free from sense appetites, he who is made perfect will never again know rebirth.

5. WISDOM

The four Holy Truths

What then is the Holy Truth of Ill? Birth is ill, decay is ill, sickness is ill, death is ill. To be conjoined with what one dislikes means suffering. To be disjoined from what one likes means suffering. Not to get what one wants, also that means suffering. In short, all grasping at any of the five Skandhas involves suffering.

What then is the Holy Truth of the Origination of Ill? It is that craving which leads to rebirth, accompanied by delight and greed, seeking its delight now here, now there, i.e. craving for sensuous experience, craving to perpetuate oneself, craving for extinction.

What then is the Holy Truth of the Stopping of Ill? It is the complete stopping of that craving, the withdrawal from it, the renouncing of it, throwing it back, liberation from it, non-attachment to it.

What then is the Holy Truth of the steps which lead to the stopping of Ill? It is this holy eightfold Path, which consists of right views, right intentions, right speech, right conduct, right livelihood, right effort, right mindfulness, right concentration.

Conditioned co-production

Conditioned by Ignorance are the Karma-formations; conditioned by the karma-formations is Consciousness; conditioned by consciousness is Name and Form; conditioned by name and form are the Six Sense-fields; conditioned by the six sense-fields is Contact; conditioned by contact are Feelings; conditioned by feelings is Craving; conditioned by craving is Grasping; conditioned by grasping is Becoming; conditioned by becoming is Birth; conditioned by birth are Decay and Death, sorrow, lamentation, pain, sadness, and despair. Thus is the origination of all this mass of suffering.

But from the utter fading out and stopping of Ignorance comes also the stopping of the Karma-formations; from the stopping of the karma-formations the stopping of Consciousness; from the stopping of consciousness that of Name and Form; from the stopping of name and form that of the Six Sense-fields; from the stopping of the six sense-fields that of Contact; from the stopping of contact that of Feeling; from the stopping of feeling that of Craving; from the stopping of craving that of Grasping; from the stopping of grasping that of Becoming; from the stopping of becoming that of Birth; from the stopping of birth comes the stopping of Decay and Death, sorrow, lamentation, pain, sadness, and despair. Such is the stopping of all this mass of Ill.

The view of self

What is the 'view of self'? Here the untaught common man, who does not see the holy men, is unacquainted with the holy

Dharma or misinformed about it, who does not see pious men, is unacquainted with the Dharma of the pious or misinformed about it, regards (1) the self as form, or (2) the self as having form, or (3) form as in the self, or (4) the self as in form. And so with feelings, perceptions, impulses, and consciousness in place of 'form'.

The absence of self in everything

'Form, brethren, is not the self. If this form, brethren, were the self, it could not turn oppressive, and one could achieve one's intention, "Let my body be thus, let my body not be thus!" It is because the body is not the self, brethren, that it turns oppressive, and that one cannot achieve the intention, "let my body be thus, let my body not be thus!" And so with feelings, perceptions, impulses, and consciousness.

'Now, what do you think, brethren, is form, or any other constituent of the "personality", permanent or impermanent?' – 'Impermanent, O Lord!' – 'Does then impermanence conduce to suffering, or to ease?' – 'To suffering, O Lord!' – 'But is it fitting to consider that which is impermanent, linked to suffering, and doomed to reversal, as "This is mine, I am this, this is myself"?' – 'No, indeed not, O Lord!' – 'Therefore, brethren, whatever form, or other skandha, there may be – past, future, or present, inward or outward, gross or subtle, low or exalted, near or far away – all that should be seen by right wisdom as it really is, i.e. that "All this is not mine, I am not this, this is not myself". The learned holy disciple who perceives this becomes disgusted with form, and everything else, up to consciousness. Disgusted, he sheds his greed for these things. His dispassion sets him free, and he then also knows that he is liberated. "Birth is extinct, the holy life completed; what had to be done has been done, there is nothing further to do" – so he wisely knows.'

The illusory nature of the world

Form should be seen as a mass of foam, because easily crushed; feeling as a water bubble, because pleasurable only for a moment; perception as a mirage, because delusive;

volitions as like the trunk of the plantain tree, because without substance; consciousness as a mock show, because deceptive.

> An artist once a picture painted
> Of such a monster that he fainted.
> So endlessly worlds transmigrate
> By false ideas infatuate.

> As stars, a fault of vision, as a lamp,
> A mock show, dew-drops, or a bubble,
> A dream, a lightning flash, or cloud,
> So should we view what is conditioned.

CHAPTER 5

DOCTRINAL DISPUTES

Although generally peaceful towards their fellow-men, the Buddhists took great pleasure in religious controversy. In India the rigidities of the caste system and the Brahmins' excessive claims to superiority were favourite targets for their invective, and also rival philosophical schools were not neglected. In this Anthology there is room only for some of the discussions which took place within the Buddhist community itself. That tolerant body had never had any central authority or well-defined creed, and so there was plenty of scope for debate. I have singled out four topics which seemed to me particularly important.

(1) The first is the Personalist Controversy. *It concerns the fundamental dogma of Buddhism, the assertion that there is no 'self'. This is the cornerstone of all Buddhist thinking. Nevertheless, among the eighteen traditional sects of the Hinayana there was one, called the 'Personalists', who dated back to about 300 B.C. and who, motivated by commonsense, maintained that in addition to impersonal events there is still a 'person' to be reckoned with. Numerically they were not at all negligible. In the seventh century Yüan Tsang counts 60,000 Personalist monks out of a total of 200,000 in the whole of India. They may well have been the weaker brethren, but apparently there were many of them. They were a constant thorn in the flesh of the other sects, and the object of ceaseless polemics on the part of the orthodox. Here I have given an abstract of the debate as it appears in Chapter 9 of the* Abhidharmakosha, *a famous fourth-century work of Vasubandhu, a leading Sarvastivadin author. Some of the arguments used must appear rather inconclusive – not necessarily from ineptitude. Opponents ought to be given some latitude, and politeness may be considered as more important than a rival's conclusive annihilation.*

(2) The second piece refers to the great division between Mahayana and Hinayana. *Hinayanists generally react to the Mahayana by silence, and their writings practically never mention it. The Mahayanists, on the other hand, were under the charge of innovation, and so they wrote much to justify their position. One of the holiest books of the*

Mahayana is the Lotus of the Good Law, *composed at various times during the first Christian centuries. It has many themes. Here we consider its discussion of the validity of the methods open to Buddhists at that time. For reasons which will become apparent from a perusal of the 'parable of the burning house', these methods are referred to as 'vehicles'. The Hinayanists here go by the name of 'The Disciples and Pratyekabuddhas', and the reader is left in no doubt about the inferiority of their teachings and the provisional nature of their attainments.*

(3) *The 'Lotus' teaches that a Buddhist should aim at becoming a 'Buddha'. On this question of 'Buddhas', Mahayanists and Hinayanists also debated the question of* how many of them there can be at a given time, *Mahayana religiosity having moved away more and more from the 'historical Buddha' Shakyamuni to 'mythical' Buddhas, such as Amitabha in the West, Akshobhya in the East, and so on. In* (3a) *the Hinayana position is stated by a Theravadin in the 'Milinda Questions'; in* (3b) *it is stated by a Sarvastivadin, and refuted from a Mahayana point of view by Nagarjuna (c. 100) in his commentary on 'The Perfection of Wisdom'. On consideration, this difference seems minor and by no means irreconcilable.*

(4) *This cannot be said of our final controversy which, though it took place within the Mahayana, shows a cleavage of opinion so deep as to exclude even mutual understanding. About A.D. 800 monks from India and monks from China met in Lhasa, and competed for the favour of its rulers. Both based their beliefs on the Sutras on 'Perfect Wisdom', but their interpretations of these holy texts were diametrically opposed. The Indians, headed by Kamalashila, viewed the progress to enlightenment as a slow and gradual process, which had to traverse a large number of precisely defined stages. It seemed to them self-evident that this should be so, and the contrary opinion of the 'Ho-shan ('religious teacher') Mahayana' appeared to them not only heretical but fundamentally unintelligible. The Ho-shan was a follower of the Southern Zen school, which about 650 had been founded by Hui-neng. They taught a 'sudden' enlightenment, and were 'Quietists' in the sense that they regarded non-action and no-thought as the sum total of the spiritual life. At Lhasa neither side understood what the other was after, but Zen was defeated, and the Indian form of the Mahayana has remained dominant in Tibet until the present day. In*

800 both sides 'memorialized' the king, and few episodes of Buddhist history are better documented than this one. Although I personally am on the side of the Indians in this dispute, I have, with commendable self-effacement, chosen my material from the Chinese dossier, which Prof. Demiéville in his Le Concile de Lhasa *(1952) has most admirably edited, translated and explained.*

I. THE PERSONALIST CONTROVERSY

Is final deliverance then possible outside this Dharma, and can it be won on the basis of non-Buddhist doctrines? – No, it cannot, for all other teachings are corrupted by false ideas about a 'self'. Instead of taking it as a mere conventional term applied to a series of impersonal processes, they believe in a self which is a substance independent of the Skandhas. But the mere belief in such a self must of necessity generate defilements. Those who hold it will be forced to pursue life in the Samsaric world, and will be unable to free themselves completely from it.

The Personalist thesis, first part: But is it not true that a Buddhist school, the Personalists, speak of a Person who is neither identical with the Skandhas, nor different from them? And is not this Person a kind of self? And yet, as Buddhists they should be able to win deliverance! – We must ask ourselves whether this Person exists as a real entity, i.e. as one of the separate elements of existence, like the elementary sight-objects, sounds, and so on, which careful analysis reveals; or whether it has a merely nominal existence, which denotes a combination of simple elements, as 'milk' is a combination of sights, smells, tastes and touchables.

The Personalist: Why should not either assumption be true? – *Vasubandhu:* If the Person is a real entity with a nature of its own, it must be different from the elementary data, just as these are different from one another. It must then be either produced by causes, or unconditioned. In the first case it is not eternal, as you maintain, and you must be able to state its conditions in detail. In the second case you adopt a clearly non-Buddhistic doctrine, and, in addition, your Person could not do anything, and would be a rather useless hypothesis. The Person is therefore unlikely to be a real entity. But if you regard it as a mere designation, then your view does not differ in the least from ours. – *The Personalist:* We claim that there is a Person; but we do not say that he is an entity. Nor do we believe that he exists merely as a designation for the Skandhas. What we say is that the word 'Person' denotes a kind of structural unity which is found in correlation with the Skandhas of one individual, i.e. with those elements which are actually present, internal to him, and appropriated by him.

The Personalist thesis, second part: The Personalist also teaches that the Person is 'ineffable', that his relation to the elements cannot be defined, that he is neither identical nor non-identical with them. He distinguishes five kinds of cognizable things – the first three are the conditioned dharmas, i.e. those past, future and present; the fourth is the Unconditioned; and the fifth is the 'ineffable', and refers to the Person. – But if the Person were quite ineffable, if nothing at all could be stated about it, then one could also not say of it either that it is the fifth category or that it is not!

The Personalist: It is perfectly true that the Person is not an object of consciousness. – *Vasubandhu:* Very well, but then one can never be aware of it; if unaware of it, one cannot cognize it; if it cannot be an object of cognition, how can its existence ever be established? And if one cannot do that, your system falls to pieces. – Vasubandhu then quotes a number of canonical texts, of which I give three here: The *Bimbisarasutra* says: 'The foolish ignorant common people, putting their trust in words, imagine that there is such a thing as a self. But there is neither "I" nor "mine". There are only dharmas, ill at ease, future, present and past.' In the *Kshudragama* the Buddha says to the Brahmin Badari: 'Badari, one who has heard the four holy truths, he can free himself from all bonds: thought alone defiles, thought alone purifies. The self has, in fact, not the nature of a self. To think that there is a self is a perverted view. There is nowhere here a living being, there is no self; dharmas alone together with their causes do exist.

No person can be found in all the Skandhas when examined. And, having seen that a person is inwardly empty, you must also see the outside world as empty. Even those who meditate on emptiness cannot be said to exist.' And another *Sutra* says: 'Five calamities result from a belief in a self: wrong opinions about the actual status of a self, an individual, a soul; non-distinction from non-Buddhists; one goes astray on a wrong road; thought does not leap forward into emptiness, finds no serenity in it, does not abide in it, does not resolve upon it; one will never be sufficiently purified to win the qualities of a saint.'

The Personalist: These texts have no authority for us. They do not form part of our Scriptures. – *Vasubandhu:* What then is the authority behind your system – your sect or the word of the Buddha? How can you claim the Buddha as your Teacher, how can you be Shakyamuni's sons, if you do not accept all the Buddha's words as binding on you? – *The Personalist:* The texts you have just quoted are not the Buddha's own words, and they are not in the Scriptures of our school. – *Vasubandhu:* That is not very convincing. For all the other schools accept these texts, and they are not in conflict either with other Sutras, or with the Dharma. This is therefore sheer effrontery on your part. And how then, incidentally, do you explain the Sutra which says: 'To mistake for a self that which is not a self, that is a perverted notion, a perverted idea, a perverted opinion.' – *The Personalist:* The Sutra only says that it is a perversion to mistake a not-self for a self; but it does not say that it is a perversion to recognize a self as a self. And also: According to your doctrines the Lord could not possibly be omniscient. You say that all thoughts and mental activities change incessantly, and that each mental act lasts only for one moment. How then can it know all the dharmas? Only an abiding Person can be omniscient. – *Vasubandhu:* May I point out that then your Person would be eternal, and that contradicts your statements that we cannot say whether he is eternal or not. And this is how we account for the Buddha's omniscience: For us the word 'Buddha' is a term denoting a series of momentary events. We do not believe that in one single moment he just knows all the dharmas simultaneously. The unique feature of his series of momentary mental actions lies in the fact that, by the mere act of turning his mind on anything, there arises immediately a correct and unperverted knowledge of any object whatever, if there should be at the same time the desire to know it. That is the sense in which we speak of 'omniscience'.

The Personalist: Why then, if the word 'person' means nothing but the five Skandhas which form the range of grasping, did the Lord teach the 'Burden Sutra', which says: 'I will teach you the burden, its taking up, its laying down, and the bearer of the burden. The five Skandhas, which are the range of grasping, are the burden. Craving takes up the burden. The renunciation of craving lays it down. The bearer of the burden is the person: this venerable man, with such and such a name, born so and so, of such and such a clan, who sustains himself on this or that food, experiences these pleasures and pains, lives for just so long, stays here for just so long, terminates his life-span in just this way.' For, if 'person' were only another name for the Skandhas, if 'person' and Skandhas were actually identical, then the burden would carry itself, and that is absurd. – *Vasubandhu:* You have misunderstood the message of this Sutra. The Lord speaks of a 'person' here only in order to conform to the usage of the world. In fact this so-called 'personality' is nothing but a series of consecutive impersonal momentary events, all of them linked to suffering. But the processes which have taken place in the past cause suffering in those which succeed them. The preceding Skandhas are therefore called the 'burden', the subsequent ones its 'bearer'.

The Personalist: Moreover, another Sutra says: 'One person, when he arises, when he is born in the world, is born for the weal of the many. Who is that one person? It is the Tathagata.' – *Vasubandhu:* Here again the Lord just conforms to the usage of the world. For that reason he treats here as a unit that which is in fact a complex; it is quite usual for people to speak of a 'word', although it is in fact a compound of syllables, or of a heap of rice, although it obviously comprises a multiplicity of grains. In addition, this Sutra says of the person that 'he arises', and that, contrary to your teaching, makes him into something conditioned. – *The Personalist:* The term 'arises' has one meaning when applied to the dharmas, another when applied to the Person. A dharma is said to 'arise' because it exists now after not having existed before. A person, however, is said to 'arise', or to 'be born' when, on rebirth in a certain form, he takes up, or acquires, certain constituents, which make him into 'this man', 'this animal', 'this ghost', and so on. It is quite usual to say of a man who has acquired a knowledge of grammar that 'a grammarian is born', or 'a grammarian has arisen', but that does not mean that he has come from nothing. The person 'arises' in the sense that he acquires at a certain time a certain series of attributes, in the above quotation those of a Buddha. – *Vasubandhu:* This explanation has been expressly condemned by the Lord. For He has said: 'There is action, and there is the retribution of action. But apart from the causally linked sequence of impersonal dharmas there is no one who acts, there is no one who gives up one set of Skandhas, and takes up others instead.' In consequence there is no person who gives up his Skandhas at death and takes up others at rebirth.

The Personalist: Nevertheless, the Person is real, for it has been said: 'To say that the self does not exist, in truth and in reality, is a wrong view.' – *Vasubandhu:* This is no proof, for it has also been said that to affirm the existence of a self is a wrong view. We Abhidharmists believe that both the general affirmation and the general negation of a self are extremist views, in accordance with the well-known saying of the *Vatsagotra-sutra:* 'Those, Ananda, who affirm a self fall into the extreme of the belief in its eternal continuation; those who deny it fall into the extreme of the belief in its eventual annihilation.'

The Personalist: If the Person does not exist, who then is it that wanders about in Samsara? It is difficult to see how the Samsara itself can wander about. – *Vasubandhu:* The correct explanation is, however, quite simple: When a flame burns a piece of wood, one says that it wanders along it; nevertheless there is nothing but a series of flame-moments. Likewise there is a continuous series of processes which incessantly renews itself, and which is falsely called a living being. Impelled by craving, this series is said to 'wander' in Samsara.

The Personalist: If the momentary processes alone exist, how can you explain these words of the Lord, when he said, on recalling one of his former lives: 'This sage Sunetra, who existed in the past, that Sunetra was I.' All the psycho-physical elements have changed, and it can therefore only be the 'person' that makes the Buddha and Sunetra identical. – *Vasubandhu:* What in fact is it that the Lord thinks of when he speaks here of 'I'? If, as you say, he means the 'person', then the past 'I' is identical with the present 'I', and your 'person' will be permanent, as against your intentions. For us, however, the Lord only meant to say that his actually present dharmas are parts of the same continuous series of dharmas as those of Sunetra. As one says: 'This fire has burned its way to here.' – In any case, you assert the existence of a real self, which is of a nature so subtle and elusive, that the Tathagatas alone can see it. In that case, the Buddhas would become believers in 'I' and 'mine', with all its pernicious consequences for the spiritual life. They will form an attachment to that part of the universe which they come to consider as their own, and in that way they will be far removed from deliverance! – *The Personalist:* It is only when, as is the habit of non-Buddhists, something which is not the true Self is mistaken for the true Self, that one will feel affection for that pretended self. If, however, one sees, as the Buddhas do, the Ineffable Person as the true self, then, because that actually is the true self, no affection for it is thereby engendered.

2. MAHAYANA POLEMICS AGAINST THE HINAYANA

The Lord thereupon emerged mindful and self-possessed from his trance, and he addressed the Venerable Sariputra as follows: 'Profound, hard to see, hard to understand is the

Buddha-cognition to which the Tathagatas have awoken. All Disciples and Pratyekabuddhas must find it hard to discern. And why? Because the Tathagatas in the course of their career have honoured countless Buddhas, and from innumerable Buddhas have they learned how to course towards the supreme enlightenment. They have arrived from afar, they have shown immense vigour, they are endowed with wonderful and astonishing dharmas, with dharmas that are hard to discern, and they also enjoin dharmas which are hard to discern.

'Hard to discern, Sariputra, is the hidden teaching of the Tathagatas. And why? Because they reveal dharmas and their causes by employing various skilful means, based on their cognition and vision. They show up causes, adduce reasons, give explanations, point to objective facts, define their terms, and use various concepts. These are the kind of skilful means which they employ to release beings who have got stuck here or there. The Tathagatas have reached the highest perfection in vision, cognition, and skill in means. They are endowed with such wonderful dharmas as the unfettered and unobstructed cognition and vision, the ten Powers, the four Grounds of Self-confidence, the eighteen special Buddhadharmas, and they possess all the cardinal virtues, even to the highest degree, all the limbs of enlightenment, the trances, the deliverances, the concentrations and Transic attainments. And manifold are the dharmas which they reveal. Greatly wonderful, truly astonishing are the Tathagatas. Enough, Sariputra let us be content with saying that the Tathagatas are supremely wonderful! And a Tathagata will naturally demonstrate a Tathagata's dharmas, those dharmas which a Tathagata cognizes. In fact, a Tathagata will demonstrate all dharmas, for he cognizes them all. What these dharmas are, how they are, of what kind they are, what mark they have, what own-being they have – all that the Tathagata alone sees before his own eyes and it is manifest to him.'

Thereupon it occurred to the great Disciples in that assembly, to Ajñatakaundinya and the others, to the 1,200 Arhats who were freed from the outflows and in full control of themselves, and to the others who belonged to the vehicle of the Disciples, whether they were monks, nuns, laymen, or laywomen, and also to those who had set out in the vehicle of the Pratyekabuddhas: 'What may be the cause, what the reason, why the Lord so excessively extols the skill in means of the Tathagatas? Why should he tell us that the dharma to which he has awoken is profound, and that for all Disciples and Pratyekabuddhas it is hard to discern? So far the Lord has proclaimed only one kind of emancipation. Should we then also acquire the Buddhadharmas, even after we have won Nirvana? We just do not understand the meaning of what the Lord has said.'

The Venerable Sariputra, reading the mind of the assembly, knew of the doubts and uncertainties present in it; he himself also had become perplexed about the Dharma, and so he said to the Lord: 'What, O Lord, is the cause, what the reason why the Lord repeatedly so greatly extols the demonstration of Dharma by the Tathagatas, their vision, cognition, and skill in means? Why does he say so emphatically that "this Dharma which I have known is very profound", that "my hidden teaching is hard to discern"? Never before have I heard such a discourse on Dharma from the Lord. Many in this assembly have their doubts and uncertainties. It were good if the Lord were to explain what the Tathagata has in mind when he so emphatically extols the profundity of the Tathagata's Dharma.' Three times the Venerable Sariputra asked the Lord. Then the Lord replied: 'Listen well, Sariputra, and be attentive! I will explain it to you!'

Scarcely had the Lord spoken when in that assembly five thousand conceited monks, nuns, laymen, and laywomen rose from their seats, saluted the Lord's feet with their heads, and left the assembly. It was the bad trait of conceit which made them believe that they had already attained what in fact they had not yet attained, that they had already achieved what in fact they had not yet achieved. At heart, however, they knew their shortcomings, and so they decided to leave the assembly. And the Lord said to the Venerable Sariputra: 'My congregation is now free of chaff. Freed from the rotten wood, its core now stands firmly established in unwavering faith. It is good, Sariputra, that those conceited people have left. Now I will explain my meaning.' 'Well said, O Lord,' said the Venerable Sariputra, and listened to the Lord in silence.

'Hear from me, son of Sari, how this Dharma has been fully known by the best of men, and how the enlightened leaders teach it through many hundreds of skilful means. Of innumerable living beings, so varied in their inclinations, I know the dispositions and conduct, for I have a knowledge of the various deeds they have done in the past, and of the merit they then acquired. With manifold explanations and reasonings I cause these beings to reach a greater spirituality; with hundreds of arguments and illustrations I gratify all beings, some in this way, some in that. At one time I have taught them the nine-fold Scripture, which is composed of the "Sutras", the "Verses", the section called "Thus was it said", the "Birth-stories", the "Marvels", the "Origins", the sections consisting of mingled prose and verse, the "Expositions", and hundreds of Similes in addition. Therein I exhibit Nirvana to those kinds of people who are content with inferior things, who are relatively ignorant, who have not for very long practised under the Buddhas of the past, and who have got stuck in the Samsaric world and suffer greatly from it. This is really only a skilful device by which the Self-Existent wishes to prepare them for the day when he can awake them to the cognition of a Buddha. But nevertheless, in these Scriptures he never tells them directly that they also ought to become Buddhas in this world. And why did he not do so? Because the Saviour speaks only after he has paid attention to the proper time for doing so, and when he has perceived that the right moment has come. To-day for some reason the moment has arrived when I can teach the real final truth. The nine-fold Scripture adjusted the teachings to those who are none too strong; I revealed them as a device by which I hoped to lead people on to the cognition of a Boon-giver, of a fully enlightened Buddha.

'But there are now here before me sons of the Buddha, who are pure in all ways, wise, virtuous, and gentle, and who have done their duties under many millions of Buddhas. To them

I now teach Sutras more advanced than the nine-fold Scripture. For they have become so perfect in their resolution and so pure in their whole being that I can announce to them that in a future period they shall become Buddhas, for the benefit and out of compassion for the world. On hearing that they shall become Buddhas who will work the weal of the world they are filled with radiant joy. When I perceive their reaction to my announcement, I am further encouraged in revealing to them new, more advanced, Sutras. Those are the true disciples of the Great Leaders who have learnt this highest Scripture of mine. One single stanza of it, learnt and borne in mind, suffices to lead them all to enlightenment. That permits of no doubt.

'There is only one single vehicle. A second does not exist, and there is no third anywhere in the world. It is only through a device of the Supreme Persons that a multiplicity of vehicles has been exhibited. It is for the purpose of revealing the cognition of a Buddha that the Saviour of the World has arisen in the world. This is his one and only task, and he has no other. The Buddhas never guide anyone to an inferior vehicle. Wherein the Self-Existent himself is established, in that very position he also establishes other beings – so that they may cognize that which he cognized, and just as he cognized it, so that they may have his powers, his trances, his deliverances, and his faculties. I would be guilty of the vice of niggardliness if, after winning the spotless supreme enlightenment, I established even one single being in an inferior vehicle. That would not be the proper thing for me to do. No niggardliness whatsoever can be found in me, no envy either, and the urge of greed has ceased in me. All evil dharmas have in me been cut out. Therefore I am a Buddha, and I have comprehended the world. When I illuminate this entire world with the splendour of my thirty-two Marks, attended by many hundreds of living beings, then I show, by what I am, the true stamp of the own-being of dharmas. And, Sariputra, I think to myself, "How can all beings be made to become bearers of the thirty-two Marks, self-luminous, knowers of the world, self-existent?" And as I look around, and reflect about this intention of mine, then, after my vow has been accomplished and I have won enlightenment, I nevertheless do not proclaim the supreme enlightenment as the aim others should strive for. Because, if I would urge beings to strive for supreme enlightenment, they would all in their ignorance become quite perplexed about my advice, and they would never grasp what I had said, however well said it might be. I must always consider what kind of people I know them to be: they have not practised for long in their past lives, they are perpetually bent on sense-pleasures and attached to sense-objects, and their minds are full of craving and stupefied by delusion. As a result of their sensuous enjoyments they tumble into the States of woe; in all the six States of existence they are perpetually harassed; again and again they augment the cemeteries; they are oppressed by ill, and their merit is but small. They are invariably entangled in the thickets of false views, and believe of something that "it is" or "is not", that "it is so" or that "it is not so". Relying on the sixty-two Heretical Views, they accept falsehood as true reality, and persist in their convictions. They are nearly incorrigible, conceited, deceitful, crooked, dishonest, badly informed, and foolish. Even in the course of countless births they could never hear and appreciate the call to Buddhahood. To them, Sariputra, I say by way of a skilful device, "Make an end of ill!" It was because I saw beings oppressed by ill, that I held out Nirvana to them, the state where ill has ceased.

'But now I teach you the real truth which is that all these dharmas have been quite calm from the very beginning, that they are at peace at all times! And the son of the Buddha who completes his practice, in a future period he shall become a Jina! It is only my skill in means which made me exhibit three vehicles. In fact, there is only one single vehicle, only one single method, and there is only one single instruction by the Leaders. Leave all doubts and uncertainties behind! And if any of you should still feel doubts, remember that the Guides of the World unfailingly speak the truth: There is only one single vehicle, and a second there is not.'

The Buddha now predicts Sariputra's future Buddhahood (see *Buddhist Texts*, 122). The Venerable Sariputra then says:

'Free from doubt I am now, O Lord, free from perplexity, now that I have heard from the Lord himself that I also am destined for the supreme enlightenment of a Buddha. But there are these 2,000 self-controlled disciples, whom the Lord has in days gone by placed on the stage of those who are in training, and they were then instructed and admonished that "this My Dharma and Discipline terminates in the meeting with a Nirvana which has utterly transcended all birth, ageing, sickness and death". And all these two thousand monks, whether they are still in training or whether they are already adepts, are the Lord's disciples, who have all of them abandoned all kinds of false views, have abandoned the view of a self, the view of becoming, the view which looks forward to the cessation of becoming. They had formed the idea that they themselves had stood on the level of Nirvana. Now they have heard from the Lord this new Dharma, which they had not heard before, and in consequence they have been assailed by doubts. Do, O Lord, please speak to these monks, so as to dispel their regrets about having misunderstood you. In that way these four classes of the assembly will become free from hesitations, free from doubts.'

The Lord replied to the Venerable Sariputra: 'Have I not explained to you before, Sariputra, that the Tathagata demonstrates Dharma in such a way that he first notes the capacities and intentions of beings, who differ so greatly in their dispositions and inclinations. Then he employs, by way of his skill in means, various methods for demonstrating his meaning, and uses many arguments, reasons, definitions, and explanations. But it is precisely the supreme enlightenment that all his demonstrations of Dharma are concerned with, and he instigates all people to use the vehicle of the Bodhisattvas. It will be best for me to tell you a parable, so that this matter might become clearer. For comparisons often help discerning people to understand the meaning of what is being taught.

'In some village, city, market town, country district, province, kingdom, or capital there lived a householder, old, advanced in years, decrepit, weak in health and strength, but rich, wealthy, and well-to-do. His house was a large one, both extensive and high, and it was old, having been built a long time ago. It was inhabited by many living beings, some two, three, four, or five hundred. It had one single door only. It was thatched with straw, its terraces had fallen down, its foundations were rotten, its walls, matting-screens, and plaster were in an advanced state of decay. Suddenly a great blaze of fire broke out, and the house started burning on all sides. And that man had many young sons, five, or ten, or twenty, and he himself got out of the house.

'When that man saw his own house ablaze all around with that great mass of fire, he became afraid and trembled, his mind became agitated, and he thought to himself: "I, it is true, have been competent enough to run out of the door, and to escape from my burning house, quickly and safely, without being touched or scorched by that great mass of fire. But what about my sons, my young boys, my little sons? There, in this burning house, they play, sport, and amuse themselves with all sorts of games. They do not know that this dwelling is afire, they do not understand it, do not perceive it, pay no attention to it, and so they feel no agitation. Though threatened by this great mass of are, though in such close contact with so much ill, they pay no attention to their danger, and make no efforts to get out."

'And this man, being strong, with powerful arms, further thinks to himself: "With my strong arms I can easily carry all these little sons of mine in one bunch against my chest out of that house." But then he had second thoughts: "This house has only one single door, and that is a narrow one; these boys, thoughtless, fickle, and childlike as they are, are sure to flutter about all over the place, and that way they may well come to misfortune and disaster in this great mass of fire." So he decided to warn them, and called out: "Come here, my boys, come out of the house! It is burning fiercely. If you do not come soon, you will all be burned in that great mass of fire, and come to misfortune and disaster!" But the young boys paid no heed to the words of that man who had only their welfare at heart. They did not become agitated, frightened, alarmed, or terrified; they did not think about their lot, they did not try to run out. They could not even appreciate or understand what the word "burning" meant. Instead, they just ran here and there, and in their foolishness repeatedly looked out at their father.

'Then this man thinks again: "This house is all ablaze, the great mass of fire is burning it down. How can I prevent further disaster for myself and my boys? Perhaps with my skill in means I can drive these boys out of the house." And that man knows the dispositions of his boys, and is aware of their interests. Now these boys have many toys to play with – beautiful, attractive, lovely, pleasing, delightful, and costly toys. And, knowing the disposition of his boys, the man said to them: "Listen, my boys! Think of your beautiful and wonderful toys, without which you would be very unhappy! Think of all the various things you have got, your bullock-carts, goat-carts, and deer-carts, which you love so much, which are so dear, pleasing, and precious to you! All of them I have put outside the door of the house, so that you can play with them. Come here, run out of the house! To each one of you I will give whatever he wants and asks for. Come out quickly, run out so that you can get them!" Thereupon those boys, when they heard their father speak of those attractive, lovely, pleasing, and delightful playthings which they delighted in, and which were what they wished for and fancied, quickly ran out of that burning house with a determined effort and in one great rush, and they pushed each other out of the way and showed little consideration for one another, because each one wanted to get there first.

'When that man saw that his boys had escaped, and were safe and sound, and knew that there was nothing to fear for them any more, he took a walk to the village square, and sat down there, jubilant and rejoicing, freed from his sorrows, worries, and fears. But the boys ran up to their father, and said: "Daddy, give us those various beautiful things to play with, those bullock-carts, goat-carts, and deer-carts!" Thereupon, Sariputra, that man gives to all his sons, in his love for his own children, the very finest of all carts, that is to say, ox-carts, swift as the wind, built of the most precious sub-

stances, with railings all round, hung with a net-work of small
bells, lofty and high, adorned with rare and wonderful gems,
embellished with jewel wreaths, decorated with garlands of
flowers, carpeted with cotton mattresses and woollen cover-
lets spread over with fine cloth, both sides padded with red
pillows, yoked to white oxen, snow-white and fleet of foot,
which were driven along by a multitude of servants. To all his
boys he gives ox-carts with fluttering banners, swift as the
wind, all of the same kind, all of the same sort. And why?
Because that man is wealthy and very rich, with an abundance
of gold, silver, and treasures stored away, and he would not
think it right to give second-rate carts to these boys. "For they
all are my own sons, they are all dear and precious to me. And
since I own all these fine carts, I should treat all the boys
equally, and not prefer one to the other. I have so great wealth
and such vast possessions that I could well give such fine carts
to all beings, how much more so to my own sons!"

'Meanwhile the boys, amazed and astonished, have climbed
on their fine carts. What do you think, Sariputra; could one
say of that man that he spoke falsely when he first held out
three kinds of carts to these boys, and later on gave all of them
the finest kind of vehicle only, the most magnificent kind of
vehicle?'

Sariputra replied: 'Not so, O Lord! Not so, O Well-Gone!
That man cannot be charged with speaking falsely, since it
was only a skilful device by which he managed to get his sons
out of that burning building, and to present them with life.
And it was only because their own bodies were first rescued
that they could later on receive all those toys to play with.
Even if the man had not given any carts at all to the boys, even
then, O Lord, he could not be charged with falsehood. It was
because he had merely considered how to save the boys by
some skilful device from that great mass of fire that he was
not guilty of falsehood. And in addition he has drawn on his
abundant wealth and possessions, and in his fondness for his
sons and in celebration of their release he has given them all
vehicles of one kind, that is to say, the finest kind of vehicles.
That man, O Lord, is certainly not guilty of falsehood!'

The Lord thereupon said to the Venerable Sariputra: 'Well said, Sariputra, well said, so it is, Sariputra, so it is as you say! And this is the meaning of the parable I have just told you: The Tathagata has himself escaped from all dangers, he is entirely and in all ways set free from all that smothers other people, from the darkening and obscuring membrane of ignorance which blinds others, and from all misfortunes, perturbations, calamities, pain, and sadness. The Tathagata is endowed with gnosis, with the ten Powers, the four Grounds of self-confidence, and the eighteen Special dharmas of a Buddha. As a result of his miraculous powers he is the world's exceedingly powerful father, great in his skill in means, and he has reached the greatest possible perfection in his cognition and vision; he is greatly compassionate, and his mind never wearies of bestowing benefits, so great is his pity. He appears in the Triple world, which is like a generally decayed old house with an old thatched roof, and aflame with the fire of a vast mass of physical and mental suffering. His purpose is to set free from greed, hate, and delusion the beings in the world who are blinded by the darkening and obscuring membrane of ignorance, and who are smothered by birth, old age, sickness, death, grief, lamentation, pain, sadness, and despair; and furthermore it is his purpose to rouse them to the highest enlightenment. When he has appeared in the world, he sees beings inflamed by the fire of birth, and so on, and cooked, scorched, and tormented by it; and he sees how they have to endure many kinds of suffering, from their efforts to acquire property as well as from the promptings of their sensuous desires. As a result of what they have sought and acquired in this life they experience manifold ills in a future life – in the hells, in the animal world, in the world of Yama; they suffer such ills as poverty among gods and men, association with undesirable things, deprivation of what they wish for. And yet, in spite of the fact that they revolve in this mass of ill, they play, sport, and amuse themselves, they are not frightened, alarmed, or terrified, they do not understand their situation, they do not think about it, they are not agitated, they do not try to escape, but are quite contented with this Triple world, which is like a house on fire, and they run about in it here and there. Although hemmed in on all sides by this vast mass of ill they do not pay any attention to the fact of ill.

'Seeing all this, the Tathagata thinks to himself: "I am indeed the father of these beings. It is I who must set them free from this vast mass of ills, it is I who must give to them the infinite and inconceivable happiness of the Buddha-cognition, which shall be their play, sport and amusement." And he further reflects that "If I, strong in cognition and magical power, but without skill in means, should promise to these beings the cognition and vision of a Tathagata, his ten Powers and his four Grounds of self-confidence, they will never set out for the sake of these dharmas. For they are bent on the five kinds of sense-objects, they are not yet freed of their fondness for the Triple world, and they will continue to be burned, boiled, scorched, and tormented by the fires of birth, and so on. Before they have run out of the Triple world, which is like a badly decayed house all in flames, they cannot possibly understand what this Buddha-cognition means." As that man in the parable, without using the strength of his arms, induces by his skill in means these boys to get out of the burning house, and thereafter gives them the finest, gives them truly magnificent vehicles; just so the Tathagata, without using a Tathagata's Grounds of self-confidence, Powers and cognition, employs his skill in means coupled with deep insight to drive beings out of the Triple world, which is like a burning house, and he holds out three vehicles to them, i.e. the vehicle of the Disciples, the vehicle of the Pratyekabuddhas, and the vehicle of the Bodhisattvas. And with the help of these three vehicles he entices beings away from the world, and he says to them: "Do not, Venerable Sirs! be satisfied in this Triple world, which is like a house on fire, with those ignoble, low and contemptible sight-objects, sounds, smells, tastes and contacts! For as long as you delight in this Triple world, for so long you burn with the thirst which accompanies the five sense-objects, you are scorched and tormented by it. Flee from this Triple world, reach out for the three vehicles, i.e. the vehicle of the Disciples, the vehicle of the Pratyekabuddhas, the vehicle of the Bodhisattvas. I give you my word on this point, I shall give you these three vehicles; climb on them so that you may escape from the Triple world!" And so as to entice them further, he adds: "These vehicles, my friends, are noble, lauded by noble men, and very lovely: play, sport and amuse yourselves with them, Venerable Sirs! and that will be a high-class form of amusement for you! You will then experience the great delight of the cardinal virtues, the powers, the limbs of enlightenment, the trances, emancipations and Transic attainments, and you shall find much happiness and joy!"

'And the more intelligent people have faith in the words of the Tathagata, who is the world's father. In their faith they apply themselves to the Tathagata's religion, and make efforts to carry out his advice. Some of them prefer to hearken (*srava*) to the authoritative voice of a teacher, and by a thorough understanding of the four holy Truths, hope to win final Nirvana for themselves. They are the ones who escape from the Triple world in the expectation of the vehicle of the Disciples (*srāvaka*), and they correspond to the boys who ran out of the burning building in the hope of getting the smallest of all carts, those drawn by deer. Others again prefer to strive for a cognition which brings self-discipline and calm, owes nothing to a teacher, and by a thorough understanding of causes and conditions (*pratyaya*) they hope to win final Nirvana for themselves. They are the ones who escape from the Triple world in the expectation of the vehicle of the Pratyekabuddhas, and they correspond to the boys who longed for the medium kind of carts, those drawn by goats. Others again prefer to strive for the cognition of the all-knowing, the cognition of a Buddha, the cognition of the Self-Existent, a cognition which also dispenses with a teacher, and by a thorough understanding of a Tathagata's cognition, Powers and Grounds of self-confidence they hope to win final Nirvana for all beings – for the sake of the many, for their welfare and happiness, out of pity for the world, for the weal, welfare and happiness of a great mass of people, be they gods or men. They are those who escape from the Triple world in the expectation of the great vehicle, and for that reason they are called "Bodhisattvas, great beings". And they correspond to the boys who longed for the finest carts, for bullock-carts.

'Just as, Sariputra, that man, when he saw that his sons had escaped from the burning house, when he knew that they were safe and sound, that they were set free and that there was nothing to fear for them any more, and when he considered his own great wealth, gave them all just one kind of vehicle, the best kind; just so, Sariputra, the Tathagata sees many millions of beings set free from the Triple world, freed from pain, fear, terror, and calamities. It is because they escaped by the door provided by the Tathagata's religion that they were freed from all pain, danger, calamity, and vexation, and that they have won the happiness of a Nirvana, which is, however, only provisional. In addition the Tathagata thinks of his vast and abundant store of cognitions, Powers, and Grounds of self-confidence, and he recollects that all these beings are his own sons, and so further leads them on to final Nirvana by the Buddha-vehicle. But he does not urge anyone to win a private Nirvana just for himself; on the contrary, he leads all those beings to a final Nirvana which is all-embracing, which is the Tathagata's own Nirvana. And, Sariputra, to all the beings who have been set free from the Triple world the Tathagata gives lovely toys of the same kind, he gives them the trances, emancipations and Transic attainments to play with, which are noble and conducive to the highest happiness. And, Sariputra, just as that man told no falsehood when, after holding out three kinds of vehicles, he gave all his boys just one kind of vehicle, a great vehicle, built of the most precious substances, adorned with all kinds of ornaments, just the best and finest vehicle of all – just so the Tathagata also has spoken no falsehood when, after first, in his skill in means, holding out the three kinds of vehicles, afterwards he leads beings to final Nirvana by the great vehicle alone. For the Tathagata, endowed with an abundant store of cognitions, Powers and Grounds of self-confidence, has the capacity to exhibit to all beings the Dharma which is connected with the cognition of the all-knowing. It is in this manner that we should under-

stand how the Tathagata, with his consummate skill in means,
demonstrates one vehicle only, i.e. the great vehicle.'

3. CAN THERE BE MORE THAN ONE BUDDHA AT A TIME?

3a. *The Hinayana position*

King Milinda said: 'The Lord, Nagasena, has said: "That is
impossible, O monks, that cannot be, that in one single world
system two fully enlightened Buddhas should simultaneously
appear – that is quite impossible." But, Nagasena, all the
Tathagatas always teach the same thirty-seven dharmas which
act as Wings to enlightenment, they explain the same four
holy Truths, they train in the same three kinds of training (in
morality, trance, and wisdom), and they all admonish us to
practise vigilance. If all Tathagatas have one and the same
teaching, doctrine, training and instruction, for what reason
should two Tathagatas not appear at the same moment? The
appearance of even one Buddha already lights up this world.
If there were still a second one, the splendour emanating from
the two would light up the world still more. And also two
Tathagatas could instruct with much more ease, could admonish with much more ease! Tell me therefore the reason
for this saying of the Lord, so that my doubts may be
dispelled!'
'This world system of ten thousand worlds can bear just
one single Buddha, can bear the virtue of just one single
Tathagata. If a second Buddha were to arise, this world
system of ten thousand worlds could not bear him. It would
shake and tremble, bend, twist, and disintegrate, be shattered,
ruined, and destroyed. It is just as with a boat which can carry
one man only. When one man has got into it, it remains steady
above the water. But if a second man should come along, as
large and weighty as the first one, and also get into it, would
then that boat be able to carry both of them?' – 'Certainly not.
But it would shake and tremble, bend, twist, and disintegrate,

be shattered, ruined, and destroyed, and it would sink down into the water.' – 'Just the same would happen with this world system if a second Tathagata were to appear. There are three further reasons why it would be unsuitable for two fully enlightened Buddhas to appear at the same moment: (1) For if they did, disputes might arise between their respective followers, and arguments about "our Buddha" and "your Buddha" would lead to the formation of two rival factions, just as it happens with the followers of two powerful ministers. (2) Moreover, the simultaneous appearance of two fully enlightened Buddhas would falsify the well-known Scripture passage which describes the Buddha as the foremost, supreme, the best, the most eminent, the utmost, the most excellent, unequalled, without an equal, matchless, without a counterpart or rival. (3) And finally, this is a natural attribute of Buddhas that only one Buddha at a time appears in the world. For what reason? Because of the greatness of the qualities of the allknowing Buddhas. Of other things also which are great in the world, there is in each case one only to be found. There is one great earth only, one great ocean, one great world-mountain Sumeru, one great space, one great Shakra, one great Mara, one great Mahabrahma. A Tathagata, Arhat, fully enlightened Buddha is great, and so there is only one in the world. Wherever any of these arise, there is no room for a second. And so also with the Tathagata.' – And king Milinda replied: 'Well said, Nagasena. So it is, and so I accept it.'

3b. The Mahayana position

The Sarvastivadin: The Buddha has said: 'Two Buddhas cannot simultaneously arise in one and the same world system, no more than two universal monarchs can co-exist at the same time'. It is therefore untrue to say that at present there are other Buddhas apart from Shakyamuni.

The Mahayanist: These are certainly the Buddha's words, but you do not understand their meaning. The Buddha wants to say that two Buddhas cannot appear simultaneously in one and the same great Tri-chiliocosm. But he does not exclude this possibility for the whole universe extending in all the ten directions. Two universal monarchs cannot appear together in the same Four-Continent world system, because each would brook no rival. And so in one Four-Continent world system there is only one single universal monarch. Just so with a Buddha and a great Tri-chiliocosm. The Sutra here draws an analogy between Buddhas and universal monarchs. If you believe, as you do, that in other Four-Continent world systems there are other universal monarchs, why do you not believe in the existence of other Buddhas in other great Tri-chiliocosms?

Moreover, one Buddha alone cannot possibly save all beings. There must therefore also be others. In fact, beings are countless and their sufferings are measureless. Countless Buddhas are therefore necessary to lead them to salvation.

The Sarvastivadin: The Sutra says that Buddhas appear as rarely as a flower on the Udumbara tree, one only from age to age, with immense intervals between. If the ten directions were full of Buddhas, then the occurrence of a Buddha would not be a rare event, one could find one easily, and could not say that Buddhas are exceedingly difficult to meet.

The Mahayanist: It is true that in one great Tri-chiliocosm the Buddhas follow each other in great intervals. But there is nothing here about the whole universe. The Buddhas are so difficult to meet because imperfect people do not know how to honour them and are lax in searching for the Path. Many of them in addition fall into the States of woe as a result of their evil deeds, and there, for aeons on end, they never see a Buddha, or hear one mentioned. It is because of the imperfection of men's hearts that the appearance of Buddhas is said to be rare.

The Sarvastivadin: If there actually were in the ten directions countless Buddhas and Bodhisattvas, why do they not come and save beings from sin and suffering?

The Mahayanist: For countless aeons these beings have heaped up sins and faults. It may be that they have also gained some merit, but that is often not sufficient for them to see a

Buddha. That is why they cannot see them. As it has been
said in these verses:

> When the reward of merit is still far away,
> When the after-effects of the sins are still felt,
> One cannot possibly see before one's eyes,
> The Lord, The Buddha, how ever great his might.
> The minds of the Buddhas, the Lords do not vary
> In their fixed intention to save all the beings.
> For all they feel love and compassion abundant,
> Desirous at all times to rescue the sufferers.
> But those to be saved must be ripened in merit,
> Their wisdom be keen, their virtue established.
> These are the conditions salvation requires,
> They must be present for freedom to burst through.

4. THE QUIETIST CONTROVERSY

From the Preface to the Chinese Memorial to the Tibetan
king:

In the year 792, our great teacher received a message from
the king which said: 'The Indian monks have claimed that the
Zen system, teaching a sudden enlightenment, which the
Chinese monks are expounding, is not at all the Lord Buddha's
teaching, and they ask for it to be suppressed.' Our teacher,
on hearing this, laughed softly, and said: 'Those Indian people
cannot be rooted very deeply in the Great Vehicle, that they
allow Mara's army to molest them! Do they not risk their own
salvation by claiming that the doctrine I teach is contrary to
the Buddha's Law?' And he asked the king to arrange a
debate, and the Indian monks to formulate their questions and
objections, so that he could reply to them. Worsted in the
debate, the Indian monks thereupon attempted to get their
own way by means of intrigues with certain Tibetan noblemen. In protest, two Tibetan followers of the Zen school
sacrificed their bodies for Dharma's sake – one burnt himself
alive, the other stabbed himself with a knife. And thirty more
Tibetan monks threatened to lay down their yellow robes and
to retire into the wilderness.

From the Ho-shan's Memorial to the Tibetan king:

Question (by Kamalashila): One might say that someone can become a Buddha only after having acquired for countless aeons an enormous amount of merit and knowledge, and that one cannot become a Buddha simply by the suppression of false ideas. For in that case, there would have been no point in speaking about the six Perfections, or the twelvefold Scripture. It would have been quite sufficient just to talk about the suppression of false ideas. Your views are therefore unreasonable.

Answer: It is because for countless aeons they have been unable to escape from false ideas that all living beings are since beginningless time impregnated with the triple poison of greed, hate, and delusion, are tied to the flood of Samsaric existence, and cannot free themselves from it. But any being who can get rid of these false ideas will win emancipation and become a Buddha.

Objection: Many aeons are needed to acquire the knowledge of all dharmas, as well as the vast mass of merit which is the result of practising all virtues. These are the prerequisites of the highest forms of meditation. The Buddhas have taught a gradual, not a sudden, method.

Answer: From a dharmic point of view, to practise and not to practise are both false ideas. As soon as false ideas are got rid of, the great knowledge is automatically realized. 'Gradual' and 'sudden' are likewise false ideas, a mere reflection of wrong and unfounded opinions.

Question: What do you mean by 'looking into your own mind'?

Answer: To turn one's vision unto the source of the mind, and completely abstain from all reflection and discursive thinking.

Question: It is said in the 'Sutra on the Ten Stages' that only on the eighth stage of their career can the Bodhisattvas have an objectless thought. How then could ordinary people, who have not even reached the first stage, obtain a thought so pure?

Answer: Why then should the Buddhas have left behind for

future generations a doctrine which teaches us to abandon all discursive ideas, if ordinary people are incapable of studying and practising that doctrine?

Question: Are then the six Perfections, and all the other moral and meditational practices which the Scriptures enjoin necessary, or are they not?

Answer: When we look at them from a vulgar and conventional point of view, the six Perfections and the other practices are useful expedients which reveal the ultimate truth. In that sense they are necessary. But from the point of view of the ultimate truth, which cannot be expressed in words, one cannot speak here of either necessity or non-necessity.

Question: Are conventional and ultimate truth the same, or different?

Answer: They are neither the same nor different. In what way are they not the same? As long as false ideas are not abandoned, one has a belief in the existence of a conventional truth different from ultimate truth. In what way are they not different? If all false ideas have been removed without residue, the identity and difference of the two kinds of truth can no longer be distinguished.

Question: If one has no thoughts, no ideas, no reflections, no mental processes – how can one have a Buddha's knowledge of everything in all its aspects?

Answer: Once the false ideas no longer arise, as soon as one abstains from all of them, the true nature which exists within the core of our own being reveals itself and omniscience together with it.

Question: If we have no other duties apart from quiet contemplation, how can we be useful to other beings?

Answer: Even without thought-processes one can be useful to other beings. For one can be like the sun or moon whose rays light up all things, like the wishing jewel which can create anything, like the great earth which has the power to produce all things.

Question: You say that beings from the very beginning have the Buddha-nature within them. How can that be proved? Also, this doctrine rather resembles that of the outsiders who believe in a self. How does your doctrine differ from theirs?

Answer: The Buddha-nature which is ours from the very beginning is like the sun which emerges from the clouds, or like a mirror which, when rubbed, regains its original purity and clarity. From the outsiders we differ in that they do not admit that the Triple world is nothing but the manifestation of Mind itself.

Question: The Scriptures teach a great number of antidotes for the removal of the poisons of greed, hate, and delusion. Why should they have been distinctly explained, if the mere withdrawal from false ideas is sufficient in itself? For specific mental illnesses specific treatments have in fact been prescribed.

Answer: The *Nirvanasutra* speaks of a medicine called Agada, a panacea which heals all sicknesses whatever they may be. Likewise with non-thought and non-reflection.

Question: Are then the various spiritual practices necessary?

Answer: A Sutra tells us that all we have to do is to abandon all discursive thinking and discrimination, and that thereby we are automatically endowed with all the spiritual practices. If one has taken hold of Suchness – and Suchness allows of no thought or discrimination – then thereby one becomes automatically possessed of all dharmas, and one may then either engage in spiritual practices or one may not. But, as long as one has missed Suchness, it is indeed necessary to practise the six Perfections and the other methods of salvation. But 'Suchness contains all the dharmas', and from its point of view no practice exists and no non-practice either.

Part Three

OTHER WORLDS AND
FUTURE TIMES

CHAPTER I

OTHER WORLDS

The horizon of Buddhists is not bounded by the limits of the sensory world, and their true interests lie beyond it. Not all forms of life fall within the range of the five senses. There are in addition the heavens and hells, in which people are rewarded and punished for their deeds, the 'intermediary state' in which they pass the interval between death and rebirth, and the 'Pure Lands' of the cosmic Buddhas.

(1) The 'gods' are in a way really 'angels', and their 'heavens' might also be called 'paradises'. Buddhist theology knows of about thirty kinds of gods, but the higher grades have a constitution so refined and a mode of life so unfamiliar that we could not easily form a concrete idea of their mode of existence. Detailed information is confined to the lowest heavens. One of these is the Paradise of Indra, also known as the heaven of the 'Thirty-three', a mythological concept borrowed from the Hindus. Its description here is taken from Ashvaghosha's poem on 'Nanda the Fair'. It tells the story of Nanda, a relative of the Buddha, who was converted and became a monk. When, longing to be back with his wife, Nanda was on the point of leaving the Order, the Buddha engendered in him distaste for his wife by showing him the celestial nymphs in Indra's heaven.

(2) The 'hells' do not imply eternal damnation, and correspond perhaps more to the 'purgatory' of the Catholics. Descriptions and pictorial representations of the hells were regarded as salutary warnings to sinners, and there are many to choose from. The one selected from the 'Middling Collection' of the Pali Canon recommended itself by its brevity. If it is to be trusted, the fate of sinners is indeed gruesome to contemplate. Some Buddhists claim that these accounts of hell should be interpreted not literally but symbolically. We must hope so.

(3) Many Buddhists further believe they possess definite knowledge of life after death, but there is no agreement here among the schools. Some assume rebirth to be instantaneous – i.e. the last act of 'deathconsciousness' in the old organism is followed immediately by a new act of 'rebirth-consciousness' in the new one. Others hold that between

*death and rebirth we spend forty-nine days in an 'intermediary state'
(Bardo in Tibetan), which is most graphically described in the
Tibetan Book of the Dead. This important book is far too long to
be included in full. For my summary I have relied on Evans-Wentz's
English translation (3rd ed., 1957), Alexandra David-Neel's
French version of a much shorter manual, and a Tibetan manuscript
in the India Office Library. This work represents Stone Age
knowledge of life after death, and many other traditions, preserved in
Egyptian, Persian, and Christian writings, corroborate its revelations.
It will seem pure nonsense to most of those who have undergone modern
compulsory education. Professor Jung, however, prized it sufficiently
to say that 'from the year of its appearance onwards the Bardo has
been my constant companion'. It is in any case a religious commonplace
that no life is well lived unless it prepares for death.*

*(4) The list of 'other worlds' envisaged by the Buddhists is not yet
exhausted. The Mahayana, as we saw in II 5, 3, taught that innumerable Buddhas exist at the same time, and it assigned them a place
in the stars outside the galactic system, where they reside in what is
known as 'Pure Lands'. The most famous of these 'Kingdoms of the
Buddhas' is that of Amitabha in the West, and many Japanese hope
to be reborn there. Our passage concerning it is taken from the
'Description of the Happy Land', a Sanskrit work of the first
century A.D.*

I. THE BLISS OF THE HEAVENS

THE Lord soon discovered that it was because of thoughts
about his wife that Nanda had strayed away into darkness.
He accordingly took him by the hand, and flew with him to
heaven, as a cormorant comes up to the surface of the water
with a fish he has caught. Their yellow robes shone like bright
gold in the clear blue sky, and they were like a pair of shel-
drakes who suddenly, with wings outstretched, rise out of a
lake in unison. And so the Lord took Nanda to the paradise
of king Indra, the bearer of the thunderbolt. There some
trees change their appearance with the six seasons, while
others display the splendid glory of all seasons all at once.

Some bear manifold garlands and wreaths, fragrant, beautiful
and already tied together, and also posies which fit the ear so
perfectly that they seem superior to ear-rings. Some trees
flower with red lotuses in full bloom, and look as if covered
with lamps; on others again grow blue lotuses in full bloom,
and they appear to have wide-open eyes. The surface of the
ponds is there always unruffled, and they abound in golden
water lilies, with stalks of lapis-lazuli, and with shoots and
stamens of diamond, well-scented and delightful to the hands.
Musical instruments of many kinds grow there, like so many
fruits, on trees which are brilliant with gems and gold, handy
for those dwellers in the heaven of the Thirty-three who wish
to use them. And, most excellent of all, the celestial coral tree
there rises up in unrivalled majesty. There are birds with
deep-red beaks, crystal eyes, tawny wings tipped with scarlet,
and feet half crimson and half white. Other gaily adorned
feathered creatures also flutter around, flame-coloured, with
faces that seem all afire. Their beauty catches the eyes of the
celestial nymphs, and their songs charm them with their
sweetness. There those who have done meritorious deeds
live happily, they do as they like, are always joyous and untroubled, for ever young and free from grief, and they shine
with their own light, each in his own station which is determined by his past deeds.

There celestial nymphs with their playfulness captivate the
wearied minds of those ascetics who had, in their life on earth,
decided to purchase Paradise by first paying the price in
austerities. They are always in the prime of their youth, and
libidinous enjoyment is their only concern. They can be used
by anyone who has done the required meritorious deeds;
and for celestial beings no fault is attached to possessing
them. They are in fact the choicest of all the rewards of
austerities.

And Nanda looked at Indra's grove, in all directions, with
eyes wide open and astonished. But the celestial nymphs
exuberantly came round him, and eyed each other in high
spirits. When he saw that world to be one long round of
merry-making, and that no tiredness, sleepiness, discontent,

sorrow, and disease existed anywhere, the world of men seemed to him no better than a cemetery, as being under the sway of old age and death, and as being always in distress. Just as the sun, when it rises, eclipses the light of a lamp lit when it was dark, so the glory of the celestial nymphs nullifies the lustre of all merely human women.

And so Nanda forgot about his wife, and wanted to have the celestial nymphs instead. In order that he might win them one day, he resumed his meditations. Ananda, however, warned him that the sojourn in Paradise is only temporary, and that the day must come when the deities fall to earth, and wail in deep distress: 'Oh, the grove of Citrarathal Oh, no more the heavenly lakel Oh, the river of heaven, no longerl Oh, how dear they were to mel'

And Ananda added: 'Just think how bitter is the pain here of people when they are about to die; how much greater must be that of those pleasure-loving beings when in the end they fall from heavenl Among mortals death is heralded by ominous symptoms; so likewise there are signs which show that a deity is about to fall; for instance, his clothes now catch the dust, his magnificent garlands wither, sweat bursts out on his limbs, and he feels no more delight in being where he is. If you compare the happiness which they have had from tasting sensuous pleasures in heaven with the suffering which their fall from it brings, then the suffering is by far the greater of the two. Recognize that Paradise is only temporary, that it gives no real freedom, holds out no security, cannot be trusted and gives no lasting satisfactionl It is better therefore to strive for final release. Even the dwellers in heaven, with all their might, come to an end. No intelligent man would set his heart on winning the right to a brief stay among theml'

2. THE TORMENTS OF THE HELLS

To begin with, the wardens of hell subject the sinner to the fivefold trussing. They drive red-hot iron stakes first through one hand, then through the other, and then through his two feet and his chest. After that they carry him along to be trimmed with hatchets. Then, head downwards, they trim him with razors. Then they harness him to a chariot, and make him pull it to and fro across a fiery expanse blazing with fire. Then those wardens make him climb up and down a huge mountain of red-hot embers, all afire, aflame, and ablaze. Next they take hold of him by his feet, and hurl him into a cauldron full of melted copper, all afire, aflame, and ablaze. In that seething foam he is thoroughly boiled, and whirled now up, now down, now to this side, now to that. With each punishment he feels sharp and bitter pains, and death does not release him until he has got rid of the after-effects of his evil deeds.

After that the wardens of hell hurl him into the Great Hell, which is :

> Foursquare, four doored, a realm quadrangular,
> Fenced all around and roofed with iron,
> Its floor one incandescent mass of molten steel,
> A hundred leagues this way and that its range extends.

The flames leap and surge right across, and fill it throughout, from right to left, and from top to bottom. And a time will come, some time, after a very long stretch of time has elapsed, when one of the four doors of the Great Hell opens up. Swiftly and nimbly he runs towards it – his skin all ablaze, his hide all ablaze, his flesh all ablaze, his sinews all ablaze, with thick smoke belching from his bones. And just when he has nearly reached the door it will close in front of him. And then, after a very long time, the Eastern door of the Great Hell will open once more, and through that door he will get out.

But next to the Great Hell there is a Hell full of Filth, and into that he falls now. Therein needle-mouthed creatures successively rip away his skin, hide, flesh, and sinews, and break open his bones, so that they can munch his marrow. Right alongside that Hell full of Filth is the Hell full of Hot Ashes, and into that he falls now and suffers dreadfully there. Next to it there is the great Forest of Sword-Trees, all afire, aflame, and ablaze. The trees tower one league high, their spikes are half a yard long, and he is made to climb up and down these trees. Right alongside is the large Sword-leaf-wood, and he is next pushed into that. Moved by the wind, the leaves cut off his hands and feet, as well as his ears and nose. Right alongside is the great Caustic River, and into that he is plunged next. And he is carried up the stream, down the stream, to and fro, again and again.

With a fish-hook the wardens after a time pull him out, put him on dry land, and ask him: 'What then, my friend, do you want now?' And he answers: 'I am hungry, Sir!' On hearing this, they prize open his mouth with a red-hot iron crowbar, and push into his mouth a red-hot ball of copper, all afire, aflame, and ablaze. And that burns his lips, mouth, throat, and chest, and passes out below, taking with it the bowels and intestines Once more the wardens ask him what he wants, and he says that he is thirsty. Again they prize open his mouth with a red-hot iron crowbar, and pour into his mouth molten lead, all afire, aflame, and ablaze. And that burns his lips, mouth, throat and chest, and passes out below, taking with it the bowels, and the intestines.

After that the wardens again push him back into the Great Hell.

For a long time now king Yama has been thinking to himself: 'Those who do evil deeds in the world, they must undergo these kinds of punishment. How much I wished that I could become a human being, at a time when a Tathagata arises in the world, an Arhat, a fully enlightened Buddha. Then I could pay homage to the Lord, and the Lord would teach me the Dharma, and I could thoroughly comprehend the Lord's Dharma!'

And, monks, I tell you all this not because I have heard it from someone else, be he a recluse or Brahmin. But only that which I myself have known, I myself have seen, I myself have discerned – only that I tell you.

Thus spoke the Lord.

3. LIFE AFTER DEATH, AND 'THE BOOK OF THE DEAD'

This is what the Lama reads to the dying person:

Preamble

I now transmit to you the profound teachings which I have myself received from my Teacher, and, through him, from the long line of initiated Gurus. Pay attention to it now, and do not allow yourself to be distracted by other thoughts! Remain lucid and calm, and bear in mind what you hear! If you suffer, do not give in to the pain! If restful numbness overtakes you, if you swoon away into a peaceful forgetting – do not surrender yourself to that! Remain watchful and alert!

The factors which made up the person known as E.C. are about to disperse. Your mental activities are separating themselves from your body, and they are about to enter the intermediary state. Rouse your energy, so that you may enter this state self-possessed and in full consciousness!

I. *The moment of death, and the clear light of Pure Reality*

First of all there will appear to you, swifter than lightning, the luminous splendour of the colourless light of Emptiness, and that will surround you on all sides. Terrified, you will want to flee from the radiance, and you may well lose consciousness. Try to submerge yourself in that light, giving up all belief in a separate self, all attachment to your illusory ego. Recognize that the boundless Light of this true Reality is your own true self, and you shall be saved!

Few, however, are those who, having missed salvation during their life on earth, can attain it during this brief instant which passes so quickly. The overwhelming majority are shocked into unconsciousness by the terror they feel.

The emergence of a subtle body

If you miss salvation at that moment, you will be forced to have a number of further dreams, both pleasant and unpleasant. Even they offer you a chance to gain understanding, as long as you remain vigilant and alert. A few days after death there suddenly emerges a subtle illusory dream-body, also known as the 'mental body'. It is impregnated with the after-effects of your past desires, endowed with all sense-faculties, and has the power of unimpeded motion. It can go right through rocks, hills, boulders, and walls, and in an instant it can traverse any distance. Even after the physical sense-organs are dissolved, sights, sounds, smells, tastes, and touches will be perceived, and ideas will be formed. These are the result of the energy still residing in the six kinds of consciousness, the after-effects of what you did with your body and mind in the past. But you must know that all you perceive is a mere vision, a mere illusion, and does not reflect any really existing objects. Have no fear, and form no attachment! View it all evenmindedly, without like or dislike!

II. *The experience of the spiritual realities*

Three and a half days after your death, Buddhas and Bodhi-sattvas will for seven days appear to you in their benign and peaceful aspect. Their light will shine upon you, but it will be so radiant that you will scarcely be able to look at it. Wonderful and delightful though they are, the Buddhas may nevertheless frighten you. Do not give in to your fright! Do not run away! Serenely contemplate the spectacle before you! Overcome your fear, and feel no desire! Realize that these are the rays of the grace of the Buddhas, who come to receive you into their Buddha-realms. Pray to them with intense faith and humility, and, in a halo of rainbow light, you will merge into the heart of the divine Father-Mother, and take up your abode in one of the realms of the Buddhas. Thereby you may still at this moment win your salvation.

But if you miss it, you will next, for another seven days, be confronted with the angry deities, and the Guardians of the Faith, surrounded by their followers in tumultuous array, many of them in the form of animals which you have never seen in the life you left. Bathed in multicoloured light they stand before you, threatening you and barring your passage.

Loud are their voices, with which they shout, 'Hit him! Hit him! Kill him! Kill him!' This is what you have to hear, because you turned a deaf ear to the saving truths of religion! All these forms are strange to you, you do not recognize them for what they are. They terrify you beyond words, and yet it is you who have created them. Do not give in to your fright, resist your mental confusion! All this is unreal, and what you see are the contents of your own mind in conflict with itself. All these terrifying deities, witches, and demons around you – fear them not, flee them not! They are but the benevolent Buddhas and Bodhisattvas, changed in their outward aspect. In you alone are the five wisdoms, the source of the benign spirits! In you alone are the five poisons, the source of the angry spirits! It is from your own mind therefore that all this has sprung. What you see here is but the reflection of the contents of your own mind in the mirror of the Void. If at this point you should manage to understand that, the shock of this insight will stun you, your subtle body will disperse into a rainbow, and you will find yourself in paradise among the angels.

III. *Seeking rebirth*

But if you fail to grasp the meaning of what you were taught, if you still continue to feel a desire to exist as an individual, then you are now doomed to again re-enter the wheel of becoming.

The judgement

You are now before Yama, King of the Dead. In vain will you try to lie, and to deny or conceal the evil deeds you have done. The Judge holds up before you the shining mirror of Karma, wherein all your deeds are reflected. But again you have to deal with dream images, which you yourself have made, and which you project outside, without recognizing them as your own work. The mirror in which Yama seems to read your past is your own memory, and also his judgement is your own. It is you yourself who pronounce your own judgement, which in its turn determines your next rebirth.

No terrible God pushes you into it; you go there quite on your own. The shapes of the frightening monsters who take hold of you, place a rope round your neck and drag you along, are just an illusion which you create from the forces within you. Know that apart from these karmic forces there is no Judge of the Dead, no gods, and no demons. Knowing that, you will be free!

The desire for rebirth

At this juncture you will realize that you are dead. You will think, 'I am dead! What shall I do?' and you will feel as miserable as a fish out of water on red-hot embers. Your consciousness, having no object on which to rest, will be like a feather tossed about by the wind, riding on the horse of breath. At about that time the fierce wind of karma, terrific and hard to bear, will drive you onwards, from behind, in dreadful gusts. And after a while the thought will occur to you, 'O what would I not give to possess a body!' But because you can at first find no place for you to enter into, you will be disatisfied and have the sensation of being squeezed into cracks and crevices amidst rocks and boulders.

The dawning of the lights of the six places of rebirth

Then there will shine upon you the lights of the six places of rebirth. The light of the place in which you will be reborn will shine most prominently, but it is your own karmic disposition which decides about your choice. The rays of lights which will guide you to the various worlds will seem to you restful and friendly compared with the blinding flash of light which met you at first.

If you have deserved it by your good deeds, a white light will guide you into one of the heavens, and for a while you will have some happiness among the gods. Habits of envy and ambition will attract you to the red light, which leads to rebirth among the warlike Asuras, forever agitated by anger and envy. If you feel drawn to a blue light, you will find yourself again a human being, and well you remember how little happiness that brought you! If you had a heavy and dull mind, you will choose the green light, which leads you to the world of animals, unhappy because insecure and excluded from the knowledge which brings salvation. A ray of dull yellow will lead you to the world of the ghosts, and, finally, a ray of the colour of darkish smoke into the hells. Try to desist, if you can! Think of the Buddhas and Bodhisattvas! Recall that all these visions are unreal, control your mind, feel amity towards all that lives! And do not be afraid! You alone are the source of all these different rays. In you alone they exist, and so do the worlds to which they lead. Feel not attracted or repelled, but remain evenminded and calm!

Reincarnation

If so far you have been deaf to the teaching, listen to it now! An overpowering craving will come over you for the sense-experiences which you remember having had in the past, and which through your lack of sense-organs you cannot now have. Your desire for rebirth becomes more and more urgent; it becomes a real torment to you. This desire now racks you; you do not, however, experience it for what it is, but feel it as a deep thirst which parches you as you wander along, harassed, among deserts of burning sands. Whenever you try to take some rest, monstrous forms rise up before you. Some have animal heads on human bodies, others are gigantic birds with huge wings and claws. Their howlings and their whips drive you on, and then a hurricane carries you along, with those demonic beings in hot pursuit. Greatly anxious, you will look for a safe place of refuge.

Everywhere around you, you will see animals and humans in the act of sexual intercourse. You envy them, and the sight attracts you. If your karmic coefficients destine you to become a male, you feel attracted to the females and you hate the males you see. If you are destined to become a female, you will feel love for the males and hatred for the females you see. Do not go near the couples you see, do not try to interpose yourself between them, do not try to take the place of one of them! The feeling which you would then experience would make you faint away, just at the moment when egg and sperm are about to unite. And afterwards you will find that you have been conceived as a human being or as an animal.

4. CELESTIAL PARADISES: THE PURE LAND OF AMITABHA

This world Sukhavati, Ananda, which is the world system of the Lord Amitabha, is rich and prosperous, comfortable, fertile, delightful and crowded with many Gods and men. And in this world system, Ananda, there are no hells, no animals, no ghosts, no Asuras and none of the inauspicious places of rebirth. And in this our world no jewels make their appearance like those which exist in the world system Sukhavati.

And that world system Sukhavati, Ananda, emits many fragrant odours, it is rich in a great variety of flowers and fruits, adorned with jewel trees, which are frequented by flocks of various birds with sweet voices, which the Tathagata's miraculous power has conjured up. And these jewel trees, Ananda, have various colours, many colours, many hundreds of thousands of colours. They are variously composed of the seven precious things, in varying combinations, i.e. of gold, silver, beryl, crystal, coral, red pearls, or emerald. Such jewel trees, and clusters of banana trees and rows of palm trees, all made of precious things, grow everywhere in this Buddha-field. On all sides it is surrounded with golden nets, and all round covered with lotus flowers made of all the precious things. Some of the lotus flowers are half a mile in circumference, others up to ten miles. And from each jewel lotus issue thirty-six hundred thousand kotis of rays. And at the end of each ray there issue thirty-six hundred thousand kotis of Buddhas, with golden-coloured bodies, who bear the thirty-two marks of the superman, and who, in all the ten directions, go into countless world systems, and there demonstrate Dharma.

And further, Ananda, in this Buddha-field there are nowhere any mountains – black mountains, jewel mountains,

Sumerus, kings of mountains, circular mountains and great circular mountains. But the Buddha-field is everywhere even, delightful like the palm of the hand, and in all its parts the ground contains a great variety of jewels and gems.

And many kinds of rivers flow along in this world system Sukhavati. There are great rivers there, one mile broad, and up to fifty miles broad and twelve miles deep. And all these rivers flow along calmly, their water is fragrant with manifold agreeable odours, in them there are bunches of flowers to which various jewels adhere, and they resound with various sweet sounds. And the sound which issues from these great rivers is as pleasant as that of a musical instrument, which consists of hundreds of thousands of kotis of parts, and which, skilfully played, emits a heavenly music. It is deep, commanding, distinct, clear, pleasant to the ear, touching the heart, delightful, sweet, pleasant, and one never tires of hearing it, it always agrees with one and one likes to hear it, like the words 'Impermanent, peaceful, calm, and not-self'. Such is the sound that reaches the ears of those beings.

And, Ananda, both the banks of those great rivers are lined with variously scented jewel trees, and from them bunches of flowers, leaves, and branches of all kinds hang down. And if those beings wish to indulge in sports full of heavenly delights on those river-banks, then, after they have stepped into the water, the water in each case rises as high as they wish it to – up to the ankles, or the knees, or the hips, or their sides, or their ears. And heavenly delights arise. Again, if beings wish the water to be cold, for them it becomes cold; if they wish it to be hot, for them it becomes hot; if they wish it to be hot and cold, for them it becomes hot and cold, to suit their pleasure. And those rivers flow along, full of water scented with the finest odours, and covered with beautiful flowers, resounding with the sounds of many birds, easy to ford, free from mud, and with golden sand at the bottom. And all the wishes those beings may think of, they all will be fulfilled, as long as they are rightful.

And as to the pleasant sound which issues from the water (of these rivers), that reaches all the parts of this Buddha-field.

And everyone hears the pleasant sound he wishes to hear, i.e. he hears of the Buddha, the Dharma, the Samgha, of the (six) perfections, the (ten) stages, the powers, the grounds of self-confidence, of the special dharmas of a Buddha, of the analytical knowledges, of emptiness, the signless, and the wishless, of the uneffected, the unborn, of non-production, non-existence, non-cessation, of calm, quietude, and peace, of the great friendliness, the great compassion, the great sympathetic joy, the great evenmindedness, of the patient acceptance of things which fail to be produced, and of the acquisition of the stage where one is consecrated (as a Tathagata). And, hearing this, one gains the exalted zest and joyfulness, which is associated with detachment, dispassion, calm, cessation, Dharma, and brings about the state of mind which leads to the accomplishment of enlightenment. And nowhere in this world-system Sukhavati does one hear of anything unwholesome, nowhere of the hindrances, nowhere of the states of punishment, the states of woe and the bad destinies, nowhere of suffering. Even of feelings which are neither pleasant nor unpleasant one does not hear there, how much less of suffering! And that, Ananda, is the reason why this world-system is called the 'Happy Land' (Sukhavati). But all this describes it only in brief, not in detail. One aeon might well reach its end while one proclaims the reasons for happiness in the world-system Sukhavati, and still one could not come to the end of (the enumeration of) the reasons for happiness.

Moreover, Ananda, all the beings who have been reborn in this world-system Sukhavati, who are reborn in it, or who will be reborn in it, they will be exactly like the Paranirmita-vasavartin Gods; of the same colour, strength, vigour, height and breadth, dominion, store of merit, and keenness of super-knowledges; they enjoy the same dresses, ornaments, parks, palaces, and pointed towers, the same kind of forms, sounds, smells, tastes, and touchables, just the same kinds of enjoyments. And the beings in the world-system Sukhavati do not eat gross food, like soup or raw sugar; but whatever food they may wish for, that they perceive as eaten, and they become gratified in body and mind, without there being any further need to throw the food into the body. And if, after their bodies are gratified, they wish for certain perfumes, then the whole of that Buddha-field becomes scented with just that kind of heavenly perfumes. But if someone does not wish to smell that perfume, then the perception of it does not reach him. In the same way, whatever they may wish for comes to them, be it musical instruments, banners, flags, etc.; or cloaks of different colours, or ornaments of various kinds. If they wish for a palace of a certain colour, distinguishing marks, construction, height, and width, made of various precious things, adorned with hundreds of thousands of pinnacles, while inside it various heavenly woven materials are spread out, and it is full of couches strewn with beautiful cushions – then just such a palace appears before them. In those delightful palaces, surrounded and honoured by seven times seven thousand Apsarases, they dwell, play, enjoy, and disport themselves.

And the beings who are touched by the winds, which are pervaded with various perfumes, are filled with a happiness as great as that of a monk who has achieved the cessation of suffering.

And in this Buddha-field one has no conception at all of fire, sun, moon, planets, constellations, stars, or blinding darkness, and no conception even of day and night, except (where they are mentioned) in the sayings of the Tathagata. There is nowhere a notion of monks possessing private parks for retreats.

And all the beings who have been born, who are born, who will be born in this Buddha-field, they all are fixed on the right method of salvation, until they have won Nirvana. And why? Because there is here no place for and no conception of the two other groups, i.e. of those who are not fixed at all, and those who are fixed on wrong ways. For this reason also that world-system is called the 'Happy Land'.

And further again, Ananda, in the ten directions, in each single direction, in Buddha-fields countless like the sands of the river Ganges, Buddhas and Lords countless like the sands of the river Ganges glorify the name of the Lord Amitabha, the Tathagata, praise him, proclaim his fame, extol his virtue.

And why? Because all beings are irreversible from the supreme enlightenment if they hear the name of the Lord Amitabha, and, on hearing it, with one single thought only raise their hearts to him with a resolve connected with serene faith.

And if any beings, Ananda, again and again reverently attend to this Tathagata, if they will plant a large and immeasurable root of good, having raised their hearts to enlightenment, and if they vow to be reborn in that world system, then, when the hour of their death approaches, that Tathagata Amitabha, the Arhat, the fully Enlightened One, will stand before them, surrounded by hosts of monks. Then, having seen that Lord, and having died with hearts serene, they will be reborn in just that world-system Sukhavati. And if there are sons or daughters of good family, who may desire to see that Tathagata Amitabha in this very life, they should raise their hearts to the supreme enlightenment, they should direct their thought with extreme resoluteness and perseverance unto this Buddha-field and they should dedicate their store of merit to being reborn therein.

CHAPTER 2

MAITREYA, THE FUTURE BUDDHA

As the years pass, the impulse of the teaching of the Buddha Shakya-muni gradually exhausts itself, and attention shifts to Maitreya, the coming Buddha, who will appear in the future, after about 30,000 years or so. At present Maitreya is believed to reside in the Tushita heaven, awaiting his last rebirth when the time is ripe. His name is derived from mitra, *'friend', 'friendliness' being a basic Buddhist virtue, akin to Christian 'love'. For centuries Iran exerted a strong influence in the North-west of India, and in the beginning Maitreya had strong affinities with Mithras. At present, many Buddhists look forward to his coming. In South Asia these eschatological hopes are little stressed, whereas in Central Asia they are a source of great religious fervour. To be reborn in Maitreya's presence is the greatest wish of many Tibetans and Mongols, and the inscription 'Come, Maitreya, come!' on the rocks of numerous mountains testifies to their longing.*

Maitreya's life is described in many documents, in Pali, Sanskrit, Chinese, and Tibetan. I have translated a typical Sanskrit version of uncertain date, which is comparatively easy to understand. It is in verse, in a rhythm similar to:

> Jerusalem, my happy home,
>   When shall I come to thee?
> When shall my sorrows have an end?
>   Thy joys when shall I see?
>
> O happy harbour of the saints!
>   O sweet and pleasant soil!
> In thee no sorrow may be found,
>   No grief, no care, no toil.
>
> There lust and lucre cannot dwell,
>   There envy bears no sway;
> There is no hunger, heat, nor cold,
>   But pleasure every way.

Thy walls are made of precious stones;
  Thy bulwarks diamonds square;
Thy gates are of right orient pearl,
  Exceeding rich and rare.

Thy houses are of ivory;
  Thy windows crystal clear;
Thy tiles are made of beaten gold;
  O God that I were there!

'THE PROPHECY CONCERNING MAITREYA'

SARIPUTRA, the great general of the doctrine, most wise and resplendent, from compassion for the world asked the Lord: 'Some time ago you have spoken to us of the future Buddha, who will lead the world at a future period, and who will bear the name of Maitreya. I would now wish to hear more about his powers and miraculous gifts. Tell me, O best of men, about them!'

The Lord replied: 'At that time, the ocean will lose much of its water, and there will be much less of it than now. In consequence a world-ruler will have no difficulties in passing across it. India, this island of Jambu, will be quite flat everywhere, it will measure ten thousand leagues, and all men will have the privilege of living on it. It will have innumerable inhabitants, who will commit no crimes or evil deeds, but will take pleasure in doing good. The soil will then be free from thorns, even, and covered with a fresh green growth of grass; when one jumps on it, it gives way, and becomes soft like the leaves of the cotton tree. It has a delicious scent, and tasty rice grows on it, without any work. Rich silken, and other, fabrics of various colours shoot forth from the trees. The trees will bear leaves, flowers, and fruits simultaneously; they are as high as the voice can reach and they last for eight myriads of years. Human beings are then without any blemishes, moral offences are unknown among them, and they are full of zest and joy. Their bodies are very large and their skin has a fine hue. Their strength is quite extraordinary. Three kinds of illness only are known – people must relieve their bowels, they must eat, they must get old. Only when five hundred years old do the women marry.

'The city of Ketumati will at that time be the capital. In it will reside the world-ruler, Shankha by name, who will rule over the earth up to the confines of the ocean; and he will make the Dharma prevail. He will be a great hero, raised to his station by the force of hundreds of meritorious deeds. His spiritual adviser will be a Brahmin, Subrahmana by name, a very learned man, well versed in the four Vedas, and steeped in all the lore of the Brahmins. And that Brahmin will have a wife, called Brahmavati, beautiful, attractive, handsome, and renowned.

'Maitreya, the best of men, will then leave the Tushita heavens, and go for his last rebirth into the womb of that woman. For ten whole months she will carry about his radiant body. Then she will go to a grove full of beautiful flowers, and there, neither seated nor lying down, but standing up, holding on to the branch of a tree, she will give birth to Maitreya. He, supreme among men, will emerge from her right side, as the sun shines forth when it has prevailed over a bank of clouds. No more polluted by the impurities of the womb than a lotus by drops of water, he will fill this entire Triple world with his splendour. As soon as he is born he will walk seven steps forward, and where he puts down his feet a jewel or a lotus will spring up. He will raise his eyes to the ten directions, and will speak these words: "This is my last birth. There will be no rebirth after this one. Never will I come back here, but, all pure, I shall win Nirvana!"

'And when his father sees that his son has the thirty-two Marks of a superman, and considers their implications in the light of the holy mantras, he will be filled with joy, for he will know that, as the mantras show, two ways are open to his son: he will either be a universal monarch, or a supreme Buddha. But as Maitreya grows up, the Dharma will increasingly take possession of him, and he will reflect that all that lives is bound to suffer. He will have a heavenly voice which reaches far; his skin will have a golden hue, a great splendour will radiate from his body, his chest will be broad, his limbs well developed, and his eyes will be like lotus petals. His body is eighty cubits high, and twenty cubits broad. He will have a retinue of 84,000 persons, whom he will instruct in the mantras. With this retinue he will one day go forth into the homeless life. A Dragon tree will then be the tree under which he will win enlightenment; its branches rise up to fifty leagues, and its foliage spreads far and wide over six Kos. Underneath it Maitreya, the best of men, will attain supreme enlightenment – there can be no doubt on that. And he will win his enlightenment the very same day that he has gone forth into the homeless life.

'And then, a supreme sage, he will with a perfect voice preach the true dharma, which is auspicious and removes all ill, i.e. the fact of ill, the origination of ill, the transcending of ill, and the holy eightfold path which brings security and leads to Nirvana. He will explain the four Truths, because he has seen that generation, in faith, ready for them, and those who have listened to his Dharma will thereupon make progress in the religion. They will be assembled in a park full of beautiful flowers, and his assembly will extend over a hundred leagues. Under Maitreya's guidance, hundreds of thousands of living beings shall enter upon a religious life.

'And thereupon Maitreya, the compassionate teacher, surveys those who have gathered around him, and speaks to them as follows: "Shakyamuni has seen all of you, he, the best of sages, the saviour, the world's true protector, the repository of the true Dharma. It was he who has set you on the path to deliverance, but before you could finally win it you have had to wait for my teaching. It is because you have worshipped Shakyamuni with parasols, banners, flags, perfumes, garlands, and unguents that you have arrived here to hear my teaching. It is because you have offered to the shrines of Shakyamuni unguents of sandalwood, or powdered saffron, that you have arrived here to hear my teaching. It is because you have always gone for refuge to the Buddha, the Dharma, and the Samgha, that you have arrived here to hear my teaching. It is because, in Shakyamuni's dispensation, you have undertaken to observe the moral precepts, and have actually done so, that you have arrived here to hear my teaching. It is because you have given gifts to the monks – robes, drink, food, and many kinds of medicines – that you have arrived here to hear my teaching. It is because you have always observed the sabbath days that you have arrived here to hear my teaching."

'And Shakra, the thousand-eyed, the resplendent king of the gods, rejoiced greatly, saluted the leader of the world, and praised him as follows: "Homage to you, O noblest of men! Homage to you, to the best of all men! Have pity on the multitude, O Lord!" And also Mara, the greatly powerful, will be there, and he also will salute the leader of the world, and praise him. And, surrounded by his retinue of gods, Brahma also will proclaim the true Dharma with his heavenly voice. And the entire earth shall be crowded with Arhats, whose outflows have dried up, who have got rid of their faults, who have shaken off all the bonds which tie them to becoming. Joyously the gods, men, Gandharvas, Yakshas, and Rakshasas worship the teacher, and so do the mighty Dragons. They also will lose their doubts, and the torrent of their cravings will be cut off: free from all misery they will manage to cross the ocean of becoming; and, as a result of Maitreya's teaching, they will lead a holy life. No longer will they regard anything as their own, they will have no possessions, no gold or silver, no home, no relatives! But they will lead a holy life of chastity under Maitreya's guidance. They will have torn the net of the passions, they will manage to enter into the trances, and theirs will be an abundance of joy and happiness; for they will lead a holy life under Maitreya's guidance.

'For 60,000 years Maitreya, the best of men, will preach the true Dharma, which is compassionate towards all living beings. And when he has disciplined in his true Dharma hundreds and hundreds of millions of living beings, then that leader will at last enter Nirvana. And after the great sage has entered Nirvana, his true Dharma still endures for another ten thousand years.

'Raise therefore your thoughts in faith to Shakyamuni, the Conqueror! For then you shall see Maitreya, the perfect

Buddha, the best of men! Whose soul could be so dark that it would not be lit up with a serene faith when he hears these wonderful things, so potent of future good! Those therefore who long for spiritual greatness, let them show respect to the true Dharma, let them be mindful of the religion of the Buddhas!'

SOURCES

I I I. *Mahavastu* I. 231–9
2a. *Suvarnaprabhasa* 206–14, 224
2b. *Jatakamala* XXVIII
p. 181, 17–p. 182, 2
p.182, 9–11, 14–19
p.183, 9–14, 21–?
p.184, 1–9
p.185, 18–p.186, 10
p.191, 20–1
3. Nagarjuna, *Maha-prajnaparamitashastra* 86c–89c

I 2 Ashvaghosha, *Buddhacarita*
1. I. 1–15
2. I. 49, 60–1, 68–77
3. II. 18–20, 24–32, 46, 56
4. III. 2–5, 26, 34–8, 40, 45–7, 54, 60–2
5. IV. 85–91, 96–100
6. V. 1–15
7. V. 16–21, 66–8
8. VI. 14–8, 21–2, 43–52
9. XII. 90–106
10. XII. 107–21
11. XIII. 1–6, 71–2
12. XIV. 1–9, 47–51, 83–108
13. XV. 1–7, 13
14. XV. 14–25
15. XV. 26–8, 31, 34, 47–51
16. XIX. 29–36
17. XX. 56–8; XXI. 1
18. XXI. 37–40, 49–53, 65
19. XXIII. 64–75; XXIV. 1–4

20. XXV. 33–4, 54–60, 62–4, 67–81
21. XXVI. 83–6, 88–106
22. XXVII. 52–3, 60–4, 70–9; XXVIII. 1–3, 53–4
23. XXVIII. 59–62

II I I. Buddhaghosa, *Papancasudani* Sutta 9, Nos. 7–10. 20–3; p. 198 ff.
2. Sarvastivada *Pratimokshasutra*: T 1436. I. II. IV. 18–20, 29; V. 1–8, 11, 29, 40, 45, 54, 59, 61, 73, 79, 85
3a. *Sutta Nipata* 964–75
3b. *Sutta Nipata* 35–9, 42, 45–6, 50–6, 59–61, 63–75
4. *Udanavarga* (a) VI Karmavarga (b) IX Shilavarga.
5. *Bya chos* (The Budda's Law among the Birds), pp. 13, 17–23, 28–9, 33–6, 46–7
6a. *Milindapañha* 242–4, 352, 357–9
6b. *Milindapañha* 177–9
II 2 I. *Milindapañha* 139–40
2. Shantideva, *Bodhicaryavatara*: VIII. 1–16, 24, 26–9, 33–4, 38–9
II 2 3. Ashvaghosha, *Saundarananadakavya* XIII. 30–56; XIV. 1–4, 6, 11–2, 17, 19–20, 22–52; XV. 1–25b, 26–63;

This brief list intends merely to help readers to identify the passages quoted. Those who want to locate their relative position within the framework of the vast canonical literature of Buddhism are referred to the lucid survey of the Scriptures, both Hinayana and Mahayana, which is contained in *A Buddhist Student's Manual*, edited by Christmas Humphreys, 1956, pp. 191–260.

GLOSSARY OF TECHNICAL TERMS

Abhidharmist: A monk who specializes in the 'higher doctrine', which consists in the analysis of the data of experience in accordance with a number of traditional categories.

Analytical Knowledges (four): Four kinds of knowledge of a very advanced kind which are needed for success in preaching and for removing the doubts of others.

Ananda: One of Shakyamuni's foremost disciples, distinguished by his devotion to the person of the Buddha.

Apsarases: Celestial nymphs.

Arhat: The highest kind of Saint, who is exempt from further rebirth.

Arhatship: The state of an Arhat.

Aryas: Sanskrit for 'Saints' or 'Holy Persons'.

Asuras: Titanic beings, for ever at war with the Gods.

Austere Practices (thirteen): Ascetic practices of special severity, by which the more zealous monks purify themselves, e.g. they sleep in a sitting position, live in cemeteries, do not eat after midday, and so on.

Avalokita: The personification of compassion in the Mahayana. Literally: 'He who looks down from on high'. Avalokiteshvara = the Lord Avalokita.

Avici Hell: One of the hot hells.

Bodhisattva: A person who wishes to win full enlightenment, or to become a Buddha. See page 20.

Brahma: A god.

Brahma-world: The heaven of Brahma.

Buddhadharmas: The attributes peculiar to Buddhas. They are usually given as eighteen (see 'Buddhist Texts', No. 140).

Deadly Sins (five): Killing (1) mother, (2) father, (3) an Arhat; (4) causing dissension in the Order; (5) deliberately causing the Tathagata's blood to flow.

Dharmas, dharmas: (1) The one ultimate Reality; (2) an ultimately real event; (3) as reflected in life: righteousness, virtue; (4) as interpreted in the Buddha's teaching: doctrine, Scripture, Truth; (5) object of the sixth sense-organ, i.e. of mind; (6) property; (7) mental state; (8) thing; (9) quality. See also page 14.

Glossary of Technical Terms

Dharmas of a Buddha, eighteen Special: See Buddhadharmas.

Dhyana: The state of Transic concentration, of which four stages are usually distinguished.

Disciple: In Mahayana texts a technical term for the followers of the Hinayana. See page 209 for its derivation.

Dragons: Nagas.

Ease: Sukha: Not so much positive happiness, as absence of suffering, annoyance and friction.

Four-Continent: Hindu geography assumes the earth to have four Continents, of which India is one.

Fruits (four): The four Saints considered at the moment when their specific achievements have come to fruition.

Gandharva: (1) a heavenly musician; (2) a being about to enter a womb.

Gnosis : Sanskrit *Jñāna* (see page 15).

Grounds of self-confidence (four): A Buddha's self-confidence is based on his infallible knowledge that (1) he knows all that is; (2) has extinguished all Outflows; (3) is acquainted with all hindrances to emancipation; and (4) all the means for attaining the extinction of suffering.

Guru: Spiritual preceptor.

Heretical Views (sixty-two): A standard list of false views, or groundless opinions, e.g. that the world is eternal, that the self comes to an end, that the Buddha exists after death, etc. (See *Digha Nikaya* I, 12–39.)

Hindrances (five): Obstacles to the attainment of trance. They are: (1) sense-desire; (2) ill-will; (3) sloth and torpor; (4) excitedness and worry; (5) doubt.

Holy: There is no real equivalent to *ārya* in English. 'Noble' is perhaps better.

Holy Persons: There are eight, i.e. the four Saints considered (1–4) at the moment when they enter their Paths, and (5–8) when they reap their fruit.

Indra: Name of a Hindu God.

Jhana: Pali for Dhyana.

Jina: 'Conqueror', an epithet of the Buddha.

Karma: A volitional action which is either wholesome or unwholesome, and in consequence either rewarded or punished.

Kasina: A meditational device.

Knowledge, three kinds of: (1) the recollection of former lives; (2) the knowledge of the rise and fall of beings; (3) the knowledge that the Outflows are extinct.

Koan: A riddle the solution of which the Rinzai branch of the Zen sect regards as a road to enlightenment.

Kos: A distance of about 2½ miles.

Koti: A huge number.

Mahabrahma: Name of a God. Literally: 'Great Brahma'.

Mantras: Words of power which work wonders.

Mara: The personification of evil. The Buddhist 'Tempter' whose baits are the sensory pleasures. Death. Sometimes identified with the five Skandhas.

Marks of a superman (thirty-two): Physical peculiarities found in a Buddha's body, as well as that of a Universal Monarch.

Mundane: Belonging to this world, and out of contact with true reality.

Muni: 'Sage'.

Naga: A serpent or dragon; a bull-elephant.

Never-returner: The third stage of the Path. He no more returns to this world, and attains Nirvana in one of the heavens.

Nirvana: The ultimate goal of all Buddhist endeavour, the extinction of craving and separate selfhood, a life which has gone beyond death.

Once-returner: The second stage of the Path. He will return to this world no more than seven times.

Outflows (four): (1) sense-desire; (2) desire for becoming; (3) wrong views; (4) ignorance. Extinction of the outflows constitutes Arhatship.

Paradise: Heaven.

Path: The straight and direct road to Nirvana. People can 'tread the Path' after they have undergone a conversion or spiritual rebirth which leads to an indifference to worldly things. Only then can the unconditioned Nirvana become an object of their thoughts and strivings.

Paths (four): Progress along the Path is divided into four stages, and one speaks of the Path of Streamwinners, Once-returners, Never-returners and Arhats respectively.

Patimokkha: Pali for Pratimoksha (see page 169).

Perfections (six): The perfection of (1) giving; (2) morality; (3) patience; (4) vigour; (5) meditation; (6) wisdom.

Person: Sanskrit *pudgala*.

Places of rebirth (five or six): Among Gods, Asuras, men, animals, ghosts, or hellish beings.

Powers (ten): This refers to a Buddha's unique intellectual powers, by which he comprehends what others cannot comprehend. For the list, see 'Buddhist Texts', No. 116.

Pratyekabuddha: A Buddha who has won enlightenment by himself, but is unable or unwilling to teach others.

Preta: A hungry ghost.

Rakshasa: A kind of demon.

Saints: Those who have won the Path. The opposite are the 'foolish common people'.

Sainthood: Arhatship.

Samadhi: Sanskrit for 'Transic concentration'.

Samsara: The world of birth and death.

Samsaric world: Samsara.

Sariputra: One of Shakyamuni's foremost disciples, distinguished by his wisdom.

Scripture, Ninefold (p. 200), or Twelvefold (p. 215): An archaic division of the Scriptures which antecedes their present form.

Sections of monastic morality (four): (1) Restraint by the Patimokka rules; (2) guarding the senses; (3) purity of livelihood; (4) circumspect use of all requisites.

Self-existent: An attribute of the Buddha.

Shakyamuni: The 'Sage of the tribe of the Shakyas'. Epithet of the 'historical Buddha'.

Shakra: A name for Indra, 'Chief of Gods'.

Siddhas: Accomplished semi-divine magicians, borrowed from Hindu mythology.

Sineru: The Pali name for the central world mountain, *Sumeru* in Sanskrit.

Skandhas (five): The constituents of the personality: (1) form = body; (2) feelings; (3) perceptions; (4) volitional impulses; (5) consciousness.

Special dharmas of a Buddha (eighteen): See Buddhadharmas.

States of existence: Places of rebirth.

States of woe: Rebirth in hell, as an animal, as a ghost, as an Asura. These rebirths are not only particularly painful, but also futile because excluding from the study of the Dharma.

Streamwinner: The first kind of Saint. He has just won the Path, thereby detaching himself from mundane existence.

Subjects of meditation (forty): A standard list from Buddhaghosa's 'Path to Purity'. See my 'Buddhist Meditation', page 14.

Subsidiary characteristics (eighty): A further list of a Buddha's physical attributes, added at a later date to the list of the thirty-two Marks.

Substrata: A technical term occasionally used for the Skandhas, which are a basis for further becoming.

Suchness: It is reached when things are seen such as they are, in their bare being, without any distortion.

Sugata: 'Well-Gone', an epithet of the Buddha.

Superknowledges (five or six): (1) wonderworking powers; (2) heavenly ear; (3) knowledge of the thoughts of others; (4) ability to recollect one's own previous births; (5) knowledge of the rebirths of other beings; (6) knowledge that the Outflows are extinct.

Supramundane: Detached from this world, moving towards contact with true reality.

Supramundane Path: The movement towards true reality takes place on the Path which can be reached only by those who have transcended the world.

Sutra: A text which claims to have been spoken by the Buddha.

Tathagata: A title of the Buddha. 'He who has thus come', i.e. as the other Buddhas have come.

Thirty-three, heaven of the: A mythological realm borrowed from Hinduism. The paradise of Indra.

Transic concentration: An attitude based on withdrawal from sense – objects, and concentration on spiritual reality. See my *Buddhist meditation* pp. 17–21.

Tri-chiliocosm: A cosmic unit, roughly corresponding to what we call a 'galactic system'.

Triple world: (1) the world of sense-desire; (2) the world of form, or fine matter; (3) the formless world.

Truths (four): See pages 186–7.

Tushita heaven: The third-lowest heaven in which Bodhisattvas await their last rebirth.

Vinaya: Discipline, or the 'Book of Discipline'.

Wings to enlightenment (thirty-seven): A list of practices which carry us to salvation.

Glossary of Technical Terms

Worldly Activity: A term of Indian philosophy, which opposes *Pravritti*, the wish to act, to *Nivritti*, inactivity, the first being pernicious, the second desirable.

Yaksha: A kind of spirit.

Yama, world of: The Underworld.

The definitions of technical terms in this Glossary are necessarily very brief, and they may fail to satisfy some readers. More information about them can be found in the Mahathera Nyanatiloka's *Buddhist Dictionary*, or in Har Dayal's *The Bodhisattva Doctrine in Buddhist Literature*, 1932.

FOR THE BEST IN PAPERBACKS, LOOK FOR THE 🐧

In every corner of the world, on every subject under the sun, Penguin represents quality and variety – the very best in publishing today.

For complete information about books available from Penguin – including Puffins, Penguin Classics and Arkana – and how to order them, write to us at the appropriate address below. Please note that for copyright reasons the selection of books varies from country to country.
